Praise for *School Libraries Supporting Literacy and W*

'Merga has managed to document the ways in w
contribute not only to the traditional aspects of literacy and research ...
enrich the community's wellbeing and social emotional health. In this trying COVID-19 period it is a timely reminder of how the library as both a physical and digital space, as well as an institution, improves the lives of all who have access. This is a work that will inspire those in the profession and encourage fellow educators and administrators to leverage the power of the library in their setting.'
Nadine Bailey, International School Teacher Librarian

'Margaret Merga's work plays an important and essential role in the advocacy and promotion of school libraries, their impact and benefits; this book is no exception. It details how school libraries with professional staff support the literacy and wellbeing of students through reading engagement, information literacy, and the creation of a welcoming and inclusive environment. It is robustly researched with personal reflections, practical strategies and realistic suggestions embedded in pedagogical approaches that make them easy to implement. This book ought to be required CPD reading, not only for library staff but also those with any sort of responsibility for the library within a school, including the decision-makers: it should be in the staff library in every school!'
Barbara Band, School Library Consultant and Trainer

'Based on her own research and that of others, Margaret Merga explores the complexities of the role of the teacher librarian and school library professional in Australia and the UK. Practical suggestions around the theme of the importance of libraries for reading, information, and student wellbeing are woven through the accessible text. Merga's comprehensive research on literacy and literature and the importance of recreational reading in the academic development of our students will provide teacher librarians with strong evidence to advocate the importance of their role. The role the school library plays in contributing to the wellbeing of students and staff is well articulated and cannot be overlooked. This is a must read for school executives and an affirming read for teacher librarians and school library staff.'
Liz Derouet, Liaison Librarian Education, University of Southern Queensland

'A must read for teacher librarians, school library professionals, principals, teachers, policy makers and anyone who cares about improving student wellbeing and literacy. Drawing from her own and international research, Merga has produced a clear and engaging exploration of the essential role that school libraries play in student literacy and wellbeing. With a practical, evidence-based approach, this book is a helpful resource for teacher librarians looking to expand their programs and cater for students with diverse needs. It is also a timely reminder of the importance of investing in school libraries staffed by qualified school library professionals, to give each child the education experience they need.'
Trish Hepworth, Director of Policy and Education, Australian Library and Information Association (ALIA)

'Margaret Merga's *School Libraries Supporting Literacy and Wellbeing* is the new testament of school libraries and librarianship! A big shout about the causality of school libraries and the value of qualified school library professionals to enrich not only reading and literacy but also students' social, emotional, health and intellectual wellbeing. Providing practical suggestions, every single page of the book is full of research-based information for those of us who want to enjoy the companionship of school librarianship . . . and

even teachers, policymakers and researchers should find this text enlightening and thought-provoking. This book made both school libraries and librarians a winner! Read this book – and learn from one of the best!'
Zakir Hossain, Teacher-Librarian/Researcher

'In this book, underpinned always by validated research, Margaret explores how the school library can help students when life gets hard, showing that literacy is a life skill, not just another academic competency and how this can be an aid to mental wellbeing in many ways. She highlights the role of the school librarian in providing practical help and support within this sphere. This is a book for all school librarians who wish to learn more about how to make our skills and environment more accessible and how to highlight these opportunities to our senior management teams. So much to explore in this valuable read.'
Sarah Pavey, Education Consultant, SP4IL and member of CILIP School Libraries Group (SLG) and CILIP Information Literacy Group (ILG)

'Dr Margaret Merga is passionate about the critical role of school libraries in literacy and wellbeing. Her drive and enthusiasm come from her own experiences as a student, educator, researcher and academic. Teacher librarians, school librarians and library staff know and understand this important role, intrinsically. We see evidence of it every single day. Drawing on a robust research base, Margaret clearly illustrates best practice in school libraries and the important multifaceted role of school library professionals. She encourages us to continually draw on current research to refine, extend and highlight exactly what we do. This book provides substantial evidence of the value of school libraries and the significant contribution they can make in the lives of our students. It is a must-read for all who value literacy and student wellbeing in our schools. School library professionals across Australia and throughout the world will treasure this book and refer to it often with keen interest, excitement, and enthusiasm!'
Kerry Pope, Head of Library Services, Toongabbie Christian College, Sydney. Co-Leader, Australian School Library Association (ASLA) Research SIG and former Vice President, Committee Chair, International Association of School Librarianship (IASL)

'This book focuses on the school library/ian roles with regard to two important issues of our time: literacy, however you define it, and the affective domain, our individual wellbeing. These dual features weave throughout the book as Margaret Merga convincingly identifies connections and a symbiotic relationship between reading/literacy and the wellbeing of students. You only need to read a few pages to be aware that you are reading the work of someone who brings considerable research, analysis and academic rigour to an enthusiasm and passion for school libraries and learning. What librarians actually do is identified holistically from the theory, good practice and the realpolitik.

In today's global village, it is necessary to look outwards, which this book does. Reflecting a traditional strength of British school librarianship – literacy/reading – in a fusion with an Australasian powerhouse of school librarianship and of innovative and good practice; in practice, the picture is rightly more mixed, and there are challenges. In essence, *School Libraries Supporting Literacy and Wellbeing* provides ways to help you break the glass ceiling that can separate school libraries/ians from the wider educational environment.'
Anthony Tilke, PhD, international school librarian, author, IB accredited workshop leader and content developer

School Libraries Supporting Literacy and Wellbeing

Every purchase of a Facet book helps to fund CILIP's advocacy,
awareness and accreditation programmes for
information professionals.

School Libraries Supporting Literacy and Wellbeing

Margaret K. Merga

facet publishing

© Margaret K. Merga 2022

Published by Facet Publishing,
7 Ridgmount Street, London WC1E 7AE
www.facetpublishing.co.uk

Facet Publishing is wholly owned by CILIP:
the Library and Information Association.

The author has asserted her right to be identified as author of this work. Except as otherwise permitted under the Copyright, Designs and Patents Act 1988 this publication may only be reproduced, stored or transmitted in any form or by any means, with the prior permission of the publisher, or, in the case of reprographic reproduction, in accordance with the terms of a licence issued by The Copyright Licensing Agency. Enquiries concerning reproduction outside those terms should be sent to Facet Publishing,
7 Ridgmount Street, London WC1E 7AE.

Every effort has been made to contact the holders of copyright material reproduced in this text and thanks are due to them for permission to reproduce the material indicated. If there are any queries please contact the publisher.

British Library Cataloguing in Publication Data
A catalogue record for this book is available from the British Library.

IISBN 978-1-78330-584-1 (paperback)
ISBN 978-1-78330-585-8 (hardback)
ISBN 978-1-78330-586-5 (PDF)
ISBN 978-1-78330-587-2 (EPUB)

First published 2022

Text printed on FSC accredited material.

MIX
Paper from responsible sources
FSC
www.fsc.org FSC® C013604

Typeset from author's files by Flagholme Publishing Services in
10/13 pt Palatino Linotype and Open Sans.
Printed and made in Great Britain by CPI Group (UK) Ltd, Croydon, CR0 4YY.

Contents

List of Tables	xi
Acknowledgements	xiii
Abbreviations	xv
Introduction	xvii
Why literacy?	xviii
Reading + literacy + wellbeing	xix
Why this book?	xxi
References	xxiii
1 What Do School Library Professionals Contribute to Student Learning and Support? A Focus on Australia and the UK	**1**
Teacher librarian and school librarian: What is the difference?	2
What teacher librarians do	4
What school librarians do	15
Things they are expected to do, be and have	22
Further thoughts	30
References	31
2 School Libraries and Reading Engagement for Literacy	**33**
Reading engagement and literacy	34
Reading for pleasure and literacy	36
Reading for pleasure and opportunity	39
Why the school library professional is a model that matters	41
Library professionals as literacy educators and supports of reading engagement	43
Australian and UK school library professionals as literacy educators	44
Australian and US school library professionals' divergence on reading for pleasure	46
Further thoughts	50
References	52

3	**Librarians Supporting Struggling Literacy Learners Beyond the Early Years**	**57**
	The challenge of low literacy	59
	Who are the struggling literacy learners?	61
	Where libraries and library professionals fit in	64
	Increasing visibility of school library professionals' role	67
	How to implement and measure the efficacy of literacy-supportive interventions	69
	Further thoughts	77
	References	77
4	**School Libraries and Reading Engagement for Student Wellbeing**	**83**
	School libraries fostering wellbeing through reading engagement	84
	Reading, emotions and escape	86
	Connecting with characters	88
	Role models	90
	Perspective-taking and personal development	91
	Pleasure in being read to	92
	Resourcing for inclusion	94
	Further thoughts	95
	References	97
5	**School Libraries, Health Resourcing and Information Literacy**	**101**
	Health literacy and information literacy	102
	Searching in the library	104
	Checking information is correct from library manager perspectives	105
	Checking information is correct from student perspectives	107
	Resourcing for teachers and parents	108
	Non-fiction books	110
	Further thoughts	112
	References	114
6	**Librarians Creating Environments for Reading and Wellbeing**	**117**
	Insights from the Project on how students value the library environment	119
	Students seeking sanctuary from weather conditions	120
	Students with developing social skills, anxiety and introversion	121
	Students seeking mentor and mentee relationships	121
	Students seeking to reset	122
	Students who love to read	123
	Students who are creative	124
	What library environments are Australian teacher librarians expected to foster?	126
	Warm and welcoming	127
	Flexible and supportive of learning	127
	Vibrant and stimulating	128
	Adaptive, safe and stimulating spaces	129
	Further thoughts	129
	References	131

7	**Challenges to Visibility and Advocacy for School Libraries and Staff**	**135**
	Challenges of the professional role and burgeoning workload	136
	Issues with training, morale and the greying workforce	137
	Challenges of deprofessionalisation	138
	Challenges of inconsistent nomenclature and shrinking staffing	140
	Challenge of conducting research and dissemination of a credible research base	144
	Challenges to the existence of a physical library	148
	Further thoughts	151
	References	151

Conclusions and Directions for Future Research	**155**
School libraries and COVID-19	155
Collaboration for learning	156
Wellbeing research that has broader generalisability and applicability	157
Workload realities	158
Establishing library and researcher partnerships	159
Capturing the evolving interests of young people: #Booktok on TikTok	159
Final thoughts	162
References	163

Appendix 1: Background and Methods of My Research Projects	**167**
2020 TikTok and young people	170
2020 School libraries promoting wellbeing in Australian primary and secondary schools	174
Semi-structured interview questions relevant to Chapter 4	175
Semi-structured interview questions relevant to Chapter 5	176
Semi-structured interview questions relevant to Chapter 6	178
2020 Library Workforce Project	179
References	189

Appendix 2: A Place to Get Away from It All: Five Ways School Libraries Support Student Wellbeing	**191**
1. They can be safe spaces	191
2. They provide resources for wellbeing	192
3. They help build digital health-literacy skills	192
4. They support reading for pleasure	193
5. They encourage healing through reading	193
References	194

Index	**197**

List of Tables

Chapter 1
Table 1	Role requirements and characteristics of the Australian teacher librarian	6
Table 2	Role requirements and characteristics of the UK school librarian	15

Chapter 2
Table 1	School library professionals as literacy educators	44
Table 2	Current RfP supportive roles and characteristics in the US and Australia	47

Chapter 3
Table 1	Plurality of perceived barriers at group and individual level and preponderance of students who have a diagnosed learning difficulty or are EAL/D learners	63

Chapter 7
Table 1	Names for school library professionals in the US, Australia and the UK	141

Appendix 1
Table 1	Research studies in literacy and/or libraries	167
Table 2	CP characteristics	172
Table 3	School and student descriptions	174
Table 4	Data on schools associated with job description documents	180
Table 5	Data on job description documents	182
Table 6	Characteristics of job description documents in the US	183
Table 7	Characteristics of job description documents in Australia	184
Table 8	Australian document characteristics	186
Table 9	UK document characteristics	188

Acknowledgements

I would like to thank Kerry Pope and Margo Pickworth for enthusiastically supporting my work during their former leadership of the Australian School Library Association. Having the opportunity to draw on your knowledge and expertise was extremely beneficial for my research, and your support during the writing of this book was invaluable.

Thanks also to my research collaborators on my libraries, literacy and wellbeing research: Saiyidi Mat Roni, Shannon Mason, Anabela Malpique, Susan Ledger, Chin Ee Loh, Cath Ferguson and Claire Gibson. I've had so much fun working with you and benefiting from your giant brains. Thanks to the University of Newcastle in New South Wales who kindly (thanks again to Susan Ledger) bestowed an honorary position on me in 2021.

Thanks to the Bupa Health Foundation, the Copyright Agency Cultural Fund, the Collier Foundation, the Ian Potter Foundation and the Association of Independent Schools of New South Wales for enabling me to conduct or support libraries, literacy and wellbeing research through generously providing funds. I would like to particularly thank Annette Schmiede, the former Executive Leader at Bupa Health Foundation, who kindly championed the wellbeing research reported in this book, and Donna Peek and Melina Georgousakis for their support and encouragement.

Thanks to Hillary Hughes, Theresa Cremin, Lyn Hay and Donna Alvermann, senior researchers and inspirational leaders in my field who have had the generosity of spirit to provide encouragement over the years, contrary to the competitive and often isolating nature of academia.

Thanks to the respondents of my studies, who I cannot identify to comply with ethics requirements.

I also want to praise and thank the professional organisations and groups that work tirelessly to promote the role of libraries in schools, including but not limited to the dynamic crew involved in the #StudentsNeedSchoolLibraries initiative in Australia and #GreatSchoolLibraries in the UK. Thanks to Barbara

Band for getting in touch and enabling me to support the important #GreatSchoolLibraries movement; you're doing great things!

Thanks to the American Association of School Librarians for the 2021 award for my paper 'addressing a persistent and recurring challenge in the field of school librarianship'. Hopefully, it will connect some US school library professionals with my work.

Thanks to the many schools that I've worked with in recent times to turn this research into practical outcomes for your students.

Many thanks to my sons Gabe and Sam for being my two favourite young humans, and to my husband Marián for kindly tolerating my many work-related disappearances and for having my back. Double thanks to Gabe for reading the first full draft of this book (as usual) and providing valuable feedback.

Thanks to Pete Baker at Facet Publishing. Working with you on this has been a smooth and pleasant process, mostly due to your great communication skills from the other side of the world. Thanks to the entire team at Facet who supported this publication, especially Julie Rowbotham for her copyediting work, and the reviewers who provided such useful feedback.

Finally, thanks to the school library professionals that constantly strive to improve students' educational and wellbeing outcomes in our schools. I greatly appreciate you.

Abbreviations

AASL	American Association of School Librarians
ACARA	Australian Curriculum, Assessment and Reporting Authority
ACILIP	Affiliate of the Chartered Institute of Library and Information Professionals
ALIA	Australian Library and Information Association
ASLA	Australian School Library Association
CILIP	Chartered Institute of Library and Information Professionals
CLPE	Centre for Literacy in Primary Education
COVID	coronavirus disease
CP	content producer
DfE	Department for Education
DIER	direct and indirect effects model of reading
EAL/D	English as an additional language or dialect
FYP	For You Page (TikTok)
GCSE	General Certificate of Secondary Education
ICSEA	Index of Community Socio-Educational Advantage
ICT	information and communication technology
ITE	initial teacher education
JDF	job description document or form
LIS	library and information science
LM	library manager
LP	Literacy Policy document
MCILIP	member of the Chartered Institute of Library and Information Professionals
NVQ	National Vocational Qualification
OECD	Organisation for Economic Co-operation and Development
PD	professional development
RfP	reading for pleasure
SLA	School Library Association
SLL	struggling literacy learner

SSSLL	Supporting Struggling Secondary Literacy Learners (project)
TLALAS	Teacher Librarians as Australian Literature Advocates in Schools (project)
TRBWA	Teacher Registration Board of Western Australia
UK	United Kingdom
URL	uniform resource locator
US	United States of America
WHS	workplace health and safety
YABBA	Young Australians Best Book Awards

Introduction

When you walk into a school library, you immediately feel that you are entering a special space with affordances that are unique to it. You might admire student art on the walls; note a cluster of students sprawled in beanbags, lost in a book; see industrious students constructing art in a makerspace, quietly laughing as part of it collapses unintentionally; or observe a group of students voraciously seeking and consuming new knowledge using information literacy skills also taught within that space. The possibilities are vast; however, what you are less likely to view are uncomfortable students wearing the pinched look of anxiety that you see on the faces of students in classrooms who are struggling and feeling that they are falling short in academic performance, social connection or other areas of concern in their young lives. The library sits as a potential sanctuary where literacy and other skills can be fostered in a supportive space.

Personally, the school library was a refuge for me as a very shy student in primary school. I have fond memories of spending many hours during recess and lunch reading books and drawing pictures of horses with my friend (singular). I can't claim to have developed my horse-drawing talent over that time (sadly, even as an adult my horse pictures still look like mice), but I gained in many other areas thanks to my school library. I had a safe place where I could be an awkward introvert away from the gaze of my more extroverted peers, and I had the chance to enjoy shared quiet companionship, which made school life much more bearable. I also had access to my favourite books, with so many worlds to explore.

Contemporary school libraries are a place for everybody, but they need to be resourced and supported to be able to act as a refuge for students. They are exciting and dynamic environments that are constantly changing in order to be responsive to evolving demands within and beyond the school community, often catering to increasingly diverse client needs with limited resources. For example, the most recent Softlink survey in the UK found that only 46% of respondents felt that their library had adequate resourcing in relation to staffing and budget (Softlink, 2021). This book is interested in how these institutions and their staff uphold and develop their traditional role as supports of literacy learning and engagement, and meet the growing demand for student wellbeing affordances, given the myriad challenges faced by schools and young people today. It will illustrate how these concerns of reading and wellbeing may be closely interrelated, drawing on recent research, and highlight how library professionals may position themselves as leaders of literacy engagement and student wellbeing within their schools.

Why literacy?

Student literacy is a perennial concern in schools and across nations, with rhetoric around slides and gains in student achievement resembling commentary on a very high-stakes version of the board game *Snakes and Ladders*. As measurement and accountability have been continually ramped up at both individual student and school levels – as seen in the increasing use of high-stakes literacy testing regimes and problematic acceptance of student scores on such tests as an unqualified proxy for student literacy performance (Cumming et al., 2019) – debates about literacy and how it can best be improved are never far from media headlines.

There is great pressure on many schools and their educators to deliver demonstrable improvement in their students' literacy performance, and in recent times, there have been growing concerns about student literacy, given its relationship with student outcomes and opportunities both within and beyond formal schooling (as reviewed in Merga, 2018). While large-scale assessments can provide insights into student learning, identifying gaps that need greater attention (Karakolidis et al., 2021), where schools narrow their focus to 'teach to the test', this further restricts curricular focus (e.g. Polesel et al., 2014; Thompson & Harbaugh, 2013). When this happens, attention to perceived peripheral concerns such as fostering students' reading for pleasure (RfP) may be minimal, potentially leaving students with limited reading models and a notion of reading as something done for the purposes of testing (Merga, 2016). Where the focus is on academic performance and testing, but the contribution of regular reading to literacy performance is poorly understood, independent reading may even be 'thought to substitute away from academic learning' (Wang et al., 2020, p. 9). School libraries can also play an important role in preventing pleasure from being divorced from students' reading experiences, as I explore in this book.

Concerns about student literacy and reading opportunities may be magnified by the impact of the COVID-19 pandemic. The pandemic and associated school closures have posed a further barrier to student literacy attainment, with projections of significant learning loss (Azevedo et al., 2020; Kuhfeld et al., 2020), though in some areas it may have enhanced the appeal of reading as a recreational activity (Sun et al., 2021). We also know that COVID-19 related learning interruptions do not impact equally on all students, further exacerbating already existing inequities in performance (Clinton, 2020). This means that the role of the library in supporting literacy and reading may be more important now than ever.

However, while research links library access to student literacy performance (Francis et al., 2010; Hughes et al., 2014; Lonsdale, 2003), and reading engagement (Mat Roni & Merga, 2019), the role of the library in fostering both literacy skills and positive attitudes towards reading may be poorly understood by school leadership and the broader community (Merga, 2019a). Further research is also needed to establish irrefutable causal links, particularly in contexts beyond the US. However, as we've explored previously, current circumstances may pose a significant challenge to this research objective (Merga et al., 2021). Furthermore, while there has been an increasing focus in recent times on the relationship between student literacy engagement and literacy learning, schools may not realise the breadth and value of the role of school library professionals in fostering reading engagement in particular (Merga, 2019b).

Reading + literacy + wellbeing

Students are much more than empty vessels to be filled with knowledge by schools. They are diverse and unique young people who need to have their social, cultural and emotional needs recognised and supported in their learning experiences. In this vein, consideration of the need to promote student wellbeing is attracting more attention in recent times, with fostering student wellbeing increasingly a key aspect of the school role. Bladek (2021) suggests that student wellbeing 'is not simply the absence of physical and mental health conditions, but a multidimensional concept that encompasses physical, social, emotional, intellectual, spiritual, and environmental aspects' (p. 3). While student wellbeing may be viewed as 'a sustainable state of positive mood and attitude, resilience, and satisfaction with self, relationships and experiences at school' (Australian Catholic University, 2008, p. 5), ideally, wellbeing initiatives undertaken at school will also have far-reaching impacts beyond the school experience.

Developing and maintaining student wellbeing is a complex and multifactorial task, as it can be shaped by a wide range of factors both intrinsic and extrinsic to students as individuals. Fortunately, the range of possible influences includes social influences such as parents, peers and school library professionals (Merga, 2020), so it is possible for you to make a valuable difference to student wellbeing. As I have explored previously in my review of the literature on how school libraries can support student wellbeing, while further research is needed in this space, to date we have 'promising findings on how school libraries operate as safe spaces for young people; promote and resource mental health and wellbeing initiatives; and, support and promote bibliotherapeutic practices and reading for pleasure' (p. 670).

Ideally, initiatives focusing on student wellbeing should seek to foster long-term benefits for students, equipping them with resources and dispositions that can have an ongoing protective effect, and fostering avid reading behaviours in young people can be a beneficial approach. Keen readers are probably already aware of the relationship between reading, literacy and wellbeing. Those of us who have been readers since a young age have enjoyed the advantage of being able to express ourselves clearly and concisely at school while others were still struggling with these skills. We have also been able to access and understand complex information through our reading skills, and our ability to speak effectively in public situations is enhanced by the broad vocabulary that we can draw from in order to express ourselves. But for many of us, reading is also a habit that brings enjoyment, respite and peace (Merga, 2017). It is an activity that can provide an escape from the challenges of the real world, the opportunity to live myriad lives and travel through time and learn from the experiences and imaginations of others.

The relationship between reading, literacy and wellbeing can also be seen in the research, and it probably extends beyond what you may have considered. For example, did you know that RfP may be associated with benefits for health-related behaviours (Mak & Fancourt, 2020a)? Furthermore, daily RfP at age seven has also been related to better prosocial behaviour and lower levels of hyperactivity and attention issues at age 11 (Mak & Fancourt, 2020b), highlighting the role of books and reading in supporting cognitive stamina, concentration and attention. It will come as no surprise to readers that RfP has been related to reduced psychological distress in college students (Levine et al., 2020), and Clark and Teravainen-Goff (2018) found that reading attitudes can be predictors of mental wellbeing. Avid readers have described using reading to regulate their emotions as a pleasurable escape (Merga, 2017), with young readers in TikTok's #Booktok community celebrating reading as affording a deeply immersive removal from the stressors of daily life (Merga, 2021).

The COVID-19 pandemic has also impacted on student wellbeing as it has brought new stressors into their lives (Bansak & Starr, 2021), highlighting the need for a greater understanding of the links between reading, literacy and wellbeing that could potentially help students cope with current and emerging challenges. It is important to note that librarians have taken considerable measures to ensure that student access to reading materials has been available during the challenges of school closures in the COVID-19 pandemic. Dearnaley (2020) gathered vignettes from school library staff in Australia that show diverse and flexible approaches to this problem, including the following from a teacher librarian in the Australian Capital Territory:

> Ensuring all families know how to access our digital collection and other wonderful resources such as the Story Box Library. Supporting staff as they learn new technology and providing one-on-one onsite and digital tutorials. Ensuring that any student who came in to collect a laptop or iPad also walked out with an armful of books. Recording staff reading picture books to share with families. Navigating the copyright information to ensure that there are no breaches during this time. Created a school library website. Have made sure all families can access our digital collection. (p. 24)

As such, school library professionals can play a very important role in supporting children and their families through challenging times.

Why this book?

The purpose of this book is to draw on a robust research base to illustrate how contemporary school libraries can support students' literacy and wellbeing to:

- support school library professionals to build a case for the importance of their role and facility, and
- audit their current offerings and adjust or extend them where applicable, based on what we know about best practice as outlined in this book.

School library professionals reading this book will hopefully feel like they are being furnished with ideas that they can use to support their advocacy and agility in strategically drawing on new research to continue to update what they do. However, as well as adding to your toolkit, the book should help you to effectively make visible what you *already* do, and how this offers benefit within your school community. While I can only deal with a relatively limited array of school library related interests in a single book, I do believe that the issues and possibilities raised here have relevance for both primary and secondary school libraries, and I report on recent research findings from both contexts, including insights that have never been shared previously.

The bulk of the research in the school library space is concentrated on the US (Everhart, 2018), meaning that school library professionals from outside this context may struggle to connect with these findings. I have endeavoured to draw on a broad base that includes – but is not concentrated on – US-based research for inclusion in this book. I urge library researchers based in the US to consider the body of research from beyond their nation; they can also learn from the mistakes and innovations of researchers and practitioners from other contexts. Internationality in school library research needs to be intentional, and the dominance of the US in the research literature means that 'research from beyond dominant geographic contexts is largely excluded from international research discourse', and 'this likely extends to limited thematic, methodological, and epistemological possibilities' (Mason et al., 2021, p. 11). To this end, this book reports on findings from a wide range of nations, such as China and Croatia, and Singapore and Sweden, in the hope that it can deliver a richness of insights into school libraries as supports of student literacy and wellbeing. I have also used online translation functions in order to include some research works published in languages that I am not proficient in, and I hope to greatly expand the number of non-English works I draw upon going forward. I have become increasingly aware that my adherence to using English-only academic literature because of my own linguistic limitations and ability to determine source credibility is inherently exclusionary, leading to the further privileging of English as *lingua franca* to the disadvantage of non-English speaking academics (Collyer, 2018).

Given the complexity of the subjects I explore, there is a good chance that the reader will want to do some further investigation in the areas of most interest to them. I recommend that you use the reference lists at the end of each chapter as a starting point to direct this further reading.

Finally, I've taken on the task of writing this book to ensure that the large volume of recent research I've conducted in school libraries finds its professional audience, so that it can support the role of school librarians throughout the world. Teresa Cremin's (2021) evocative reflection on her journey as a reader and reading researcher really resonated with me; she notes that 'when I am reading, researching, talking or writing about reading for pleasure – that volitional act of engagement with texts which offers me such satisfaction – I feel most "at home" as an educator, a researcher and a human' (para. 3). I also get a lot of joy out of having a highly pragmatic purpose in order to support the real and immediate needs of school library professionals for advocacy materials that can establish recognisable credibility by drawing on reputable and current research. As such, I hope this book is useful for you.

References

Australian Catholic University. (2008). Scoping study into approaches to student wellbeing. https://docs.education.gov.au/system/files/doc/other/appendix_1_literature_review.pdf

Azevedo, J. P., Hasan, A., Goldemberg, D., Iqbal, S. A., & Geven, K. (2020). *Simulating the potential impacts of COVID-19 school closures on schooling and learning outcomes: A set of global estimates*. The World Bank.

Bansak, C., & Starr, M. (2021). Covid-19 shocks to education supply: How 200,000 US households dealt with the sudden shift to distance learning. *Review of Economics of the Household*, 19(1), 63–90.

Bladek, M. (2021). Student well-being matters: Academic library support for the whole student. *The Journal of Academic Librarianship*, 47(3), e102349.

Clark, C., & Teravainen-Goff, A. (2018). *Mental wellbeing, reading and writing: How children and young people's mental wellbeing is related to their reading and writing experiences*. National Literacy Trust.

Collyer, F. M. (2018). Global patterns in the publishing of academic knowledge: Global North, Global South. *Current Sociology*, 66(1), 56–73.

Clinton, J. (2020). *Supporting vulnerable children in the face of a pandemic*. Centre for Program Evaluation, Melbourne Graduate School of Education, University of Melbourne.

Cremin, T. (2021). Reflecting on my journey as a reader and a reading researcher. In S. M. Morris, L. Rai, & K. Littleton. *Voices of Practice*. PressBooks (online). https://voicesofpractice.pressbooks.com/chapter/reflecting-on-my-journey-as-a-reader-and-a-reading-researcher

Cumming, J. J., Van Der Kleij, F. M., & Adie, L. (2019). Contesting educational assessment policies in Australia. *Journal of Education Policy*, 34(6), 836–857.

Dearnaley, M. (2020). A snapshot of a school library during Covid-19: Students need school libraries campaign. *Access*, 34(2), 22–25.

Everhart, N. (2018). Making the case for diversity in school library research. *School Libraries Worldwide*, 24(2), i–iv.

Francis, B. H., Lance, K. C., & Lietzau, Z. (2010). *School librarians continue to help students achieve standards: The third Colorado study. Closer Look Report*. Colorado State Library, Library Research Service.

Hughes, H., Bozorgian, H., & Allan, C. (2014). School libraries, teacher-librarians and student outcomes: Presenting and using the evidence. *School Libraries Worldwide*, 20(1), 29–50.

Karakolidis, A., Duggan, A., Shiel, G., & Kiniry, J. (2021). Educational inequality in primary schools in Ireland in the early years of the National Literacy and Numeracy Strategy: An analysis of National Assessment data. *Irish Journal of Education*, 44(1), 1–24.

Kuhfeld, M., Soland, J., Tarasawa, B., Johnson, A., Ruzek, E., & Liu, J. (2020). Projecting the potential impact of COVID-19 school closures on academic achievement. *Educational Researcher, 49*(8), 549–565.

Levine, S. L., Cherrier, S., Holding, A.C., & Koestner, R. (2020). For the love of reading: Recreational reading reduces psychological distress in college students and autonomous motivation is the key. *Journal of American College Health.* https://doi.org/10.1080/07448481.2020.1728280

Lonsdale, M. (2003). *Impact of school libraries on student achievement: A review of the research.* Australian Council of Educational Research.

Mak, H. W., & Fancourt, D. (2020a). Reading for pleasure in childhood and adolescent healthy behaviours: Longitudinal associations using the Millennium Cohort Study. *Preventive Medicine, 130,* e105889.

Mak, H. W., & Fancourt, D. (2020b). Longitudinal associations between reading for pleasure and child maladjustment: Results from a propensity score matching analysis. *Social Science & Medicine, 253,* e112971.

Mason, S., Merga, M. K., Canché, M. S. G., & Roni, S. M. (2021). The internationality of published higher education scholarship: How do the 'top' journals compare? *Journal of Informetrics, 15*(2), https://doi.org/10.1016/j.joi.2021.101155

Mat Roni, S., & Merga, M. K. (2019). Using an artificial neural network to explore the influence of extrinsic and intrinsic variables on children's reading frequency and attitudes. *Australian Journal of Education, 63*(3), 270–291.

Merga, M. K. (2016). 'I don't know if she likes reading': Are teachers perceived to be keen readers, and how is this determined? *English in Education, 50*(3), 255–269.

Merga, M. K. (2017). What motivates avid readers to maintain a regular reading habit in adulthood? *Australian Journal of Language and Literacy, 40*(2), 146–156.

Merga, M. K. (2018). *Reading engagement for tweens and teens: What would make them read more?* ABC-CLIO/Libraries Unlimited.

Merga, M. K. (2019a). Do librarians feel that their profession is valued in contemporary schools? *Journal of the Australian Library and Information Association, 68*(1), 18–37.

Merga, M. K. (2019b). *Librarians in schools as literacy educators.* Palgrave Macmillan.

Merga, M. (2020). How can school libraries support student wellbeing? Evidence and implications for further research. *Journal of Library Administration, 60*(6), 660–673.

Merga, M. K. (2021). How can TikTok inform readers' advisory services for young people? *Library & Information Science Research.* https://doi.org/10.1016/j.lisr.2021.101091

Merga, M. K., Mat Roni, S., Loh, C., & Malpique, A. (2021). Revisiting collaboration within and beyond the school library: New ways of measuring effectiveness. *Journal of Library Administration. 61*(3), 332–346.

Polesel, J., Rice, S., & Dulfer, N. (2014). The impact of high-stakes testing on curriculum and pedagogy: A teacher perspective from Australia. Journal of Education Policy, *29*(5), 640–657.

Softlink. (2021). *2020 School Library Survey*. https://www.softlinkint.com/assets/img/content/2020_School_Library_Survey_United_Kingdom_-_Report.pdf

Sun, B., Loh, C. E., & Nie, Y. (2021). The COVID-19 school closure effect on students' print and digital leisure reading. *Computers and Education Open*, e100033.

Thompson, G., & Harbaugh, A. G. (2013). A preliminary analysis of teacher perceptions of the effects of NAPLAN on pedagogy and curriculum. *Australian Educational Researcher, 40*(3), 299–314.

Wang, H., Guan, H., Yi, H., Seevak, E., Manheim, R., Boswell, M., & Kotb, S. (2020). Independent reading in rural China's elementary schools: A mixed-methods analysis. *International Journal of Educational Development, 78*, e102241.ibrarians do

1

What Do School Library Professionals Contribute to Student Learning and Support? A Focus on Australia and the UK

What do school library professionals contribute to student learning and support? It will come as no surprise to you that the answer is a lot!

This is the longest chapter in the book, simply because school library professionals make a substantial and multifaceted contribution to student learning and support, but we need to start here and be expansive. The book is interested in the role of school libraries and their professional staff in supporting literacy and wellbeing, so it is important that these specific aspects of the role of school library professionals are considered within this broader frame of their role. Furthermore, school libraries and their staff are expected to contribute to student learning in contemporary schools, though the relationship between libraries and student achievement may not be well understood, so this chapter can also be used by school library professionals seeking to articulate some of the diverse facets of their role, as I will explore further in this chapter.

Associations between school libraries and student achievement have been extensively explored over time (Farmer, 2006; Lance & Kachel, 2018; Merga, 2019). While we can always do with more and higher quality research from diverse contexts (Stefl-Mabry et al., 2019), the evidence we have suggests that school libraries and their professional staff can make an important difference in the lives of young students. Although studies have often focused on the impact of libraries and library access on student performance in literacy testing (Francis et al., 2010; Hughes et al., 2014), this is only part of the whole picture around what libraries have to offer. This chapter takes a close look at the specific roles of teacher librarians in Australia and school librarians in the UK, exploring what they specifically do to enhance student learning, relating these practices to the research we already have around best practice and student learning.

Teacher librarian and school librarian: What is the difference?

First, I need to be clear that I do not conflate the roles teacher librarian and school librarian, even though I use the term *school library professional* commonly in this book to refer to both. Teacher librarians in Australia and school librarians in the UK obviously work in different national contexts and schooling systems, with different curricular and regulatory constraints, and they may have different professional standards and requirements.

In Australia, teacher librarians are conceptualised as follows.

> A qualified teacher librarian is defined as a person who holds recognised teaching qualifications and qualifications in librarianship, defined as eligibility for professional membership for the Australian Library and Information Association (ALIA).
>
> Within the broad fields of education and librarianship, teacher librarians are uniquely qualified. This is valuable because curriculum knowledge and pedagogy are combined with library and information management knowledge and skills.
>
> Teacher librarians support and implement the vision of their school communities through advocating and building effective library and information services and programs that contribute to the development of lifelong learners.
>
> (Australian School Library Association (ASLA), 2019, paras. 1–3)

In my experience with the ASLA, I have seen that Australian teacher librarians are very protective of their titles, as they hold tertiary qualifications in both education and librarianship. In my observation, teacher librarians are not protective of their titles in order to feel superior or promote division and exclusivity; rather, they have justifiable concerns that their roles will be replaced by staff who often have qualifications in neither area, but who are cheaper to employ due to remuneration structures in Australian schooling systems. For example, a recent study focused on South Australia found that while '94% of schools have someone to manage the library collection and to select resources', in only '23% of schools the person in this role is a qualified teacher librarian' (Dix et al., 2020), and Erickson (2019) reported on a small sample of Canadian paraprofessionals managing their school libraries. Teacher librarians are devalued despite the fact that they 'have the capacity to provide tailored lessons and classroom support for their school communities, saving time and potentially decreasing workloads for classroom teachers' (Willis, 2020, p. 15). I explore the issue of deprofessionalisation further in Chapter 7.

The School Library Association (SLA) supports and advocates for school library professionals in the UK, and they also provide some information around expectations of the role. Their website states that 'the School Library Association believes that the School Librarian/Library Manager has an essential and unique specialist role to play in supporting pupils' learning and their development into effective, independent learners and readers' (SLA, n.d.-a, para. 1). Furthermore, it contends that the School Librarian should be:

- a partner with teaching staff in the education process
- a partner in supporting individual learning behaviours
- an acknowledged expert in resource and information provision and management
- a leader and partner with teaching staff in the collaborative design and implementation of information literacy programmes throughout the school
- a leader in creating and developing a climate to promote and support reading for pleasure across the school
- an acknowledged partner with all departments to effectively support and resource each key stage
- a partner in out of hours learning.

(SLA, n.d.-a, para. 2)

Their website also contains a job description for the primary school librarian role, which details its core purpose, specific responsibilities and person-specific criteria (SLA, n.d.-b).

In the UK, the Chartered Institute of Library and Information Professionals (CILIP) is the library and information association involved with librarians' professional registration. On their webpage on school librarians, CILIP states that 'the school library or learning centre will house books and journals alongside internet access and audio-visual materials and the librarian is responsible for promoting the use of the service and engaging with teaching and management staff to ensure this'. Qualifications and capacities are also mentioned, as they note that 'an accredited degree or postgraduate qualification in library and information science is usually required and for some roles a teaching qualification is also beneficial', and that 'many employers also look for CILIP Chartership or a willingness to work towards Chartership'. Furthermore,

> You'll need to be adept at teaching information literacy skills and encouraging and assessing reader development through activities like shadowing the Carnegie Medal for children's and young people's fiction. Sometimes the librarian is also responsible for the virtual learning environment.
>
> (CILIP, n.d., para. 2)

Interestingly, while the UK school librarian is expected to be 'adept at teaching', the limited available research suggests that it is rare for them to be a qualified teacher (Streatfield et al., 2011). Furthermore, having a teaching qualification as well as a qualification in librarianship may not necessarily be deemed desirable by UK school librarians.

For example, a small study by Brackenbury and Willett (2011) found that school librarians were typically viewed as support staff, with respondents disappointed to be viewed in this light 'when they had either worked hard for academic qualifications in order to be able to call themselves a librarian or had contributed to the teaching and learning outcomes of the school by teaching "library lessons"' (p. 241). In response,

> interviewees were asked whether the situation would improve if librarians received dual training, and came with teaching qualifications, as well as library qualifications. It was felt that this idea might help more librarians to be considered as teaching staff, which was evidently an issue for many of the librarian interviewees, but the responses to this suggestion were very mixed. For example, one interviewee suggested that if somebody had a teaching qualification then they would immediately be given additional teaching duties at the expense of their library responsibilities; and another suggested that having two qualifications would lead to substantially enhanced salary expectations (with the possible implication that these would not be met). (p. 242)

While a larger scale study is needed to explore whether these views hold broader generalisability, given the challenges faced by Australian teacher librarians, these concerns raised by UK-based school librarians relating to workload allocation and remuneration seem justified. As I explore further in this chapter, it could still be beneficial for a formal education qualification to be made part of the UK workforce education norms, but that is not as simple a contention as one might imagine, given the Australian experience (as explored further in Chapter 7).

What teacher librarians do

While professional associations produce valuable and comprehensive documents on the scope of teacher librarian roles, and what proficiency looks like across the dimensions of the role (e.g. ASLA, 2014), until recently, little was known about what schools actually expect from their teacher librarians in Australia, and school librarians in the UK. In 2020, I undertook a comprehensive analysis of job description documents or forms (that I will refer to hereafter as JDFs) from a corpus of current JDFs. For information on the methods I used, please refer to the explanation of the 2020–2021 Library Workforce Project in Appendix 1 of this book.

I was inspired to undertake this research when I spoke with teacher librarians in 30 schools as part of the 2018 Teacher Librarians as Australian Literature Advocates in Schools (TLALAS) project. In our discussions around what teacher librarians do in their daily practice, it became very clear to me that the role was incredibly complex, and I felt this was far more so than commonly recognised by those outside the library. What was interesting was that in many cases, the teacher librarian I was interviewing said that they themselves were unaware of how much they were doing, and how diverse the role was, until they heard themselves articulating this in our interview. Clearly, many school library professionals are just getting on with enacting really complex roles without time to weigh and consider the extent and complexity of what they are offering their schools.

I was convinced that in order to value the role, we need to understand how it is expressed in diverse schooling contexts. With access to schools limited in 2020 and complicated by school closures due to the COVID-19 pandemic, I could not travel to schools and observe what was being done in libraries. Therefore, collecting data about the expected role of these library professionals from JDFs that were designed by schools and made freely available online appeared to be a pragmatic starting point, given the constraints in place at that time.

As per Table 1 on the following pages, I reported on the role requirements and characteristics of the Australian teacher librarian that occurred frequently in the documents (in at least 25% of them) as I wanted to be able to show what teacher librarians are *typically* expected to do. Of course, this means that many common roles and expectations were excluded (Merga, 2020b). Perhaps unsurprisingly, the only role requirement or characteristic to be featured across all documents in the 40-document corpus was 'teaching and facilitating learning', highlighting that schools employing teacher librarians were looking for *educators* first and foremost. The text examples in the table are taken from the documents so that the reader can see an example of how this aspect looked in one of the original documents. These text examples may have been lightly edited where necessary for readability without impacting on meaning (Merga, 2020b).

Clearly, the role of teacher librarian involves mastery over a vast array of skills, knowledge and capabilities.

Table 1 *Role requirements and characteristics of the Australian teacher librarian*

Aspect	Aspect count	Aspect scope	Text example
Teaching and facilitating learning	40	Plan for teaching. Use a variety of teaching strategies. Teach in library areas (e.g. literature, literacy, information literacy, digital citizenship) and core curriculum areas (e.g. English). Teach both groups and individuals.	'Employ a variety of teaching strategies to effectively implement the curriculum and actively engage students in the learning process. Participate in the preparation and maintenance of teaching resources and learning materials. Provide regular, timely and positive feedback to each student on their progress'.
Collaboration and teamwork	37	Assist staff with resourcing, and plan units of work with colleagues. Incorporate information literacy and literacy skills into units of work. Collaborate to create and resource reading programmes. Work as part of a team with other library staff. Model strong collaborative skills for the learning of colleagues.	'A successful teacher librarian is an enabler, collaborating with and supporting teachers to incorporate information literacy, literature, print and digital resources in curriculum delivery'.
Collection and resource building and provision	36	Purchase resources and texts for the library that are responsive to teacher and student needs and interests. Review and weed the collection to ensure materials available retain relevance and appeal. Establish plans and processes for the development and resourcing of the library collection over time. Develop resources to create quality learning experiences for students. Encourage all library users to participate in collection development. Provide staff with quality resources to support teaching. Facilitate external access to library resources through development of online library portals and catalogues. Enable effective access to and use of digital resources.	'Liaise with subject coordinators regarding the purchase of resources for the library. Approve orders for books and/or other resources. Obtain resources in areas where they are lacking'.
Literacy education	36	Plan and facilitate contemporary student-centred reading programmes. Link literary texts with curriculum units where appropriate. Collaborate with other teaching staff to promote literacy and literature. Provide training and information for staff and parents in reading, literacy and literature.	'Promote an understanding of the essential relationship between reading ability and academic success. Promote and foster an environment where students are engaged in reading, viewing, listening and creating for understanding and enjoyment.

Continued

Table 1 *Continued*

Aspect	Aspect count	Aspect scope	Text example
Literacy education (continued)		Support teachers to enhance student literacy skills. Develop strategies to foster a love of reading and literature for leisure. Promote a diverse range of text types and themes, from varied cultural perspectives. Conduct book talks, make recommendations and guide students' recreational reading choices. Promote the benefits of regular reading for academic performance. Plan, promote and conduct displays and events to encourage reading. Promote literature to staff. Draw on a range of resources to make informed choices about collection development and publicise and promote new acquisitions. Possess an extensive knowledge of children's literature across a breadth of genres. Read junior and young adult fiction acquisitions. Foster and maintain a school culture that promotes reading and literature. Provide an environment conducive to reading. Model reading engagement and enjoyment.	Provide an environment that encourages a habit and love of reading and of sharing children's literature . . . (Have) an extensive literature repertoire and knowledge of how to promote and foster reading. (Have) extensive knowledge of children's literacy. (Be) passionate about developing a love of reading in students'.
Support information skills in staff and students	36	Perform background curation of sources for research classes and create research guides. Teach information skills such as search strategies, note taking, referencing and bibliography. Contribute to parent information literacy skills sessions. Teach students critical information literacy skills such as evaluating information and sources. Plan and deliver training and support in inquiry-based learning. Support the delivery of quality online information services. Support the Information and Communication Technology (ICT) staff with troubleshooting. Promote understanding and compliance around issues of academic integrity and plagiarism, copyright and digital rights management, research ethics and online safety. Develop resources to support information skills in staff and students. Provide dyadic assistance with student searching.	'You will also guide students to become information literate individuals through the development and facilitation of the information literacy scope and sequence that fosters a love of inquiry. Plan and deliver an information literacy program across the Kindergarten to Year 6 curriculum and actively engage with the Junior School to develop, organise and manage information resources and identify the user needs or areas of potential collaboration. Using Kindergarten to Year 6 Scope and Sequence and the information literacy scope and sequence as a guide, develop the Library collection and promote independent thought'.

Continued

Table 1 Continued

Aspect	Aspect count	Aspect scope	Text example
Library and learning environment	34	Create and maintain a library learning environment that is friendly, well-ordered, welcoming, flexible, productive, vibrant, stimulating, inclusive, positive and safe. Provide displays that make the space a showcase for students' learning achievements. Provide a space that accommodates students with diverse needs and interests.	'Engage and challenge learners within a supportive, information-rich learning environment. Creating a stimulating and helpful environment for students, including showcasing student learning achievements. Provide and develop flexible learning spaces that accommodate different uses and needs; class presentations, group work, teaching areas, leisure reading. Maintain the Library as a welcoming, dynamic, inclusive and engaging learning environment'.
Communication and interpersonal skills	32	Communicate effectively and professionally with colleagues, students and parents. Establish and maintain effective lines of communication and follow up processes that support the information needs of colleagues, parents and students. Demonstrate a high level of written and verbal communication skills and interpersonal skills.	'Establish and maintain effective lines of communication and follow up processes that support the information needs of colleagues, parents and students'.
Administration and day-to-day tasks	31	Attend and organise meetings. Create and manage budgets. Be actively involved in committees. Shelve books and perform stocktake. Assist students with borrowing, reservations, and reference and resourcing queries. Support cataloguing, acquisitions and the building of digital content. Keep accurate and timely records. Assist student printing, photocopying and scanning inquiries. Open and close the library as required.	'Undertake required administrative tasks including the organisation of meetings and learning teams, program budgeting, resourcing, correspondence, learning area-based competitions and enrichment opportunities, allotment consultation, records and back up and supervision of support staff where relevant'.
Events and displays	31	Create dynamic visual displays in the library. Organise special events and activities that relate to and support student learning. Promote events and displays within the school and community as applicable.	'Maintain and create displays promoting children's literature, including new and older publications, current events, series and themes in literature. Facilitate participation in the YABBA Awards. Arrange both incursions and excursions for authors, illustrators and other speakers to broaden students' knowledge of literature'.

Continued

Table 1 Continued

Aspect	Aspect count	Aspect scope	Text example
Delegated and unspecified responsibilities	29	Perform unspecified duties at the request of school leadership.	'Other duties may be required, at the direction of the Head of Information Services and/or Headmaster. From time to time it may be necessary to modify this role statement to meet the needs of the school. Any proposed changes will be discussed with the relevant member of staff'.
Curriculum development and knowledge	28	Be actively involved in school-based curriculum design, implementation and support. Have strong knowledge of the state/territory curriculum. Remain abreast of curriculum developments. Contribute to curriculum evaluation.	'Teaching staff will exhibit an ability to plan and manage the learning process by developing and creating innovative curriculum programs that meet the personal, social, emotional, physical, mental and spiritual needs of their students'.
Professional development of self and others	28	Develop knowledge through professional reading, communication with colleagues and attendance at approved professional development activities. Present at and/or attend conferences. Hold active membership of professional associations. Provide ongoing professional development for staff in areas such as literacy, information literacy and literature. Promote educational developments, disseminate curriculum information and facilitate the incorporation of new ideas. Support the establishment of a vibrant professional learning community. Upgrade formal professional qualifications where required. Maintain professional accreditation with recognised professional associations. Be subject to performance appraisals.	'Participate in, and contribute to, training and professional development of staff and students in various facets of library operation'.

Continued

Table 1 Continued

Aspect	Aspect count	Aspect scope	Text example
Qualifications, memberships and registrations	28	Hold qualifications in teacher librarianship and be registered to teach. Be eligible for membership of Australian Library and Information Association (ALIA). Hold a current Working with Children Check and First Aid accreditation. Undertake a Police Check. Show evidence of current mandatory reporting training.	'Be a qualified Teacher Librarian or working towards this qualification with experience in education and have or working towards the appropriate qualifications recognized by ALIA (Australian Library and Information Association). Have a current Working With Children's Check. Be registered with the Teacher Registration Board of Western Australia (TRBWA)'.
Support the school ethos	28	Perform formal and informal pastoral care roles as required. Support the religious ideology of the school. Participate in religious rituals, retreats and spirituality programmes. Support students' spiritual and personal development.	'A willingness to actively support the Christian ethos of the school and to respect the rights, dignity and worth of all members of the school community'.
Library systems skills and management	24	Manage, establish and monitor the physical and ICT systems in the library. Develop information systems and services responsive to student and teacher needs. Have a strong knowledge of library management systems.	'To coordinate library staff (teaching and education support) and effectively manage the resources, borrowing system and facility of the Library'.
Provide ICT support for staff and students	24	Imbed ICT across the curriculum. Teach ICT skills, and provide ICT support. Train staff in ICT use. Remain knowledgeable of developments in digital information technologies. Be proficient in the use of assistive technologies for inclusive education.	'Be proactive in responding to users' changing needs and effectively manage users' expectations. Provide training and assistance to students and staff in the effective use of systems and information retrieval processes'.
Co-curricular and extracurricular responsibilities	23	Supervise and provide coaching or supportive input in sporting or cultural co-curricular activities. Be available outside standard school hours, including holiday periods, to support students. Attend school functions, social activities, meetings and parent/teacher nights. Make presentations when necessary. Initiate and support the development of new initiatives such as book clubs.	'Teaching staff are expected to participate in a range of duties beyond classroom responsibilities. These duties may include, but are not limited to, participation in relevant meetings and professional learning activities, playground duties and co-curricular duties and will involve application of discipline, participation in relevant meetings and professional learning activities, playground duties and co-curricular duties and

Continued

Table 1 *Continued*

Aspect	Aspect count	Aspect scope	Text example
Co-curricular and extracurricular responsibilities (Continued)			will involve application of discipline, participation in the College's program for spiritual and pastoral care and various other duties. Some of the duties will need to be undertaken at times other than during the school day including on weekends'.
Child safety and wellbeing	22	Administer First Aid as required. Show care for student welfare and develop supportive relationships with them. Promote students' physical, emotional and mental wellbeing. Show understanding of and commitment to legal and moral obligations relating to child safety. Hold current First Aid accreditation. Complete training in and adhere to mandatory reporting requirements.	'Safeguard and promote the safety, welfare and wellbeing of children and young people. Providing First Aid assistance as required'.
Personal ICT skills	22	Have advanced ICT skills. Have good understanding of learning technologies and their application to enhance learning. Be committed to continual development of ICT skills. Build knowledge in new and emerging technologies.	'Remain up to date and use a variety of traditional and emerging technologies to deliver a range of innovative library services and programs'.
Adhere to and implement policies	21	Implement a range of school specific policies on discipline, uniform, behaviour, study, safety and attendance. Adhere to broader state policies and legislation.	'Knowing and implementing the College Strategic Plan, school policies and other legislative requirements including those that ensure child safety. Using the (School) Transformation Model in order to facilitate change management initiatives for the betterment of the College'.
Collaboration and communication with parents and community	19	Encourage parental involvement with the school. Build productive partnerships and a strong connection with the school community. Liaise and communicate with parents as primary stakeholders in their child's education. Engage parents and community members as library volunteers.	'The Teacher-Librarian/Literacy Specialist will build a co-operative partnership with parents, teachers, students and the (School) community in working towards the achievement of the (school's) aims . . . Encouraging the appropriate involvement of parents and other community members in the life of the (School)'.

Continued

Table 1 Continued

Aspect	Aspect count	Aspect scope	Text example
Document and develop policies, plans and procedures	18	Develop, document and evaluate library policies, goals and objectives in line with the school's strategic goals. Develop short-term and long-term strategic and operational plans for the library learning environment. Organise and implement efficient procedures for the delivery of library services and resource selection. Amend policies, plans and procedures as required in response to changing needs.	'Contribute to the development of library policy, procedures and processes and provide recommendations to the Library Manager for change when appropriate'.
Meet diverse student needs	18	Cater to diverse student skills, abilities, knowledge and interests. Support students with special needs. Help to identify students needing teaching adjustments.	'Plan taking into consideration the needs, interests and developmental stage of children e.g. cognitive, physical, social, emotional, language and perceptual needs as well as socio-economic, cultural and religious background of all children'.
Supervision and duty of care	18	Perform yard duties and undertake teaching and non-teaching supervisory duties. Supervise students with diverse needs or behavioural issues.	'(Provide) supervision of students during lunch times and after school until 4.30pm. (Care) pastorally for students with special or other needs who regularly spend time in the Library or need time out from the classroom'.
Resilience	17	Have capacity to deal with multiple tasks. Manage time effectively. Show flexibility and perform under pressure.	'Remain flexible in regard to rosters, desk duties, borrower services and circulation tasks. (Show) flexibility with a high degree of motivation for the role. (Have a) track record of being approachable with an empathetic work ethic. (Be) adaptable and able to work well under pressure'.

Continued

Table 1 Continued

Aspect	Aspect count	Aspect scope	Text example
Workplace health and safety (WHS)	17	Perform WHS duties as required, including evacuation drills. Adhere to and ensure that library spaces are compliant with WHS policies, plans and procedures. Promote a healthy and positive workplace culture. Report any safety issues as per policy.	'Contribute to a healthy and safe work environment for self and others and comply with all safe work policies and procedures'.
Increase the use of library	16	Develop frameworks to optimise library use. Promote library services within the school. Run engaging orientation programmes for new users. Promote library-based events and report about such activities to the school community.	'Promotion of library activities and services throughout the (School) community utilising tools such as the (School) newsletter, webpage and mobile applications'.
Student assessment and reporting	16	Have knowledge of and apply current assessment theory and processes. Use various applicable modes of assessment. Provide regular, timely, constructive and clear feedback to students and families about student performance. Provide formal reports on student progress. Meet reporting requirements as per school policy and deadlines. Provide transparent guidance around assessment criteria. Identify learner needs through assessment. Set developmentally appropriate assessments.	'Use a variety of relevant and appropriate assessment and evaluation techniques to regularly assess student progress. Provide regular, timely, and positive feedback to each student on their progress. Provide formal, interim, and semester reports to parents and students that conform to the (School) Reporting Style Guide'.
Engage students in learning	15	Build relationships with students drawing on current teaching and learning practices.	'Actively engages students in the planning and learning process, perceiving that learning is an active and collaborative venture, both between the teacher and students. Considers the students' own experience to be a fundamental and especially valuable resource'.

Continued

Table 1 Continued

Aspect	Aspect count	Aspect scope	Text example
Experience	15	Have previous experience as a teacher librarian working in a school library. Have experience working with the Australian Curriculum and state/territory specific curriculum requirements. Have previous experience demonstrating leadership and collaboration. Have experience in a primary/secondary education setting. Have experience working with a particular sex (single-sex schools). Have experience with managing physical and digital collections. Have experience supporting inquiry-based learning.	'Demonstrated experience in leading a library/resource centre is desirable, including supervision and development of staff, systems management and resource management. Experience working successfully and collaboratively with other team members'.
Leadership	15	Contribute to the broader curriculum leadership of the school. Model strong and effective leadership practices.	'The Teacher Librarian will provide leadership in relation to the successful operations of the library, its services to the (School) community and management of an effective library team'.
Staff leadership and co-ordination	15	Co-ordinate the roles and duties of library staff and volunteers.	'Provide guidance and support to library staff to ensure that the day-to-day administration of the school information centre is efficient and that systems, resources and equipment are well maintained'.
Data collection, management and reporting	14	Evaluate library performance by collecting and analysing performance data to inform planning. Monitor and report on student borrowing patterns. Report on the library's support for teaching and learning, highlighting significant developments and identifying future needs. Ensure that confidential information is handled appropriately.	'Measure library resources, facilities, programs and services against current policies, standards document and benchmarks'.

Continued

Table 1 *Continued*

Aspect	Aspect count	Aspect scope	Text example
Behaviour management	13	Set and maintain clear behavioural expectations for students. Use appropriate behaviour management strategies to facilitate student learning and ensure student safety.	'Employ behaviour management strategies which ensure a safe, orderly and successful learning environment'.

(Adapted from Merga, 2020b).

What school librarians do

As I have already explained, teacher librarians in Australia cannot just be conflated with school librarians in the UK due to contextual and other differences. In order to understand the role of school library professionals in the UK, I collected a corpus of the same size (40 documents), which I then analysed to identify recurring roles. In order to be included, role requirements and characteristics of the UK school librarian needed to be mentioned in 40% of the sample; this difference was shaped by the word-count limitations of the journals where I published my findings.

There were many rich and interesting similarities between the UK and Australian roles. There were also some clear differences between the roles (e.g. the expected Australian emphasis on teacher librarian as educator) as well as more subtle differences, with collaboration far more likely to be expected in the Australian role. Perhaps UK school librarians are more likely to work independently or in smaller teams.

Table 2 *Role requirements and characteristics of the UK school librarian*

Aspect	Aspect count	Aspect scope	Text example
Literacy and reading supportive activities and dispositions	37	Support literature selection. Have a broad and current knowledge of literature. Promote and model reading for pleasure. Devise and support reading and literature events. Work closely with students to support reading and literacy skill development. Promote a whole-school reading culture. Implement and support reading programmes.	'Lead role in encouraging and promoting reading for pleasure throughout the school. Reading for purpose and pleasure is our aim: you will work with students and staff to ensure that students engage in challenging texts that stretch and challenge them – most importantly, they enjoy. Organise promotions and special events (e.g. author events, shadowing book awards,

Continued

Table 2 *Continued*

Aspect	Aspect count	Aspect scope	Text example
Literacy and reading supportive activities and dispositions (Continued)			World Book Day). Recruit and train student literary quiz teams. Lead or help run reading groups. Develop reading lists for each year group. Love reading and have a passion for passing this love on to others. (Have) an interest in children's and teen fiction and willingness to read widely to keep current'.
Experience	34	Required or desired experience could include demonstrable experience using library management information systems and software, working in a library, collaborating for learning, working in a school context, using ICT for learning and information retrieval and other relevant ICT applications, working with young people, providing staff and/or student training, fostering reading engagement, using specific reading support programmes or methods, management and leadership, behaviour management, budget and administration, digital copyright and licensing, constructing and promoting displays and customer service.	'Experience of working in a library, preferably in a school or college environment. Experience of utilising ICT and skills to access and retrieve information. Experience of working with young people and meeting their particular needs and requirements'.
Administration and management	33	Perform diverse administrative tasks. Keep accurate records. Maintain and manage library data systems. Perform circulation functions on the Library Management System. Manage the library budget. Attend meetings. Schedule and co-ordinate student access and activities in the library.	'To carry out efficiently the various necessary administrative functions including school requirements in relation to the proper and accurate keeping of records'.
Communication	33	Have excellent oral and written communication skills and the ability to adapt communications for a range of audiences and stakeholders. Be proficient in communication across mediums. Communicate in a professional and timely manner. Ability to understand required policies and procedures.	'Keep the Headteacher, Teaching and Learning Leader, school governors and parents informed about the needs and development of the library and information service in the school. Excellent communication skills, both oral and written, and the ability to adapt to very different audiences'.

Continued

Table 2 *Continued*

Aspect	Aspect count	Aspect scope	Text example
Relationships and interpersonal skills	33	Work well as part of a team. Foster and strengthen relationships both within and beyond the school community. Demonstrate excellent customer service skills.	'Encourage and actively promote the engagement of parents/carers in their children's learning and assist with parental events including parents' evenings. Have the ability to engage constructively with and relate to a wide range of young people and their families with diverse social and ethnic backgrounds. Demonstrate excellent interpersonal skills and solution focussed approach to professional relationships. Have the ability to consult and negotiate with external agencies to reach the best outcome for the school'.
Collection building, management and accessibility	32	Monitor the collection to ensure continued relevance and condition, making repairs and additions as required in response to school and student needs. Weed the collection as required. Take preservation measures (e.g. book covering). Consult with staff to support collection building. Source suppliers for securing quality resources. Ensure the collection is reflective of contemporary views on issues relating to diversity. Catalogue the collection and promote its easy access by staff and students. Manage interlibrary loans.	'Identifying and buying quality resources for the school library and classroom libraries to deliver the National Curriculum and primary strategies and support equality and diversity issues. Selecting resources from the Schools Library Services. In consultation, select, acquire, maintain and withdraw library stock, ensuring a balance between subject and ability levels and show an active engagement in diversity and equality issues'.
Library promotion and induction	32	Provide orientation in library services for staff and students to promote library use. Promote new and existing resources. Promote the library through internal and external social media. Liaise with stakeholders to improve the library's collection and services. Promote the library in the broader community, including meeting parents and visitors. Raise the appeal and profile of the library.	'With the library team, develop displays to promote the library's resources and services. Promote the Library online internally (e.g. School Portal) and externally on social media. Promote awareness and usage of online subscription resources among students and staff. Encourage pupils and staff in the academic research and study in the library'.

Continued

18 SCHOOL LIBRARIES SUPPORTING LITERACY AND WELLBEING

Table 2 Continued

Aspect	Aspect count	Aspect scope	Text example
Undertake professional development	31	Attend training sessions to enhance knowledge and skills and maintain compliance with policies and procedures. Keep abreast of developments in technology, professional practice and educational research relevant to the school library. Maintain productive memberships in professional associations. Show keen commitment to ongoing professional development.	'Participate in training and other learning activities and performance development as required. Keep up to date with current trends and initiatives and newly released publications in order to select Library resources. Attend courses as appropriate'.
Events and displays	30	Devise and support diverse library activities and events. Create engaging library displays.	'To mount displays and organise competitions, activities and themed events to maintain pupil interest'.
Qualifications*	30	Required or desired qualifications could include minimum GCSE Grade C or above in English and Maths or equivalent, an appropriate advanced level qualification, National Vocational Qualification (NVQ) Level 2, NVQ Level 3, NVQ Level 4, current First Aid certification, degree-level qualification in Library/Information Studies or first degree with postgraduate library qualification, being Chartered or working towards Chartership, certificates within education, completion of Department for Education (DfE) Teacher Assistant Induction Programme, professional certification in librarianship such as ACILIP or MCILIP, specific training in Children's Librarianship.	'Have a minimum of NVQ3 level relevant library and information qualifications or equivalent experience. Ideally be a fully qualified Chartered Librarian or equivalent experience'.
Initiative, organisation and resilience	29	Shows innovation and initiative. Is well-organised with strong time-management and planning skills. Is resilient and flexible, and adaptive to change. Has strong problem-solving skills. Creative and able to work with high autonomy. Shows attention to detail. Is optimistic and positive in outlook.	'Making things happen – the drive, motivation and commitment to initiate, focusing on delivering outcomes and being proactive rather than reactive. Embracing change and coming up with new ways of working for the good of the students and the school. Having a positive outlook. Showing resilience – responding positively to pressure, remaining emotionally stable and positive when faced with

Continued

Table 2 Continued

Aspect	Aspect count	Aspect scope	Text example
Initiative, organisation and resilience (Continued)			challenges. Manage time and space effectively, keeping a balance of time spent in direct services to patrons and time spent on administrative tasks'.
Supervision and extracurricular duties	27	Supervise students in the library. Lead or support extracurricular activities running at lunchtime or outside normal school hours. Provide supervision cover for absent colleagues. Attend school events, parent engagement sessions and professional development opportunities, outside normal school hours. Perform allocated lunchtime supervision duties.	'Supervise students using the library area when on duty before school, during lunchtime and/or after school hours. Be involved in extracurricular activities, e.g. open days, presentation evenings. Supervise small groups of students undertaking a teacher-led learning activity by co-ordinating and explaining basic instructions for the activity. Assist in the supervision and training of volunteer helpers/student library monitors'.
Information and communications technology (ICT) knowledge and skills	26	Have strong ICT skills and a commitment to maintaining and developing these skills. Have strong knowledge of library database systems and supporting online services. Expertise in using ICT to support information acquisition. Have working knowledge of current social media platforms and ICT resources. Ability to draw on knowledge and skills to provide information on the latest research applications and new technology in teaching and learning.	'Be confident, knowledgeable and competent in the use of ICT skills. Have the ability to manage and disseminate information in a range of different media'.
Student wellbeing	26	Provide First Aid as required. Provide pastoral support, including as a pastoral tutor or student mentor. Safeguard student welfare, pastoral care, health and safety. Ensure that the library environment is safe. Be compliant with all policies and procedures designed to maintain and promote student wellbeing.	'Support and contribute to the school's responsibility for safeguarding pupils. Have the ability to develop a culture of mutual respect with the pupils'.

Continued

Table 2 *Continued*

Aspect	Aspect count	Aspect scope	Text example
Facilitate information literacy	25	Have strong research and information literacy skills. Develop information literacy skills of students and staff. Create and deliver training sessions in core information literacy, and related study and research skills. Support teachers' implementation of research-based curriculum. Encourage students to be ethical and critical users of information. Maintain a high level of resource awareness.	'The main purpose of the role is to ensure that pupils and staff are effective users of ideas and information. Empower students to be critical thinkers, enthusiastic readers, skilful researchers, and ethical users of information. Instil a love of learning in all pupils and ensure equitable access to information. To support learners to identify, locate and access the information they require'.
Manage and enhance library environment	25	Establish and maintain a library environment that is conducive to learning. Provide an attractive, safe, inclusive, stimulating and welcoming learning space. Manage all matters relating to the technological affordances, security, fittings and furnishings of the library environment.	'You will develop and maintain the library as a vibrant area for individual study and to support learners and learning areas in their work. Maintain the Library in good order and create/maintain a quiet, controlled atmosphere conducive to study and learning'.
Other duties	22	Perform duties not specified in the job description as directed by leadership.	'The aim of the job description s to indicate the general purpose and level of responsibility of the post. Please be aware that duties may vary from time to time without changing their character or general level of responsibility. Duties may be subject to periodic review by the Principal (in consultation with the post holder) to reflect the changing work composition of the business. This is an outline job description only and the post holder will be expected to undertake the duties commensurate within the range and grade of the post or any other reasonable duties as directed by the Principal'.
Alignment with school ethos and policies	21	Align the school library with the ethos and policies of the school. Maintain awareness of and compliance with school policies. Contribute to promotion of the school ethos.	'Provide the expertise necessary to ensure that library provision is aligned with the mission, goals, and objectives of the school and materials are appropriate for use'.

Continued

Table 2 *Continued*

Aspect	Aspect count	Aspect scope	Text example
ICT resourcing and training	21	Operate and maintain ICT equipment/software. Develop and maintain the library's online presence. Organise, direct and participate in appropriate ICT training for staff and pupils. Curate web-based learning resources. Provide technical support for use of ICT resources in the library in liaison with other appropriate staff. Maintain electronic records. Contribute to the school's digital literacy strategy. Build the ICT resource collection in consultation with staff.	'Responsibility for optimising the use of IT services within the school; this is to include on-line view data systems and the compilation of in-house databases as appropriate. Development of training packages for staff and pupils on the use of IT as an effective information retrieval tool'.
Behaviour management	19	Promote a productive working environment through use of appropriate behaviour management strategies. Deal promptly with behavioural incidents, adhering to policy. Recognise and reward good behaviour.	'Promote good pupil behaviour, dealing promptly with conflict and incidents in line with established policy and encourage pupils to take responsibility for their behaviour. Issue student rewards and recognition in line with the school policy'.
Instruction	19	Deliver training sessions to staff and students. Demonstrate instructional effectiveness in small-group, large-group, and one-to-one instruction and interventions. May be required to assess student performance. Use strategies to support students to achieve learning goals. Play a role in evaluating student skills and knowledge, such as determining reading skill levels.	'Plan and lead reading lessons, including targeted interventions and monitoring of the impact of the lessons and interventions. Provide individualised progress reports for students to be shared within the pastoral structures of the school. Provide support to students with their learning'.
Staff and volunteer supervision and support	19	Train and supervise staff and volunteers to support them to perform routine library tasks. Be involved in the appointment of suitable support staff and volunteers. Recognise and reward volunteers for their contributions, including student library monitors. May act as a line manager for library staff.	'Supervising and train staff, parents, volunteers and pupil librarians working in the Library, as required. Training Library Support Team staff in basic cataloguing and processing duties, as required, ensuring that correct quality control procedures are in place and applied'.

Continued

Table 2 *Continued*

Aspect	Aspect count	Aspect scope	Text example
Collaboration for learning	17	Collaborate with colleagues to support student learning. Work closely with teachers to ensure that students have access to study packs and resources that enhance learning.	'Work Collaboratively • Ability to engage and work with colleagues in the library section and wider School community. • Work closely with the E-learning team on projects and events, and in daily operations. • Liaise closely with appropriate teaching staff to develop resource collections for particular collections, when required'.
Curriculum support	17	Contribute to the development of teaching programmes, particularly those related to information literacy, library skills and reading. Work with staff to provide materials to support curriculum and ensure that these materials are readily accessible. Engage external providers such as authors to provide learning opportunities that enhance learning. Maintain current knowledge of evolving resource possibilities to meet curriculum needs.	'Support the delivery of the curriculum for year groups, individual subjects and individual pupils, enabling pupils to perform independent research'.
Educational knowledge	16	Have understanding of education systems, curriculum and policies. Have knowledge of current educational initiatives in library and information services. Have understanding of child development and learning. Ideally have knowledge of learning theory and teaching methods.	'Knowledge and understanding of teaching and learning, of educational issues and the National Curriculum as they relate to the provision of learning resources . . . Awareness of child development and the role of reading in the educational development of the child'.

*Qualifications specifically pertained to educational attainment in primary, secondary, tertiary or workplace learning contexts.

(Adapted from Merga, 2020a)

Things they are expected to do, be and have

It's now worth looking more closely at the many similarities between the roles, while recognising the subtle differences between them. While I explore the two samples, it's important to remember that while they were both rich and current, given the nature of the analysis, we cannot suggest that the findings I share here are broadly generalisable, and analysis of JDFs certainly doesn't tell us much about the actual realities of the role in different schools.

It is certainly likely that in some contexts, the actual role bears very little resemblance to what appeared in the JDF, so further research is needed.

Furthermore, I need to point out that these documents were not analysed concurrently; if they were, it is likely that categories would have been differently appointed. Given this caveat, I focus on the commonalities, with limited attention to some potential differences more for the purposes of future research or workforce implications, rather than to proclaim them universal.

As I explore herein, the roles clearly have a lot in common, and on this basis, I refer to teacher librarians and school librarians as *library professionals* for ease of nomenclature when referring to this collective group. I discuss aspects of the roles here in no particular order.

General teaching and learning support

It might be expected that the Australian teacher librarians would be the only ones doing 'teaching' due to their educational qualifications, but the reality indicated by these documents is that UK school librarians are typically involved in some form of teaching too. Behaviour management expectation was only common in the UK context. However, this role sat just outside the salience of the Australian documents, suggesting that it was also often required. While Australian teacher librarians were typically involved in curriculum development and knowledge, UK school librarians provided curriculum support and were required to have educational knowledge. Professionals across both contexts were required to be involved in their own professional development, though Australian teacher librarians were more likely to be asked to also facilitate the professional development of others, and both also had responsibility for extracurricular duties. While there was far greater emphasis in the Australian contexts in meeting diverse student needs as *learners*, as well as student assessment and reporting, it is clear that UK school librarians are already typically expected to play a role in instruction and instruction support.

There may be minor differences in what constitutes teaching and instruction; these terms are typically conflated and used interchangeably. Further research is needed to capture the extent to which UK school librarians are teaching in some form; however, the findings I present in this chapter strongly suggest that based on the recent data, while it is a given that all teacher librarians will be expected to teach, school librarians may also have a noteworthy instructional role that may be poorly recognised and rewarded in their current positioning as a support role, rather than an educational role.

Literacy engagement and learning

I look at this in depth in Chapter 3, and as I explore in detail, library professionals are expected to foster student literacy as well as reading-supportive activities and dispositions. Arguably, this is one of the most expected, traditional roles of school library professionals, but as I will explain further in Chapter 3, this role is comparatively neglected in the JDFs of US library professionals (Merga & Ferguson, 2021). It seems that it cannot be taken for granted that this is something that all library professionals throughout the world are still expected to do as one of the competing demands of their role, though it is certainly a core part of the role of school library professionals in Australia and the UK.

Interpersonal skills

Library professionals are expected to have strong interpersonal skills, demonstrating a commitment to collaboration and teamwork to support student learning. They need to be competent communicators, well-organised and able to work with high autonomy. This flies in the face of the traditional caricature of the school library professional as an anti-social individual who goes around 'shushing' people; these days, to get the job and do it well, school library professionals need to be warm individuals with the ability to communicate effectively. They need to be able to build relationships with very diverse stakeholders in student learning, including students, parents, teachers, school leaders and members of the broader community, which relates to their capacity to build and support school culture, which I discuss further herein.

Given the complexity of the role that I have illustrated in this chapter, I find it interesting to note that *both* the Australian and UK documents included a notable emphasis on the need for resilience. As the role of school library professionals continues to diversify through job creep, they are certainly going to need all the resilience they can draw upon. Further requirements are likely to be continually absorbed into professional expectations, and given the challenges faced by libraries in recent times, initiated or compounded by the COVID-19 pandemic, the trait of resilience may be increasingly required.

However, I feel that while attention is already being given to the impact of COVID-19 on the wellbeing of educators (Allen et al., 2020; Kim & Asbury, 2020), the same attention is not being given to teacher librarians as educators, or school librarians as support staff, so we need this research now. Resilience is important, but as job pressures increase and other pressures continue to arise over time, relying on the trait of resilience is simply not enough.

Library professionals will also need support. They will need to have their role understood, and their concerns listened to, and access to the same support services available to educators (where these are forthcoming). The last thing I want to see is school library professionals burning out because their workload is too overladen to be achievable, only to be told the problem isn't the excessive and diverse workload, it's their lack of resilience. I've seen this kind of narrative play out in my various roles in academia, which is also well-known for its workload issues, and it doesn't end well; *Nature*'s website recently posted a piece on pandemic burnout in academia (Gewin, 2021), and I wouldn't be surprised to see school-based educators experiencing similar issues. However, we need the research scrutiny to keep across the possibilities of these kinds of issues emerging for school library professionals. In a book about libraries and wellbeing, we can't ignore the wellbeing of school library professionals.

Resource provision

Library professionals are collection-building experts, but they also have a broader role to play in resource provision. Working closely with teachers, library professionals ensure that the resources available in the library are fit for both current and future purposes, weeding the collection regularly to ensure that students are exposed to the most accurate information and recent works of fiction that hold the appeal of currency.

In this regard, this aspect of the role also overlaps with literacy engagement and learning. One aspect that is also related to student wellbeing that was more strongly featured in the UK documents than their Australian counterparts was ensuring 'the collection is reflective of contemporary views on issues relating to diversity' (Merga, 2020b, p. 6). With growing interest in using diverse texts in Australian schooling contexts (e.g. Adam & Barratt-Pugh, 2020), it can be hoped that this aspect of the resource provision role will assume greater prominence in the future.

Information skills

While I look at information skills in greater depth in Chapter 5, where I explore school libraries, health resourcing and information literacy, I note here that library professionals play an important role in supporting informational skills and facilitating information literacy. Furthermore, this role is not only concerned with enhancing the information skills of students; staff may also have their information skills developed by library professionals.

Technology skills

Although technology skills often overlapped with information literacy and skills, library professionals were supposed to both have, and continually develop, their personal Information and Communication Technology (ICT) knowledge skills, and provide support and training in ICT skills. In Australia in particular, they were often expected to troubleshoot and provide ICT support for staff and students, and this reminded me of conversations I'd had with teacher librarians who found themselves spending a lot of time supporting students with issues with iPads and resetting student passwords.

It's also important that the breadth of ICT skills requested not be lost in the summative nature of my reporting here; library professionals were supposed to be experts in learning technologies, devices, diverse applications, database systems and supporting online services, and social media platforms among others, and the knowledge and skills needed often explicitly encompassed *both* current and future technologies, highlighting the need for continual upskilling and agility in this space.

Whether it is actually realistic to expect library professionals to maintain a high standard of ICT skills across the competing demands of their role is another question, and one that warrants further exploration. In a recent UK report of schools that had an on-site designated school library area, 'less than half report that their main member of library staff has undertaken some form of CPD (continuing professional development) relevant to librarianship in the past year (44%)' (BMG Research, 2019, p. 1). If training may not always be forthcoming, this places the burden of remaining abreast squarely on the shoulders of the school library professional. While schools may demand and expect their library professionals to be across evolving technology to perform their library role, there may not be sufficient time and resourcing to support this goal, which could put considerable pressure on school library professionals.

Library environment creation and support

I will address how library professionals create environments supportive of reading and wellbeing in depth in Chapter 6, so here I will just briefly explain that the influence of library professionals on their library environments is significant. They manage the space to enhance learning, promote student comfort, and allow for diverse activities such as reading for pleasure and makerspace work (Merga, 2021a), and therefore this role clearly intersects with many other roles listed here.

School culture

Like all educators and support staff, library professionals are expected to support the culture of their schools and align their values and practices with school policies. However, more attention should be given to the broader role that library professionals may play in developing and promoting a positive school culture. Relating to interpersonal skills, library professionals may collaborate with and communicate with parents and stakeholders from the community, and they may also play a transformative role in promoting a reading culture within their school.

While there is a wealth of anecdotal and personal advocacy stories about the role of library professionals as leaders of school cultural change, further research is needed to identify how common it is for library professionals to play a significant role in leading and supporting the promotion of school cultures. Our previous work has positioned school library professionals as key informants around enabling and constraining factors influencing the establishment of a school reading culture (Merga & Mason, 2019), which is logical given that a school reading culture is centrally concerned with inspiring students to read (Loh et al., 2017), and as I explore in detail in Chapter 2, this is what library professionals do.

I've started to make some further inroads, recently analysing school-level literacy policies and plans in Australia and the UK, to explore the extent to which libraries (and by extension their staff) are recognised as influencing students' literacy attainment and attitudes. I found that UK documents were far more likely to promote the role of their library as influencing the school's literacy affordances and culture than their Australian counterparts (Merga, 2021b). However, more work needs to be done in this space.

Administration and management

The administrative tasks undertaken by library professionals were also complex and extensive, and included but were not limited to general administration; administration of library systems (which also links with ICT skills); library management; policy development, adherence and implementation; and workforce management of library staff and volunteers. My previous research has found that the administrative aspect of the workload could be daunting, and that 'particularly where limited support staff are available, librarians feel overwhelmed by their diverse and demanding workload, and spend large volumes of time performing low-level rote tasks related to administration' (Merga, 2019, p. 134). This pressure is not without its consequences, as it was felt to reduce 'time available to support children's literature and literacy learning' (Merga, 2019, p. 134).

Library promotion

Library professionals inducted students into the library and promoted increased use of the library. Activities and strategies that promote the contribution of the library and that seek to heighten its use can clearly be beneficial as they can maximise the value of the library resource. Library promotion can also be key to professional survival, as such advocacy can help school libraries and their staff weather budget cuts and other resourcing constraints that can heighten their precarity. Aharony (2009) noted that 'nowadays in the information age librarians should be empowered, decisive and less introverted in order to survive, to market their libraries and in order to justify their professional position', and this has 'implications for libraries' survival in the twenty-first century' (p. 48).

Student wellbeing

While the role of the library professional in supporting student wellbeing is explored extensively in Chapters 4, 5 and 6, it is also worth noting here that at least to some extent, this wellbeing role is present in JDFs, so it is clearly part of library professionals' expected job requirements. Furthermore, in JDFs this also overlaps with considerations around library environment, and general teaching and learning support. Child safety, student wellbeing, supervision and duty of care were key role features across contexts.

Qualifications and experience

Library professionals across both contexts were commonly asked for qualifications and experience. This is interesting, given that as I discussed earlier in this chapter and in further detail in Chapter 7, the qualified Australian library workforce is being eroded as library roles, including those of library leadership, may be increasingly occupied by unqualified staff (Dix et al., 2020), though further research is urgently needed to confirm the generalisability of these South Australian findings.

While there was some diversity in the qualifications expected of Australian teacher librarians, the expectations of school librarians in the UK were widely varying; as seen in Table 2, they spanned from a minimum GCSE Grade C or above in English and Maths or equivalent to university degree-level qualification. I find this extremely interesting and would love to do further work on the qualifications and professional expectations of the library profession, because as I've briefly touched on in the introduction to this chapter, they have implications for what library staff are actually qualified to do in librarianship and/or education capacities, as well as for what constitutes fair remuneration.

While some UK librarians have expressed understandable reluctance towards the inclusion of an educational qualification in school librarian professional learning, it could be a good idea for the following reasons. UK librarians are often expected to play an educational role as part of their role scope (refer to Table 2). Furthermore, that the only role requirement or characteristic that featured across all documents in the Australian 40-document corpus was 'teaching and facilitating learning', suggests that positioning the UK school librarian as a qualified educator could be a notable selling point, but I caution that further research with UK schools would be needed to confirm that this appeal crosses contexts, and that it does not actually reduce the employment prospects of UK school librarians in line with the reservations outlined earlier in this chapter.

Other duties

Built into the JDFs was the expectation that the school library professional be prepared to be very flexible in allowing additional aspects to be added to their roles. Both roles commonly included delegated and unspecified responsibilities and duties. It will be important to capture what exactly these are, how they may change over time, and how they might be responsive to specific contextual needs, both present and forthcoming, to see if a consistent subset of 'hidden' roles emerges. Judging from the current vast scope of the library professional role, this requirement that the school library professional role continues to absorb a growing breadth of expectations needs to be monitored.

This is commonly known as job creep or role creep, and I've previously suggested that 'as teacher librarians often experience role creep, and pick up additional aspects of their role, it may pay for them to audit the full scope of their role' (Merga, 2019, p. 227). This can help them to push back with leadership when they are asked to take on new roles that make their workload untenable, and help them to ensure they are being fairly paid for their work. It can also help them to keep track of what they are doing, as previously discussed.

The risk here is that library professionals may fail to be sufficiently self-protective and continue to accept new facets to their role, which could potentially lead to burnout and redirection away from other valuable facets of the role. As noted by Ettarh (2018) in discussion of librarians in general (not specific to school library contexts), 'with the expansion of job duties, and expectation of "whole-self" librarianship, it is no surprise that burnout is a common phenomenon within libraries' (p. 13). If further research indicates that these other duties are regularly being added, it is easy to see how this can result in overwork, 'working more than is desirable for wellbeing' (Kossek, 2016, p. 261). It seems appropriate to also include this consideration in this book as workforce wellbeing should also be a priority.

Further thoughts

First and foremost, it can be clearly seen that the roles of both Australian teacher librarian and UK school librarian are valuable and highly complex, involving mastery over disparate skills and knowledge. They have a number of core commonalities that justify the combining of the professions in discussion in this book under the umbrella term *library professionals*, while also having some interesting differences.

The nature of this analysis means that this is more accurate a representation of what *schools expect* than what library professionals *actually do* in their role, which could greatly diverge from what is stated in JDFs, as partly alluded to in the common expectation of unspecified responsibilities and other duties. We need research that looks at the extent to which JDFs genuinely reflect the role and characteristics of school library professionals. While I have looked at Australia and the UK here, it would be great for school library researchers reading this book in other contexts to undertake this research, as a large international corpus of research in this area would enable us to more effectively learn from each other, and have a greater understanding of which issues hold international relevance.

At the very least, this chapter can be used to raise awareness of current challenges and issues facing the profession, and to raise attention to the importance of school library workforce wellbeing. On a practical level, it enables both teacher librarians and school librarians to draw on the aspect scopes in order to illustrate what they do for the purposes of meeting their job review requirements and applying for new or promotional opportunities. Next time you are asked about what you do, you can draw on some of the aspect scopes to show that the skills and knowledge you are expected to display but also consistently maintain are broad and deep. The function of this chapter establishes important unifying commonalities, while at the same time situating further discussion on the literacy and wellbeing supportive role of school library professionals within the broader work expectations that they must meet.

References

Adam, H., & Barratt-Pugh, C. (2020). The challenge of monoculturalism: What books are educators sharing with children and what messages do they send? *The Australian Educational Researcher, 47*(5), 815–836.

Aharony, N. (2009). Librarians' attitudes towards marketing library services. *Journal of Librarianship and Information Science, 41*(1), 39–50.

Allen, R., Jerrim, J., & Sims, S. (2020). How did the early stages of the COVID-19 pandemic affect teacher wellbeing? *Centre for Education Policy and Equalising Opportunities (CEPEO) Working Paper*, No. 20-15.

ASLA. (2014). Evidence guide for teacher librarians in the proficient career stage. https://asla.org.au/resources/Documents/Website%20Documents/evidence_guide_prof.pdf

ASLA. (2019). What is a teacher librarian? https://asla.org.au/what-is-a-teacher-librarian

BMG Research. (2019). National survey to scope school library provision in England, Northern Ireland, and Wales. https://d824397c-0ce2-4fc6-b5c4-8d2e4de5b242.filesusr.com/ugd/8d6dfb_8b81a7c94c2c4c4a970265496f42307a.pdf

Brackenbury, H. L., & Willett, P. (2011). Secondary school librarians as heads of department in UK schools. *Library Management, 32*(4/5), 237–250.

CILIP. (n.d.). School librarians. https://www.cilip.org.uk/page/SchoolLibrarians

Dix, K., Felgate, R., Ahmed, S. K., Carslake, T., & Sniedze-Gregory, S. (2020). *School libraries in South Australia. 2019 Census.* Australian Council for Educational Research. https://doi.org/10.37517/978-1-74286-583-6

Erickson, N. (2019). I may not be a librarian, but I'm running the school library: Understanding the work identity of library paraprofessionals. In J. L. Branch-Mueller (Ed.) *Proceedings of the 48th Annual Conference of the International Association of School Librarianship and the 23rd International Forum on Research in School Librarianship.* IASL. https://journals.library.ualberta.ca/slw/index.php/iasl/article/download/7428/4303

Ettarh, F. (2018). *Vocational awe and librarianship: The lies we tell ourselves.* In the Library with the Lead Pipe. http://www.inthelibrarywiththeleadpipe.org/2018/vocational-awe

Farmer, L. S. (2006). Library media program implementation and student achievement. *Journal of Librarianship and Information Science, 38*(1), 21–32.

Francis, B. H., Lance, K. C., & Lietzau, Z. (2010). *School librarians continue to help students achieve standards: The third Colorado study. Closer Look Report.* Colorado State Library, Library Research Service.

Gewin, V. (2021). Pandemic burnout is rampant in academia. *Nature.* https://www.nature.com/articles/d41586-021-00663-2

Hughes, H., Bozorgian, H., & Allan, C. (2014). School libraries, teacher-librarians and student outcomes: Presenting and using the evidence. *School Libraries Worldwide*, *20*(1), 29–50.

Kim, L. E., & Asbury, K. (2020). 'Like a rug had been pulled from under you': The impact of COVID-19 on teachers in England during the first six weeks of the UK lockdown. *British Journal of Educational Psychology*, *90*(4), 1062–1083.

Kossek, E. E. (2016). Managing work-life boundaries in the digital age. *Organizational Dynamics*, *45*(3), 258–270.

Lance, K. C., & Kachel, D. E. (2018). Why school librarians matter: What years of research tell us. *Phi Delta Kappan*, *99*(7), 15–20.

Loh, C. E., Ellis, M., Paculdar, A. A., & Wan, Z. H. (2017). Building a successful reading culture through the school library: A case study of a Singapore secondary school. *IFLA Journal*, *43*(4), 335–347.

Merga, M. K. (2019). *Librarians in schools as literacy educators*. Palgrave Macmillan.

Merga, M. K. (2020a). What is the literacy supportive role of the school librarian in the United Kingdom? *Journal of Librarianship & Information Science*. https://doi.org/10.1177/0961000620964569

Merga, M. K. (2020b). School librarians as literacy educators within a complex role. *Journal of Library Administration*, *60*(8), 889–908.

Merga, M. K. (2021a). Libraries as wellbeing supportive spaces in contemporary schools. *Journal of Library Administration*, *61*(6), 659–675.

Merga, M. K. (2021b). The role of the library within school-level literacy policies and plans in Australia and the United Kingdom. *Journal of Librarianship and Information Science*. https://doi.org/10.1177/09610006211022410

Merga, M. K., & Ferguson, C. (2021). School librarians supporting students' reading for pleasure: A job description analysis. *Australian Journal of Education*. https://doi.org/10.1177/0004944121991275

Merga, M. K., & Mason, S. (2019). Building a school reading culture: Teacher librarians' perceptions of enabling and constraining factors. *Australian Journal of Education*, *63*(2), 173–189.

School Library Association (SLA). (n.d.-a). The role of the school librarian. https://www.sla.org.uk/support-for-secondary-schools

School Library Association. (SLA). (n.d.-b). Job description: Primary School Librarian. https://www.sla.org.uk/filedownload/a7af37538b123120be55ca9debd0b2242da13865/ad42399dad4ef065ec57971e1ac208ee88b4c762

Stefl-Mabry, J., Radlick, M., Mersand, S., & Gulatee, Y. (2019). School Library Research. *Journal of Thought*, *53*(3/4), 19–34.

Streatfield, D., Shaper, S., Markless, S., & Rae-Scott, S. (2011). Information literacy in United Kingdom schools: Evolution, current state and prospects. *Journal of Information Literacy*, *5*(2), 5–25.

Willis, J. (2020). The future for school librarians. *Independent Education*, *50*(1), 14–15.

2
School Libraries and Reading Engagement for Literacy

Think about all the ways you have communicated with others over the last couple of days. Almost certainly, this has involved a combination of reading, writing, listening and speaking skills that you may take for granted.

For example, that text message response you sent from your phone drew on your writing skills, but you also needed good reading comprehension to understand the meaning behind the message you were responding to. Add differences in writing styles, literacy skills, first language structures and norms, and discourse features as just some of the many complex factors that shape the message that is sent, and how it is received. This is the reality of the tacit complexity underpinning every communication you are involved in.

Furthermore, we have linguistic features such as sarcasm, which must be detected in order for the recipient to understand the communication intends the very *opposite* of what is professed; we don't even always say or write what we mean. Technological advances have not diminished the need for strong literacy skills, and it can be argued that the need for students to have strong literacy is actually growing in contemporary times.

Literacy is one of the most important skills for contemporary communication and optimisation of an individual's academic, vocational and social opportunities (e.g. Lane & Conlon, 2016). In their report on literacy and numeracy skills and labour market outcomes for the Productivity Commission in Australia, Shomos and Forbes (2014) contended that higher literacy skills 'are associated with better labour market outcomes (employment and wages)' (p. vi), and therefore raising the literacy levels within a population delivers economic benefits.

The practical barriers of low adult literacy may be poorly understood by those with functional literacy, and our recent research explored how literacy interventions in adulthood can support these lifelong learners to master skills that literate adults take for granted, such as reading street signs and filling out forms required in the course of a work role (Ferguson & Merga, 2021). Low literacy can exclude us from vital health communications that can impact on both individual and community health, such as government-issued health information during the pandemic. We recently found that given that around two in every five Australians struggle with literacy, government-issued health information available online was too complex for many Australians to understand (Ferguson et al., 2021).

As it is so important, there is a strong need for schools to equip students with these essential skills. Given the world we currently live in, there are also accountability measures for schools, requiring them to pay close attention to fostering student literacy and to measure and track progress at school, national and international levels of comparison.

Reading engagement and literacy

Encouraging young people to love reading and supporting them to build their literacy skills are part of the educative role of teacher librarians and school librarians (referred to collectively in this chapter as in others as *library professionals*). As I will illustrate in this chapter, a key role of library professionals is fostering *reading engagement*, a term that has been conceptualised and operationalised in divergent ways in the literature over the years, often encompassing behavioural, affective and cognitive elements (e.g. Barber & Klauda, 2020). It can be linked to various theories of motivation, such as expectancy value theory (e.g. Durik et al., 2006), and it has been framed in a variety of diverse and often complex and multifactorial forms. For example, Guthrie et al. (2013) conceptualise 'reading engagement in its behavioural form, consisting of actions and intentions to interact with text for the purposes of understanding and learning', contending that 'engagement is the act of reading to meet internal and external expectations' (p. 10).

While there is no one universally accepted definition for reading engagement, for pragmatic purposes, reading engagement can be simplistically described as referring to positive attitudes towards reading, and frequency of engagement in the practice of reading, which influence and are influenced by student literacy skill attainment (Merga, 2018a). In this basic model, ascribing reading engagement would depend on a person's response to the questions 'Do you like reading?' and 'How often do you read for enjoyment?', which are interrelated but distinct questions about attitudes and frequency. For the everyday person, this kind of very basic conceptualisation of reading engagement makes sense on a practical level. Applying it to anything from skateboarding to Sudoku, if we enjoy something, we are likely to do it more often, and this practice will help us to both build and maintain our skills in the activity. Unsurprisingly, reading makes us better readers, just as running makes us better runners.

It is also important to note that frequency of reading cannot be seen as a *sole* measure of a person's reading engagement, as attitude must be taken into account. This is because some students love reading but work long hours in paid employment, are involved in sibling care, have competitive martial arts lessons or have a range of other time constraints that may severely limit their reading opportunities. I remember interviewing an exhausted student who just kept buying books that she never had time to read because she was balancing multiple part-time jobs with full-time schooling. Other researchers have also found that some young people had a strong desire to read but poor time availability to do this (e.g. Bjørgan, 2018).

Social influences in young people's lives, such as library professionals, teachers, parents and friends, can all potentially influence their level of reading engagement, and if you reflect on your own experiences as a young person, most of you will be able to identify people who have changed the way you look at reading. In my study of avid book readers, I found that most avid readers (64.3%) felt that there had been a positive influence on their reading, though this could take many different forms. For example, some were influenced by just watching an adult model keen reading, some developed a shared social habit with parents or friends, and some were read to as children, fostering an early love of books and reading (Merga, 2017b). Of course, it is not only social influences that make a difference; many factors influence reading engagement, and for a detailed explanation you could refer to my previous book on the research on promoting reading engagement in young people beyond the early years (Merga, 2018a). However, it is certainly the case that as a social and educative influence in the lives of your students, you can make an important difference to young people's reading engagement.

This facet of your job as a school library professional is a literacy-supportive role, given the growing body of research contending that reading engagement, expressed as a regular reading habit and positive attitudes towards reading, is extremely important for building and maintaining young people's literacy skills. Reading frequency is related to reading achievement (e.g. Scholes, 2021), and advantages and skills in literacy are compounded as young people move through the years of schooling, but 'apart from the effects of reading skills on practice', researchers have 'found that how much children read in middle childhood affects reading skills later on. It seems that the habit of engaging in regular reading activities stems from being interested in reading' (Van Bergen et al., 2020, p. 15). Children are more likely to read when they have positive attitudes towards reading, and this reading frequency in turn is related to literacy skill development and maintenance, particularly in relation to reading comprehension (e.g. Locher & Pfost, 2020), with Becker et al. (2010) finding that 'children who see reading as a desirable activity tend to read more frequently and thus develop better reading skills' (p. 781).

Reading frequency is naturally related to reading volume, though they are not identical. For example, a student may read daily, but only read small amounts during that time, whereas another student may confine their reading to the weekend, where they read larger volumes of text than the daily reader when we look at reading volume across the week. The available research suggests that 'reading volume (print exposure) has a positive effect on students' reading achievement. Once they acquire minimal competence as readers, their reading volume becomes a predictor of their gains in reading achievement' (Allington & McGill-Franzen, 2021, p. 6). This means that when you encourage and support young people to read often and for longer periods, you are playing a key role in supporting their reading achievement.

Reading for pleasure and literacy

As briefly touched on earlier in this book, Reading for Pleasure (RfP) can be defined as 'volitional reading in which we choose to engage' (Kucirkova & Cremin, 2020, p. 2), that is, the reading of self-selected materials that we do for enjoyment. RfP can occur in diverse contexts including classrooms, where it may seem a little out of place, as these are contexts where reading might be more typically undertaken for the purposes of instruction or information. Providing opportunities for young people to enjoy RfP can be positioned as a 'somewhat "fluffy" pedagogy more suitable for capable readers', and this negative view towards RfP 'is perpetuated in policy discourse and the dominant body of Australian literacy research' (Vanden Dool & Simpson, 2021, p. 9).

This negative positioning ignores the evidence, and a substantial body of research links RfP opportunity with improved attitudes towards reading (e.g. Yoon, 2002). Reading enjoyment and attitude is furthermore related to crucial literacy skills such as reading comprehension (Rogiers et al., 2020; Torppa et al., 2020), and given that this is one of the facets of literacy skill that many schools regularly measure in their students for national and international testing regimes, this 'fluffy' practice suddenly takes on an importance that should not be ignored in contemporary schools.

And yet, the benefits of RfP may be poorly understood in many schools, and therefore RfP may struggle to compete with more didactic, 'teacherly' activities in lesson planning. Westbrook et al. (2019) describe a notion that

RfP is not seen to be 'teaching reading, whereas analysing every part of a text equates to developing reading skills', which ignores the reality that such 'analysis slowed the reading considerably to the detriment of volume of text read' (p. 64). Students need explicit reading instruction, but they also badly need opportunities for sustained and uninterrupted text exposure. With classrooms not necessarily spaces that can accommodate activities that may lack the *appearance* of didactic learning, school libraries clearly emerge as the most potentially friendly spaces towards RfP that are not intensely instructor mediated.

Providing time for RfP should be a whole-school priority, given that the benefits of RfP extend beyond literacy-specific language subjects such as English or language arts, to other learning areas such as mathematics (Clavel & Mediavilla, 2020; Sullivan & Brown, 2015; Wang et al., 2020). Having a school library professional within the school can help the development of this kind of supportive culture, getting buy-in from teachers across subject areas. This is partly because of their expertise, but also because they typically sit outside the silos that can develop around the subject areas, particularly in secondary school.

We want our young people to make a positive contribution to their societies and to be active and socially aware citizens. The RfP of fiction may offer benefits for social-emotional learning (Aerila et al., 2021), and support the development of prosocial skills such as empathy (Stansfield & Bunce, 2014). Recent research suggests that these benefits may also be conferred for those who may struggle with these skills, including those on the autism spectrum (Chapple et al., 2021). These benefits can be clearly linked to curricular priorities. For example, in Australia, the reading of fiction aligns with the Australian Curriculum general capabilities that are expected to be developed across subject areas and schooling years including, but not limited to, 'Personal and social capability', 'Ethical understanding' and 'Intercultural understanding' (Australian Curriculum, Assessment and Reporting Authority, n.d.).

Furthermore, schools throughout the world are interested in developing healthy behaviours in their young students, and more recently attention has been given to links between higher frequency of RfP in childhood (age 11) and greater health-protective behaviours in later years (age 14). While further research should be conducted in this space, regular RfP is associated with less likelihood of consuming cigarettes and alcohol and a greater chance of regularly eating fruit (Mak & Fancourt, 2020a). Daily RfP in childhood (age 7) has been linked with a lower occurrence of attentional issues and better prosocial behaviour in later childhood (age 11) (Mak & Fancourt, 2020b). As I explore in more detail in Chapters 4, 5 and 6 of this book, reading may also offer mental health benefits (e.g. Levine et al., 2020), as well as supporting general health and wellbeing.

RfP should be a whole-school priority that is fostered as part of a positive school reading culture. This positive school reading culture can be defined as one in which there is a commonality of 'beliefs and behaviours that indicate that reading is highly valued by all stakeholders and wherein the students practice the daily habit of independently reading inside and outside of the school' (Grace, 2021). However, declines in young people's attitudes towards reading, which have been observed in Australia (Darmawan, 2020) and elsewhere (Clark & Teravainen-Goff, 2020; Parsons et al., 2018), bring into question the effectiveness of schools in establishing these positive cultures and practices. Pandemic conditions may have had a slightly positive impact on reading engagement in recent times, with the most current UK findings indicating that children's reading enjoyment 'increased during lockdown (from 47.8% pre-lockdown to 55.9% post-lockdown), having reached a 15-year low before lockdown' (Clark & Picton, 2020, p. 2). However, more needs to be done to foster reading engagement and greatly increase the number of students frequently involved in the beneficial practice of RfP.

While traditionally RfP may have been cast as something more typically enjoyed by girls, it can be enjoyed regardless of gender. While there is much discussion of the need for 'boy-friendly' books and literacy instruction which can position young males as inevitably and homogenously reluctant and disengaged, many boys can and do find reading enjoyable, including the reading of fiction (Merga, 2017a; Scholes et al., 2021). Library professionals, teachers and parents should be careful not to project their stereotypes around boys' reading behaviour on their young and impressionable students, given that gender-related differences are likely to be more a product of socialisation and upbringing (e.g. Baker & Milligan, 2016) than innate and immutable characteristics. Attention to enhancing boys' attitudes towards reading could be integral to improving their literacy performance and closing the often-cited gap between girls' and boys' literacy skill attainment (Logan & Johnston, 2009; Merga, 2017a).

I also need to note here that as far as the research is concerned, books, and fiction books in particular, are more consistently associated with literacy benefit than the reading of other text types (Jerrim & Moss, 2019) such as emails (Pfost et al., 2013), text messages (Zebroff & Kaufman, 2016) and comic books (OECD, 2010). Jerrim et al. (2020) found that 'it is not only whether young people read or not that matters – but also what they read', and that 'as per some previous research, we find little evidence that reading newspapers, comics and magazines have positive benefits for young people's academic achievement', whereas 'in contrast, the association between reading books/novels and young people's academic progress at school is quite strong' (p. 529). Fortunately, the view that boys typically prefer to read non-fiction rather than fiction has been challenged by the data in recent times (Merga, 2017a), so it is certainly possible to connect boys with the kinds of fiction that can be appealing for their interests, just as it is with girls.

While I point out the continued importance of books and book reading, I do not suggest that students have nothing to gain from reading graphic novels, online news articles or diverse other text types. Personally, I was so addicted to graphic novels as a young person that I wrote my Honours dissertation on Kishiro's *Battle Angel Alita* (Gunnm) manga series, so I can certainly see enjoyment value that can be gained from reading diverse text types, in addition to the possibilities of enhancing cultural competence and facets of visual literacies. Furthermore, while the reading of fiction is more commonly associated with literacy benefit than the reading of informational texts, this book mounts an argument in Chapter 5 for the value of non-fiction books as a key health information resource for young people.

I report on the research findings to assert that at this stage, we have compelling evidence that books should remain an important part of young people's reading diet, and that in terms of literacy attainment, other text types should not entirely supplant books. However, it is important to note that these books need not be 'highbrow' literature. While more research is needed in this area, Martin-Chang et al. (2020) found that familiarity with popular young adult fiction was positively associated with teenagers' reading and spelling achievement and reading speed.

Reading for pleasure and opportunity

Students in schools today have a wide range of competing demands on their time. As I mentioned previously, even students who love reading may not have time to do it often, and we can't assume that young people are typically exposed to extended reading experiences in the course of their schooling. This is concerning, given that research has linked time spent reading at school with growth in reading skills (e.g. Taylor et al., 1990). While we need more research in this area, Vinterek et al. (2020) have contended that the Swedish school system

> does not manage to ensure equal opportunities for students to develop their reading literacy in middle and lower secondary school. On the contrary, the trend is that students' changing leisure-time media habits are mirrored by an equally diminishing amount of school-related reading, resulting in a drastic decrease in young people's engagement with long and continuous texts. (p. 13)

While there is a lack of similar research in other contexts, this finding may potentially resonate with you as a school library professional in other places.

As such, we can't assume that students are getting enough exposure to text to advance their reading skills in the school day, and there is a need to maintain a commitment to designated time for sustained RfP, such as in silent reading opportunities and provision of access to books. Unfortunately, as previously mentioned, RfP may be seen as a 'fluffy' pedagogy, and perhaps this is one of the reasons why we see a reduced commitment to providing opportunities for silent reading as students move through the years of schooling (Merga, 2013). Even where on the surface time seems to be made for RfP, this does not always translate to opportunity for RfP in practice; even where commitment to silent reading in the classroom is made, this is often replaced in practice by competing tasks necessitated by a crowded curriculum (Merga, 2018b). Furthermore, Hempel-Jorgensen et al. (2018) found that RfP may not always be implemented following best practice, finding a 'restrictive and restricting nature of pedagogy in relation to children's volition and social interaction as readers in the observed classrooms' (p. 92).

For students to read self-selected materials, one of the key tenets of reading for enjoyment, they need to be able to access the library during class time. Unfortunately, access to books through library visits in class time also drops as students move through the years of schooling (Merga & Mat Roni, 2017). COVID-19 related school closures may also have significantly limited access to books for students in recent times, and 40% of primary school children in England 'have not been able to take books home and have either had to rely on having their own books at home or solely on electronic versions of texts' (Center for Literacy in Primary Education (CLPE), 2021, p. 3). Unfortunately, 'the younger the child, the less likely they have been able to take books from school home' (p. 4), meaning that beginning readers from homes that lack rich book resources are most likely to be disadvantaged during school closures.

Even where library time for students is set within the school timetable, student access to libraries is still not a given, and opportunities for RfP are not necessarily available, even putting aside the interruptions of the COVID-19 related school closures. As I found in my research, 'weekly timetabling of library sessions does not guarantee the fostering of reading opportunity or engagement' (Merga, 2019, p. 83). Some school library professionals struggle to even see students for library orientation and induction, let alone reading opportunities, with an Australian teacher librarian working in secondary school explaining how she had observed that classroom teachers have become less supportive of facilitating library induction by making their students available.

At the beginning of the year, I used to give library orientations. And the last couple of years, I've had a couple of classes of Year 7s where they've said, 'No, we can't even get through what we're meant to get through, let alone anything else'. (p. 82).

This means that some students are moving from primary school to high school without even being familiarised with what their new libraries offer or how to use them. This must impact on their ability to make the most of the school library resource. School library professionals may need to mount strong arguments with their leadership team to ensure that this is supported by all concerned educators within the school. Given all the complex and costly literacy 'solutions' flung at schools, far more attention needs to be given to the simple and research-supported practice of ensuring students have opportunities to read sustained texts for pleasure in their school libraries.

RfP and related access to books should not be undervalued. Students must have access to *library time* that is *reading time*, and this time should not be impinged upon by other curricular demands as though RfP does not constitute a beneficial and educative experience. It is time to stop allowing this practice to be framed as simply some kind of filler activity to calm students down after lunch, and instead, we need to increase awareness of its importance for young people.

Why the school library professional is a model that matters

When we look at the kinds of people who exert influence on the decision-making of young people, we might not put school library professionals near the top of the list. Surely parents, peers and other teachers may have a greater influence, given that they usually get to spend far more time with our students. However, when it comes to fostering positive attitudes towards RfP and modelling keen engagement of reading, we cannot assume that this job will be done by others.

Research supports the contention that fostering reading engagement in young people is not safely in the hands of other social influences such as parents and teachers. Not all parents can provide models of engaged reading within the home, and not all classroom teachers are keen readers or see fostering reading engagement as part of their job (e.g. Garces-Bacsal et al., 2018). In their study of primary school teachers in the UK, Cremin et al. (2008) found that teachers may have limited knowledge of writers and children's literature, particularly in relation to literature with strong representative diversity, observing that it is questionable whether they know a sufficiently diverse range of writers to enable them to foster reader development and make informed recommendations to emerging readers with different needs and interests. The lack of professional knowledge and assurance with children's literature which this research reveals and the minimal knowledge of global literature indicated has potentially serious consequences for all learners. Particularly those from linguistic and cultural minority groups who may well be marginalised unless teachers' own reading repertoires can be expanded. (p. 458)

While there is a popular notion that every teacher is a teacher of reading (Alvermann & Moje, 2018), and that teachers are readers, Australian research has indicated that young people may not necessarily see their teachers as readers at all (Merga, 2016). Similarly, US research suggests that not all pre-service teachers 'come to English education programs with positive reading identities nor do all develop identities as reading teachers' (Kerkhoff et al., 2020, p. 208). Therefore, it cannot be assumed that classroom teachers have the time, knowledge base and/or motivation to ensure their students view them as keen reading models.

Similarly, parents are also not always willing or able to be effective models in this regard, and our research found that even though girls typically read more often than boys, they also received more encouragement to read (Merga & Mat Roni, 2018a).

Even where teachers and parents have supported reading engagement, this support can prematurely end with *expired expectations* and *orphaned responsibility*. While you may have come across these terms before, I'll provide a quick summary of what I mean by them in the context of this book.

First, expired expectations refers to where parents or teachers stop encouraging young people to read for pleasure once they have learned to read on their own. This curtailing of expectations may inadvertently communicate to the young person that reading is no longer important, and I've had young people tell me that this was the point that they realised that a regular reading habit was no longer necessary. Students who perceive expired expectations may stop reading for enjoyment, replacing it with other leisure activities now that reading is no longer expected or supported.

Second, orphaned responsibility occurs where parents assume it is the *teacher's* job, and teachers assume it is the *parent's* job to encourage young people to read (Bunbury, 1995; Merga & Mat Roni, 2018a) once young people can read on their own. This is obviously problematic when it occurs because it becomes no one's responsibility, hence the term orphaned responsibility.

Again, in the absence of encouragement and expectations, it is easy for young people to perceive that reading is no longer a valuable pastime for them. There are many other leisure practices that also afford pleasure and offer other rewards such as social connection, and therefore if reading is to compete with an activity such as computer games for young people's time, which could offer lower cognitive demands for more immediate rewards, it needs to at least be encouraged and supported. While research suggests that 'video games do not have or have very little relations with cognitive and school tests' (Lieury et al., 2016, p. 1587), 'in contrast, reading activities are positively associated with cognition and school tests' (p. 1588). However, it is not a given that young people understand the comparative benefits of RfP.

As such, communication of the importance of reading should not be lost to young people as they move through the years of schooling. Given that we know that children who think that reading is important read more frequently than those who do not (Fraguela-Vale et al., 2016; Merga & Mat Roni, 2018b), we cannot afford to have no one cheerleading for reading in young people's lives. As such, the potential contribution of the school library professional in building reading engagement and literacy skills through a clearly diverse and typically research-supported array of strategies should not be underestimated. In some children's lives, they may be the *only* person fulfilling this role.

Library professionals as literacy educators and supports of reading engagement

Now that we have established that reading engagement is beneficial, and that RfP counts as a valuable learning activity when implemented following best practice, it is time to take a close look at what library professionals do as literacy educators and supports of reading engagement. As with the previous chapter, here I draw on the data and some of the findings from the 2020–2021 Library Workforce Project, and you can learn more about the research methods employed in Appendix 1. In brief, this project involved individually analysing current job description forms or documents (referred to as JDFs) of teacher librarians from Australia, and then those of school librarians in the UK, in relation to their expected reading educator and reading engagement role. It also then involved comparatively analysing JDFs from Australia and the US in relation to the RfP supportive roles and characteristics of library professionals in these contexts.

While the Australian and UK documents were not analysed at the same time, there were clear similarities that emerged between the two roles, as you can see in Tables 1 and 2. While as expected, dual librarianship and education qualified Australian teacher librarians were far more likely to be termed literacy educators than their UK school librarian counterparts, school librarians in the UK were still expected to work closely with students to support reading and literacy skill development as well as implement and support educational reading programmes. Library professionals in both contexts were expected to be reading models, promote RfP, have a broad and current knowledge of literature, support student choice and promote a whole-school reading culture.

Australian and UK school library professionals as literacy educators

Table 1 draws on data from my recent JDF analysis to show the similarities in literacy educator role between Australian and UK school library professionals. That these analyses were not concurrent needs to be taken into account when looking at the relationships between the subthemes, as I would need to analyse them concurrently to derive conclusive results, but clearly there are similarities worth noting and exploring further. The table also includes the Australian data on what the scope looks like for each subtheme related to the literacy education and support role, and it also includes an example from the text of a JDF document to give the reader a sense of the kinds of wording used in articulating the role.

Table 1 *School library professionals as literacy educators*

Subtheme Australia	Related UK subtheme(s)	Australian scope content	Australian text example
Teaching for reading engagement and literacy	Work closely with students to support reading and literacy skill development. Implement and support reading programmes.	Plan and facilitate contemporary student-centred reading programmes. Link literary texts with curriculum units where appropriate. Collaborate with other teaching staff to promote literacy and literature. Provide training and information for staff and parents in reading, literacy and literature. Support teachers to enhance student literacy skills. Develop strategies to foster a love of reading and literature for leisure.	'Develop and lead programs to promote and improve literacy through reading. Support teachers to increase literacy and reading comprehension at all levels'. (S19)

Continued

Table 1 *Continued*

Subtheme Australia	Related UK subtheme(s)	Australian scope content	Australian text example
Text and reading promotion and student choice	Devise and support reading and literature events. Support literature selection.	Promote a diverse range of text types and themes, from varied cultural perspectives. Conduct book talks, make recommendations and guide students' recreational reading choices. Promote literature to staff. Promote the benefits of regular reading for academic performance. Plan, promote and conduct displays and events to encourage reading.	'Conduct Book Talks and recommend suitable reading material in order to inspire, engage and guide readers'. (S26)
Collection knowledge, building and curation	Have a broad and current knowledge of literature	Draw on a range of resources to make informed choices about collection development and publicise and promote new acquisitions. Possess an extensive knowledge of children's literature across a breadth of genres. Read junior and young adult fiction acquisitions.	'Use a range of publishers, literature websites and journals to make informed choices about collection development for young adults'. (S29)
Whole-school reading culture	Promote a whole-school reading culture.	Foster and maintain a school culture that promotes reading and literature.	'Develop a community-wide reading culture through the regular and active promotion of literature'. (S24)
Reading environment	No comparable subtheme.	Provide an environment conducive to reading.	'Provide an environment and atmosphere that is attractive and welcoming to boys and conducive to reading'. (S22)
Modelling	Promote and model reading for pleasure.	Model reading engagement and enjoyment.	'Ideally, the position of Teacher Librarian would be a member of staff who could represent and advocate for the quality teaching of English in all its forms, and the joyful association of reading and learning'. (S20)

(Adapted from Merga, 2020a, 2020b)

It can be seen that both Australian teacher librarians and UK school librarians were expected to play an important role as literacy educators and supports as articulated by schools through their JDFs, and these data in Table 1 suggest that it is common for school library professionals, at least in these nations, to be expected to model RfP; promote a whole-school reading culture; have a broad and current knowledge of literature that they can draw on to connect young people with books; devise and support reading and literature events; support student choice in literature selection; and work closely with students to support reading and literacy skill development. As such, in both contexts, Australian- and UK-based school library professionals can make an important contribution to students' reading engagement and related literacy performance.

Australian and US school library professionals' divergence on reading for pleasure

Are their similar expectations of Australian and US school library professionals when it comes to fostering RfP in their students?

After noticing the interesting commonalities between the reading engagement supportive role of Australian- and UK-based school library professionals, we decided to explore JDFs from Australia and the US with analysis focused on their role as supporters of RfP. As such, this was a more focused version of previous work, which looked at the whole role and the literacy educator aspect more generally, and did not compare nations concurrently.

We genuinely went into this analysis expecting to find strong similarity between Australia and the US in relation to this aspect of the role, given that:

- their professional standards may be quite similar in that both are typically dual qualified, though this may not always be the case in reality (as I explored in Merga, 2019), and
- there are some other similarities between the two education systems within which the school libraries operate, with Australia influenced by both the US and the UK (Dinham, 2015).

To investigate this question, US JDFs and a larger body of Australian JDFs that featured in the previous analysis (Merga, 2020a) were concurrently analysed to explore the current RfP supportive roles and characteristics in the US and Australia.

As you can see in Table 2, we were wrong; the differences between the two nations are notable, with 44.4% of US documents having no mention of an RfP supportive activity with reference to RfP, compared to 16.4% of

READING ENGAGEMENT FOR LITERACY   47

Table 2 Current RfP supportive roles and characteristics in the US and Australia

Role/characteristic in the US and Australia	% of total (N=126 US and N=61 Australia)	Aspect statement	Text examples
No mention of RfP	44.4%	No mention of an RfP supportive activity with reference to RfP.	Not applicable
No mention of RfP	16.4%	No mention of an RfP supportive activity with reference to RfP.	Not applicable
Fosters RfP and love of literature	31.7%	Empower and motivate students and staff to be enthusiastic readers. Promote a lifelong habit of reading. Encourage appreciation of literature, including diverse genres, text types and perspectives. Model a positive attitude towards reading.	'Empower students to be critical thinkers, enthusiastic readers, skilful researchers, and ethical users of information. To instil a love of reading and learning in all students and ensure equitable access to information . . . The school librarian supports students' success by guiding them in reading for understanding, for exposure to diversity of viewpoints and genres, and for pleasure'.
Fosters RfP and love of literature	62.3%	Promote and foster enjoyment of RfP for students with diverse interests and abilities. Encourage staff to read for pleasure. Encourage staff and students to have a lifelong love of literature. Have knowledge, skills and strategies for encouraging RfP.	'A focus on reading and a love of literature has for many years been a key feature of the culture of (School), and naturally, the Library plays a significant role in fostering and maintaining that emphasis and expectation. One of the most important points in our School's framework is: "At the heart of everything we do sits a love and appreciation of reading; it enables us to explore, investigate and expand on understandings and create new ideas"'.
Create reading contexts and cultures	14.3%	Create an inviting reading environment that promotes and enables RfP. Create book displays designed to increase student interest in reading. Promote a school-wide reading culture among students and staff.	'Maintains a comfortable environment conducive to learning and promotes an appreciation of literature and reading'.

Continued

Table 2 Continued

Role/characteristic in the US and Australia	% of total (N=126 US and N=61 Australia)	Aspect statement	Text examples
Create reading contexts and cultures	34.4%	Promote a school-wide culture of enthusiasm for reading. Provide a library environment that is conducive to and encouraging of reading. Create environmental features such as displays that promote reading and enjoyment of literature.	'Promote and foster an environment where students are engaged in reading, viewing, listening and creating for understanding and enjoyment. Provide an environment that encourages a habit and love of reading and of sharing children's literature'.
Knowledge of literature and collection with appeal	12.7%	Use students' interests to inform collection building. Have strong knowledge of current children's literature. Have extensive knowledge of current popular, young adult and classical literature.	'Recommends, promotes, and purchases resources based on student interest, skill/reading level, and curriculum requirements'.
Knowledge of literature and collection with appeal	42.6%	Have extensive knowledge of a wide range of literature, including but not limited to children's and young adult literature. Regularly read new literature. Seek opportunities for professional development in children's literature to further enhance knowledge of literature. Use a range of sources and tools to keep abreast of emerging works to provide a relevant, engaging and evolving collection.	'Provide an extensive collection of quality fiction and non-fiction to meet the needs of a wide and diverse range of boys of varying reading abilities and interests. Liaise with numerous book sellers/bookshops and develop relationships with various bookshops to ensure the School is provided with the most up to date books available, the most comprehensive range and the best new titles'.
Events and promotional activities and initiatives	11.9%	Conduct events, promotional activities and initiatives to encourage RfP. Organise book clubs, reading-related contests, book talks, author visits, reading promotions and various other programmes to encourage students to read.	'Promote a lifelong love of reading and a robust reading culture through regularly scheduled book clubs, book talks, mock Newbery Awards, displays, etc. Play an active role in special events such as book fairs and author visits'

Continued

Table 2 *Continued*

Role/characteristic in the US and Australia	% of total (N=126 US and N=61 Australia)	Aspect statement	Text examples
Events and promotional activities, initiatives and programmes	36.1%	Promote enjoyment of reading through events and promotional activities, initiatives and programmes. Collaborate with partners such as teachers and parents in fostering students' reading enjoyment through programmes and initiatives.	'Develop reading programs that encourage students to read widely on a regular basis. Collaborate with teachers to develop literature based reading programs. Develop activities to promote a love of reading and literature appreciation, such as: Book Week, author, illustrator or storyteller visits, literary activities'.
Connecting students with reading materials	10.3%	Connect students with appropriate and appealing reading materials through discussion about books and supporting selection. Provide book matching through counselling and recommendations to meet student interests. Create reading lists and reading suggestions. Support families to maintain student reading over the summer vacation period.	'Provides reference and readers' advisory services to the general student population, including students who have special learning needs or specialized intellectual interests. Prepares lists of topical and new materials to support class assignments and to promote interest in reading'.
Connecting students and staff with reading materials	32.9%	Connect students with reading materials appropriate to their interests and abilities through guidance and recommendations. Teach students the habits and practices of self-directed reading. Promote and resource staff recreational reading.	'Conduct Book Talks and recommend suitable reading material in order to inspire, engage and guide readers'.
Modelling and individual reader identity	23.0%	Be an avid reader. Display personal characteristics and avid reader ideation and practices. Share enthusiasm and passion for reading that inspires others.	'Have a passion for reading, literature and technology in education. Love of literature'.

(Adapted from Merga & Ferguson, 2021)

Australian documents. For ease of readability, Australian findings are presented in grey cells, with US findings in white cells.

It seems that when it comes to the valuing of RfP, schools' expectations of US school library professionals *do* differ from those of their Australian counterparts. This has interesting implications for workforce mobility; if you are a school library professional outside the US who values fostering RfP, the US might not be the right place for you to work, because your employer may not value this, given that nearly 45% did not articulate any expectation of this facet of the role. Given the detailed presentation of the benefits of RfP given in this chapter, it also raises questions about US school library professionals' role as a literacy support.

Another interesting difference was that while nearly a quarter of Australian documents talked about the school library professional as a reading model, with a *reader identity*, the same expectation was not there in the US documents. As such, if you are a school library professional who does not enjoy reading, or identify as a reader, you may be far more likely to find satisfying work in the school library market in the US rather than in Australia, where a passion for reading is more likely to be expected.

I would love to learn more about the reasons behind the differences in this facet of the role in Australian and US school library professionals. The American Association of School Librarians' (AASL) (2020) revised position statement on the school librarian's role in reading *clearly* endorses a role for fostering reading engagement. It promotes an expectation that 'the school librarian creates a rich reading environment and culture within school libraries and school communities to nurture learners' journeys in finding their passion for reading and lifelong learning' (p. 2). As such, there seems in many cases to be a concerning divide between professional expectations articulated by AASL as the professional body and what schools want in regards to the role as detailed in their JDFs, which is particularly strange given the educational importance of this facet of the role which I have explained both in this chapter and the following chapter. This is all the more confusing given that, as noted by Reed and Oslund (2018), the US has seen 'professional and national mandates for literacy instruction to be part of the school librarian's instructional role' (p. 15). Perhaps at a school level, literacy instruction is not seen to include fostering engagement for literacy-supportive practices, or perhaps more recent emphases and initiatives in the ever-changing climate of US education have superseded this focus.

Further thoughts

The number one takeaway message from this chapter is that this multifaceted aspect of the school library professional role cannot afford to be sacrificed among the growing demands faced by the professions. We need school library professionals as visible and active experts focusing on building reading engagement and fostering RfP. RfP should be recognised as an important and literacy-supportive activity, and we need to keep encouraging and supporting our children to be readers both in the early years of schooling and beyond. As the key active advocates for RfP in schools – and in some cases, the only positive reading models in young people's lives – this is a responsibility for school library professionals, though one that may not be valued equally across the school library professional roles in diverse nations, as seen in the analysis of Australian and US JDFs.

In this vein, the second key message would be that, as also seen in the previous chapter, while there are certainly similarities between the library professions in Australia, the UK and the US, there are also important differences that should not be ignored. If US classroom educators also do not have the time, knowledge and/or inclination to foster RfP in their students, who is taking on this role in the US if not the school library professionals? Why is this aspect of the role so much more likely to be expected in the Australian context than in the US one?

Furthermore, it is crucial that current research looks at the extent to which these literacy educator roles (or lack thereof) reflect what is actually done by school library professionals within their schools. While I hope that the reason that the RfP component is absent from so many US JDFs is because it is *tacit* and commonly in practice, I worry that it is absent because it has been devalued, poorly understood and crowded out of the school library professional role. Even if schools are expecting this facet of the role without stating it, if they are not bothering to articulate this aspect of the role in their JDFs, do they really understand the value of it?

And in this regard, we return full circle to the need for advocacy. School library professionals and their organisations need to make sure that school leaders understand that their fears of underperformance in literacy at the local, national and international level can, to some extent, be assuaged by allowing students who have independent reading skills *more time to read*, and opportunities to read for pleasure. While you and I know that reading frequency is related to literacy skill development and maintenance, it is surprising how many school administrators are unaware of this research.

Allowing opportunities for RfP in the library is not typically a complex intervention, even though it may be poorly understood and valued. In many cases, it just involves better use of resources that are already available (the school library professional and the library). Furthermore, as I explore in the following chapter, even where students *are* struggling with independent reading skills, school library professionals may play an important role in building their reading skills and related engagement. As such, the library and the school library professional can be central to reading engagement and related literacy attainment for *all* students.

References

Aerila, J. A., Lähteelä, J., Kauppinen, M. A., & Siipola, M. (2021). Holistic literature education as an effective tool for social-emotional learning. In J. Tussey & L. Haas (Eds.), *Handbook of research on supporting social and emotional development through literacy education* (pp. 26–49). IGI Global.

Allington, R. L., & McGill-Franzen, A. M. (2021). Reading volume and reading achievement: A review of recent research. *Reading Research Quarterly, 56*, S231–S238.

Alvermann, D. E., & Moje, E. B. (2018). A relational model of adolescent literacy instruction: Disrupting the discourse of 'every teacher a teacher of reading'. In D. E. Alvermann, N. J. Unrau, M. Sailors, & R. B. Ruddell (Eds.), *Theoretical models and processes of literacy* (pp. 1072–1103). Taylor & Francis.

American Association of School Librarians (AASL). (2020). *The school librarian's role in reading: Position statement.* http://www.ala.org/aasl/sites/ala.org.aasl/files/content/advocacy/statements/docs/AASL_Position_Statement_RoleinReading_2020-01-25.pdf

Australian Curriculum, Assessment and Reporting Authority. (n.d.). *General capabilities.* https://www.australiancurriculum.edu.au/f-10-curriculum/general-capabilities

Baker, M., & Milligan, K. (2016). Boy-girl differences in parental time investments: Evidence from three countries. *Journal of Human Capital, 10*, 399–441.

Barber, A. T., & Klauda, S. L. (2020). How reading motivation and engagement enable reading achievement: Policy implications. *Policy Insights from the Behavioral and Brain Sciences, 7*(1), 27–34.

Becker, M., McElvany, N., & Kortenbruck, M. (2010). Intrinsic and extrinsic reading motivation as predictors of reading literacy: A longitudinal study. *Journal of Educational Psychology, 102*(4), 773–784.

Bjørgan, J. B. (2018). *Strukturendringer i den litterære offentligheten. En analyse av unge voksnes lesevaner og bruk av litterære arenaer* [Master's thesis, The University of Bergen]. https://bora.uib.no/bora-xmlui/bitstream/handle/1956/18620/Strukturendringer-i-den-litter-re-offentligheten-JBj-rgan-2018.pdf?sequence=1

Bunbury, R. M. (1995). *Children's choice: Reading at home or at school.* Deakin University Press.

Center for Literacy in Primary Education (CLPE). (2021). *Reading for pleasure in 2020.* https://clpe.org.uk/publications-and-bookpacks/research/clpe-reading-pleasure-2021

Chapple, M., Williams, S., Billington, J., Davis, P., & Corcoran, R. (2021). An analysis of the reading habits of autistic adults compared to neurotypical adults and implications for future interventions. *Research in Developmental Disabilities, 115*, e104003.

Clark, C., & Picton, I. (2020). *Children and young people's reading in 2020 before and during the COVID-19 lockdown.* National Literacy Trust research report. Retrieved from https://files.eric.ed.gov/fulltext/ED607776.pdf

Clark, C., & Teravainen-Goff, A. (2020). *Children and young people's reading in 2019.* National Literacy Trust research report. Retrieved from https://cdn.literacytrust.org.uk/media/documents/Reading_trends_in_2019_-_Final.pdf

Clavel, J. G., & Mediavilla, M. (2020). The intergenerational effect of parental enthusiasm for reading. *Applied Economic Analysis.* https://doi.org/10.1108/AEA-12-2019-0050

Cremin, T., Mottram, M., Bearne, E., & Goodwin, P. (2008). Exploring teachers' knowledge of children's literature. *Cambridge Journal of Education, 38*(4), 449–464.

Darmawan, I. G. N. (2020). The changes in attitudes of 15-year-old Australian students towards reading, mathematics and science and their impact on student performance. *Australian Journal of Education, 64*(3), 304–327.

Dinham, S. (2015). The worst of both worlds: How the US and UK are influencing education in Australia. *Education Policy Analysis Archives, 23*(49), 1–20.

Durik, A. M., Vida, M., & Eccles, J. S. (2006). Task values and ability beliefs as predictors of high school literacy choices: A developmental analysis. *Journal of Educational Psychology, 98*(2), 382–393.

Ferguson, C. & Merga, M. K. (2021). How can an adult literacy tutoring program help participants build confidence and meet their goals? *Australian Journal of Language and Literacy, 44*(1), 75–83.

Ferguson, C., Merga, M., & Winn, S. (2021). Communications in the time of a pandemic: The readability of documents for public consumption. *Australian and New Zealand Journal of Public Health, 45*(2), 116–121.

Fraguela-Vale, R., Pose-Porto, H., & Varela-Garrote, L. (2016). Tiempos escolares y lectura. *Ocnos. Revista de estudios sobre lectura, 15*(2), 67–76.

Garces-Bacsal, R. M., Tupas, R., Kaur, S., Paculdar, A. M., & Baja, E. S. (2018). Reading for pleasure: Whose job is it to build lifelong readers in the classroom? *Literacy, 52*(2), 95–102.

Grace, R. A. (2021). *Improving students' K-prep reading scores by investigating the reading culture at Harrison Independent School* [Doctoral dissertation, Liberty University]. ScholarsCrossing. https://digitalcommons.liberty.edu/doctoral/2834

Guthrie, J. T., Klauda, S. L., & Ho, A. N. (2013). Modeling the relationships among reading instruction, motivation, engagement, and achievement for adolescents. *Reading Research Quarterly, 48*(1), 9–26.

Hempel-Jorgensen, A., Cremin, T., Harris, D., & Chamberlain, L. (2018). Pedagogy for reading for pleasure in low socio-economic primary schools: Beyond 'pedagogy of poverty'? *Literacy, 52*(2), 86–94.

Jerrim, J., & Moss, G. (2019). The link between fiction and teenagers' reading skills: International evidence from the OECD PISA study. *British Educational Research Journal, 45*(1), 181–200.

Jerrim, J., Lopez-Agudo, L. A., & Marcenaro-Gutierrez, O. D. (2020). Does it matter what children read? New evidence using longitudinal census data from Spain. *Oxford Review of Education, 46*(5), 515–533.

Kerkhoff, S., Broere, M., & Premont, D. (2020). Average and avid: Preservice English teachers' reading identities. *English Teaching: Practice & Critique, 19*(2), 197–215.

Kucirkova, N., & Cremin, T. (2020). *Children reading for pleasure in the digital age: Mapping reader engagement*. Sage.

Lane, M., & Conlon, G. (2016). *The impact of literacy, numeracy and computer skills on earnings and employment outcomes*. OECD Education Working Papers, No. 129, OECD Publishing. http://dx.doi.org/10.1787/5jm2cv4t4gzs-en

Levine, S. L., Cherrier, S., Holding, A. C., & Koestner, R. (2020). For the love of reading: Recreational reading reduces psychological distress in college students and autonomous motivation is the key. *Journal of American College Health*. https://doi.org/10.1080/07448481.2020.1728280

Lieury, A., Lorant, S., Trosseille, B., Champault, F., & Vourc'h, R. (2016). Video games vs. reading and school/cognitive performances: A study on 27000 middle school teenagers. *Educational Psychology, 36*(9), 1560–1595.

Locher, F., & Pfost, M. (2020). The relation between time spent reading and reading comprehension throughout the life course. *Journal of Research in Reading, 43*(1), 57–77.

Logan, S., & Johnston, R. (2009). Gender differences in reading ability and attitudes: Examining where these differences lie. *Journal of Research in Reading, 32*(2), 199–214.

Mak, H. W., & Fancourt, D. (2020a). Reading for pleasure in childhood and adolescent healthy behaviours: Longitudinal associations using the Millennium Cohort Study. *Preventive Medicine, 130*, e105889.

Mak, H. W., & Fancourt, D. (2020b). Longitudinal associations between reading for pleasure and child maladjustment: Results from a propensity score matching analysis. *Social Science & Medicine, 253*, e112971.

Martin-Chang, S., Kozak, S., & Rossi, M. (2020). Time to read young adult fiction: Print exposure and linguistic correlates in adolescents. *Reading and Writing, 33*(3), 741–760.

Merga, M. K. (2013). Should Silent Reading feature in a secondary school English programme? West Australian students' perspectives on Silent Reading. *English in Education, 47*(3), 229–244.

Merga, M. K. (2016). 'I don't know if she likes reading': Are teachers perceived to be keen readers, and how is this determined? *English in Education, 50*(3), 255–269.

Merga, M. (2017a). Do males really prefer non-fiction, and why does it matter? *English in Australia, 52*(1), 27–35.

Merga, M. K. (2017b). Becoming a reader: Significant social influences on avid book readers. *School Library Research, 20,* 1–21.

Merga, M. K. (2018a). *Reading engagement for tweens and teens: What would make them read more?* ABC-CLIO/Libraries Unlimited.

Merga, M. (2018b). Silent reading and discussion of self-selected books in the contemporary classroom. *English in Australia, 53*(1), 70–82.

Merga, M. K. (2019). *Librarians in schools as literacy educators.* Palgrave Macmillan.

Merga, M. K. (2020a). School librarians as literacy educators within a complex role. *Journal of Library Administration, 60*(8), 889–908.

Merga, M. K. (2020b). What is the literacy supportive role of the school librarian in the United Kingdom? *Journal of Librarianship & Information Science.* https://doi.org/10.1177/0961000620964569

Merga, M. K., & Ferguson, C. (2021). School librarians supporting students' reading for pleasure: A job description analysis. *Australian Journal of Education.* https://doi.org/10.1177/0004944121991275

Merga, M. K., & Mat Roni, S. (2017). Choosing strategies of children and the impact of age and gender on library use: Insights for librarians. *Journal of Library Administration, 57*(6), 607–630.

Merga, M. K., & Mat Roni, S. (2018a). Parents as social influences encouraging book reading: Research directions for librarians' literacy advocacy. *Journal of Library Administration, 58*(7), 674–697.

Merga, M. K., & Mat Roni, S. (2018b). Children's perceptions of the importance and value of reading. *Australian Journal of Education, 62*(2), 135–153.

Organisation for Economic Co-operation and Development (OECD). (2010). *PISA 2009 results: Executive summary.* OECD Publishing.

Parsons, A. W., Parsons, S. A., Malloy, J. A., Gambrell, L. B., Marinak, B. A., Reutzel, D. R., & Fawson, P. C. (2018). Upper elementary students' motivation to read fiction and nonfiction. *The Elementary School Journal, 118,* 505–523.

Pfost, M., Dörfler, T., & Artelt, C. (2013). Students' extracurricular reading behavior and the development of vocabulary and reading comprehension. *Learning and Individual Differences, 26,* 89–102.

Reed, K. N., & Oslund, E. L. (2018). School librarians as co-teachers of literacy: Librarian perceptions and knowledge in the context of the literacy instruction role. *School Library Research, 21.* https://files.eric.ed.gov/fulltext/EJ1202900.pdf

Rogiers, A., Van Keer, H., & Merchie, E. (2020). The profile of the skilled reader: An investigation into the role of reading enjoyment and student characteristics. *International Journal of Educational Research, 99,* 101512.

Scholes, L. (2021). Year 3 boys' and girls' enjoyment for reading across economic demographics in Australia: Implications for boys and students from lower SES communities. *International Journal of Inclusive Education.* https://doi.org/10.1080/13603116.2021.1941319

Scholes, L., Spina, N., & Comber, B. (2021). Disrupting the 'boys don't read' discourse: Primary school boys who love reading fiction. *British Educational Research Journal, 47*(1), 163–180.

Shomos, A., & Forbes, M. (2014). *Literacy and numeracy skills and labour market outcomes in Australia.* Productivity Commission. https://www.pc.gov.au/research/supporting/literacy-numeracy-skills/literacy-numeracy-skills.pdf

Stansfield, J., & Bunce, L. (2014). The relationship between empathy and reading fiction: Separate roles for cognitive and affective components. *Journal of European Psychology Students, 5*(3), 9–18.

Sullivan, A., & Brown, M. (2015). Reading for pleasure and progress in vocabulary and mathematics. *British Educational Research Journal, 41*(6), 971–991.

Taylor, B. M., Frye, B. J., & Maruyama, G. M. (1990). Time spent reading and reading growth. *American Educational Research Journal, 27*(2), 351–362.

Torppa, M., Niemi, P., Vasalampi, K., Lerkkanen, M. K., Tolvanen, A., & Poikkeus, A. M. (2020). Leisure reading (but not any kind) and reading comprehension support each other: A longitudinal study across grades 1 and 9. *Child Development, 91*(3), 876–900.

Van Bergen, E., Vasalampi, K., & Torppa, M. (2020). How are practice and performance related? Development of reading from age 5 to 15. *Reading Research Quarterly.* https://doi.org/10.1002/rrq.309

Vanden Dool, C., & Simpson, A. (2021). Reading for pleasure: Exploring reading culture in an Australian early years classroom. *Literacy.* https://doi.org/10.1111/lit.12247

Vinterek, M., Winberg, M., Tegmark, M., Alatalo, T., & Liberg, C. (2020). The decrease of school related reading in Swedish compulsory school: Trends between 2007 and 2017. *Scandinavian Journal of Educational Research.* https://doi.org/10.1080/00313831.2020.1833247

Wang, H., Guan, H., Yi, H., Seevak, E., Manheim, R., Boswell, M., & Kotb, S. (2020). Independent reading in rural China's elementary schools: A mixed-methods analysis. *International Journal of Educational Development, 78*, e102241.

Westbrook, J., Sutherland, J., Oakhill, J., & Sullivan, S. (2019). 'Just reading': The impact of a faster pace of reading narratives on the comprehension of poorer adolescent readers in English classrooms. *Literacy, 53*(2), 60–68.

Yoon, J. C. (2002). Three decades of sustained silent reading: A meta-analytic review of the effects of SSR on attitude toward reading. *Reading Improvement, 39*(4), 186–196.

Zebroff, D., & Kaufman, D. (2016). Texting, reading, and other daily habits associated with adolescents' literacy levels. *Education and Information Technologies, 22*(5), 2197–2216.

3
Librarians Supporting Struggling Literacy Learners Beyond the Early Years

When you read the title of this chapter, as a school library professional, certain students that you've worked with over the years probably came to mind as struggling literacy learners (SLLs). You have been in close proximity to the challenges they have faced as they have fallen further and further behind their higher-achieving peers as they move through the years of schooling, struggling to develop the literacy skills that support academic achievement.

I know there has been dissent about using the term 'struggle' in recent times, and I recognise that it can contribute to a homogenising deficit discourse that can obscure the strengths and differences within this group, but I am strategic in my choice of this term. First, like Lupo et al. (2019), I believe that 'struggle is not a bad word, as there are benefits of overcoming the struggle of reading difficult texts with the right type of support' (p. 558). Second, and perhaps most importantly, I am also concerned about more positively naming or framing these students in the literature, because on a pragmatic level it is already very hard to access sufficient support to meet the needs of these students (as we explore in detail in Merga et al., 2020a). Any change of nomenclature that downplays the difficulties these students experience could have the effect of further decreasing the likelihood that educators and schools will get adequate resourcing to support their needs, which as I explore herein, are complex and varied.

However, I know that these students are far more than this label. They have diverse intellectual capacities, as even highly intelligent students can fall into the SLL category when they experience issues that act as a barrier to their achievement, and each of these SLLs may also have diverse aspirations, talents and backgrounds. I conflate them as SLLs not to erase their uniqueness but rather to argue that there is a pressing need to concentrate resourcing on the needs of these students.

While SLLs are still forging basic but essential literacy skills, the focus of their learning experiences in school increasingly shifts to higher-order skills that they may not be able to access due to gaps in these foundational literacy skills. This has been likened to a Matthew Effect, where the rich get richer and the poor get poorer; for example, in the case of reading,

> if the development of vocabulary knowledge substantially facilitates reading comprehension, and if reading itself is a major mechanism leading to vocabulary growth – which in turn will enable more efficient reading – then we truly have a reciprocal relationship that should continue to drive further growth in reading throughout a person's development.
>
> (Stanovich, 2009, p. 36)

The Matthew Effect results in a spread of literacy achievement between high-ability students and SLLs so large that it can pose a great challenge for mainstream teachers seeking to meet the learning needs of all of the students in their classrooms.

For example, findings based on Victorian students in Australia, gleaned through analysis of student assessments of literacy and numeracy, describe a growing gap. They suggest that

> the spread of student achievement more than doubles as students move through school in Australia. The middle 60 per cent of students in Year 3 are working within a two-and-a-half-year range. By Year 9, the spread for these students is five-and-a-half years. The top ten per cent of students are about eight years ahead of the bottom ten per cent.
>
> (Goss & Sonnemann, 2016, p. 4)

As such, meeting the needs of students with a substantial achievement gap in one mainstream classroom is one of the biggest challenges that educators face today.

In the previous chapter, I briefly detailed some of the benefits of literacy skills in relation to how they can be enhanced through reading engagement, which in turn can be strongly mediated by school library professionals. In this chapter, I will give greater attention to how *school library professionals* such as teachers and school librarians may support SLLs beyond the early years, and why this role can be so beneficial.

The challenge of low literacy

First, we know that in current times, the need for advanced literacy skills is strong, given the ubiquity of technologically mediated communication. In order to succeed in the modern world, our students need to be equipped with robust literacy skills:

> The nature of reading has evolved significantly over the past decade, due to changes in technology, the use of electronic devices and the increasing need for readers to engage in a greater variety of reading tasks, such as triangulating different sources, navigating through ambiguity, distinguishing between fact and opinion, and constructing knowledge.
>
> (Sizmur et al., 2019, p. 32)

When students' literacy skills are not developed, or they stagnate, this can have major implications for their lives both within and beyond school. We know that lack of literacy skills limits opportunity in school (Daggett & Hasselbring, 2007), the workplace (Kirsch et al., 2002), and broader society (Keslair, 2017), and it can constrain students' earning potential and employment prospects (McIntosh & Vignoles, 2001) and employment into adulthood (Australian Bureau of Statistics (ABS), 2013; OECD & Statistics Canada, 2000). As such, one of the most important interventions for levelling the playing field that can impact on the school years and beyond involves building young people's literacy skills regardless of the level of literacy attainment they have when they enter into formal schooling.

While concerns have been raised over falling literacy in various contexts, in Australia in recent times, the number of SLLs seems to be growing, which means that the number of young people who will struggle to cope with the literacy demands needed in everyday life in adulthood can be expected to grow likewise. Nearly one in five Australian teenagers could now be considered an SLL due to low literacy performance (Thomson et al., 2016), and according to the most recent available PISA findings, this situation is not improving over time; between 2000 and 2018, Australia's performance in reading literacy decreased 'from 528 points in 2000 to 503 points in 2018' (Thomson et al., 2019, p. xv) and 'the proportion of low performers in Australia has increased by 7 percentage points between 2000 and 2018' (p. 32). Furthermore,

> Internationally, the OECD has identified Level 2 as the level of proficiency on the PISA performance scale at which students demonstrate reading literacy competencies that will enable them to actively participate in life situations. 80% of Australian students attained this level compared to 88% in 2000. In Australia, Level 3 has been identified as the National Proficient Standard in reading

literacy. 59% of Australian students attained this standard compared to 69% in 2000.

(Thomson et al., 2019, p. 32)

This is concerning, given that Australia already has more than seven million adult Australians with literacy levels that are below what is needed to function with ease in current life (ABS, 2013).

SLLs are not only an issue for Australian schools. The performance of SLLs is also of broader international concern, given that 'the proportion of low performers, both girls and boys, increased between 2009 and 2018, on average across OECD countries' (Schleicher, 2019, p. 18). While some nations may hesitate to turn their focus on their lower-performing students, due to concerns that this may be to the detriment of higher-performing students, 'PISA results show that countries can pull up low performers without adversely affecting other students' (p. 18), suggesting that this fear is unlikely to be justified. England has also not seen improvements in the literacy performance of its SLLs, though it has a smaller achievement gap between high- and lower-performing students than both Australia and the US. Most recent findings indicate that 'England had 17% of pupils working at the lower proficiency levels (below Level 2)' (Sizmur et al., 2019, p. 49), which is more positive than many nations, but still shows room for progress. Recent findings from Chile suggest that nearly half of Chilean tenth graders are reading below grade level, and that socio-economic status can be an influential factor; furthermore, Chileans do not typically identify as frequent readers (Cubillos Guzmán, 2021). We need to focus on our SLLs, and give them the attention and support they need to achieve their goals.

Student literacy is about far more than can be captured in a single high-stakes literacy assessment. While high-stakes literacy test results need to be used with great caution as an indicator of overall national student literacy attainment (Niyozov & Hughes, 2019), in the absence of an alternative measure to track the prevalence of SLLs, these results are presented here with this clear caveat. It would be great to be able to avoid these kinds of measurement systems altogether, but the reality is that schools may struggle to get adequate resourcing to support their SLLs, and these data are badly needed to make the argument that SLLs are not neglected in budgetary considerations at national, state and local levels (Merga et al., 2020a).

This said, weighing the pig does not make it fatter, and no amount of measurement and indicators of SLLs will lead to any material change without a robust focus on their needs, and allocation of resourcing linked to best practice for supporting SLLs. This includes investment in school libraries and their staffing.

Who are the struggling literacy learners?

It is a useful starting point to gauge the kinds of specific challenges that these learners are facing in order to develop appropriate strategies to assist them. In 2019, I undertook the Supporting Struggling Secondary Literacy Learners (SSSLL) project; identifying these challenges had been in the back of my mind since a serendipitous discussion with an early career teacher at a conference where I was presenting. At morning teatime, I grabbed some delicious cake and took the opportunity to meet some classroom teachers to learn more about the issues currently preoccupying them. I was involved in initial teacher education at that time, and I always liked having the chance to ask early career teachers if there was anything missing from their initial teacher education in relation to literacy that I could increase in my programme. This young teacher explained that the biggest issue he faced was the SLLs in his mainstream English classrooms. He felt that he lacked the knowledge and skills to create effective interventions in his rural context that met the diverse issues faced by these students. This resonated with my own early experiences as an English teacher.

When I looked more closely at the issue, I was overwhelmed by the number of one-size-fits-all solutions to supporting SLLs being marketed to schools that did not align with my own experience or the experiences of educators that I've spoken with over the years. These range from computer applications that are marketed to solve the issues of SLLs, scripted reading programmes that position students as a homogenous group of empty vessels that all learn the same way and at the same rate, and educational products that focus on *one* aspect of literacy (such as phonics) and position this as the solution for *all* students.

Many scholars, and I would argue most educators who work closely with young people, would agree that literacy skills are very complex, and the needs of SLLs are not often identical. Therefore, it seems implausible that simplistic solutions would fit the needs of every child. For example, Kim's (2020) direct and indirect effects model of reading (DIER) illustrates the complexity of skills involved in the reading process:

> According to DIER, the reading process draws on a complex array of language, cognition, knowledge, and skills, including word reading, listening comprehension, text reading fluency, background knowledge (content knowledge and discourse knowledge [e.g., genre knowledge including text structure, register knowledge]), reading affect or socio-emotions (e.g., motivation, attitude, self-concept, self- efficacy, anxiety), higher order cognitions and regulation (e.g., inference, perspective taking, reasoning [see Note 1], monitoring, and setting goals), vocabulary, grammatical (morphosyntactic and

syntactic) knowledge, phonology, morphology, orthography, and domain-general cognitions (e.g., working memory [see Baddeley, 2012] and attentional control [attentional control includes both cognitive or inhibitory control and behavioural control]. (p. 469–470)

As such, it just doesn't seem realistic for schools to seek to address the issues of SLLs through just buying an application or programme focused on one or a few of these skills.

Drawing on my previous experiences as an English teacher, as well as the research literature, I expected to find that there were many external factors that also impacted on literacy skill development. The most obvious one of these is absenteeism. Where students do not regularly attend your school, it doesn't matter what rich classroom learning experiences teachers put in place for them to bridge their literacy gaps, or how much money the school throws at a new 'solution'; if they are not there, they are not going to be exposed to them. It was time to find out if we were the outliers, or if SLLs are actually, as I suspected, felt to be a heterogeneous group with diverse issues, experiences and difficulties.

I was also interested to find that it is relatively rare for researchers to actually ask classroom teachers and other school-based educators such as teacher librarians about the SLLs that they work with on a daily basis; I found this odd as these are qualified educators with expertise in literacy, whose valuable insights should be tapped in order to give researchers the real picture of what it means to support an SLL in today's classrooms. This raises another issue; so much research in education about educators does not draw on the knowledge bases of educators, and I feel that researchers need to get better at giving voice to these experts in their research.

In this study, I was lucky to have 315 classroom teachers of English in mainstream Australian classrooms respond to my survey on the SSSLL project, which collected both qualitative and quantitative data on English teachers' strategies, preparedness and challenges for supporting SLLs to achieve their literacy goals. As the survey responses began to roll in, it quickly became apparent that many teachers are really struggling to meet the needs of SLLs in mainstream classrooms. Findings suggested that, as per Table 1, the sheer breadth of barriers faced at both individual and group levels can be staggering. It is also very important to note that many young people who struggle with literacy do not fall into English as an additional language or dialect (EAL/D) or diagnosed learning difficulty categories. This distinction needs to be made as in Australia, as well as some other contexts, additional support for schools and teachers can be contingent on students' alignment with these categories, so this means that many teachers are not

Table 1 Plurality of perceived barriers at group and individual level and preponderance of students who have a diagnosed learning difficulty or are EAL/D learners

Agreement	in sample (N = 315)	in sample (%)
Agreement with diverse barriers at group level (Group)		
Strongly agree	185	58.73
Somewhat agree	105	33.33
Neither agree nor disagree	17	5.40
Somewhat disagree	5	1.59
Strongly disagree	3	0.95
Agreement with diverse barriers at individual level (Individual)		
Strongly agree	212	67.30
Somewhat agree	93	29.52
Neither agree nor disagree	5	1.59
Somewhat disagree	3	0.95
Strongly disagree	2	0.63
Agreement with SLLs typically having learning difficulty (Diagnosed)		
Strongly agree	23	7.30
Somewhat agree	131	41.59
Neither agree nor disagree	55	17.46
Somewhat disagree	82	26.03
Strongly disagree	24	7.62
Agreement with SLLs typically being EAL/D		
Strongly agree	16	5.08
Somewhat agree	62	19.68
Neither agree nor disagree	38	12.06
Somewhat disagree	93	29.52
Strongly disagree	106	33.65

(Adapted from Merga, 2019a)

eligible for additional support for many of the SLLs that they work with as they do not fit these categories.

While according to Table 1, one-size-fits-all approaches are unlikely to uniformly work at either individual or group levels, what I found most interesting was the respondents' written descriptions of what this diversity looked like in their mainstream secondary English classrooms. For example, one respondent details a range of complex issues:

> EAL/D, Intellectual impairment, Speech language impairment, low attendance, multiple primary schools, ADD, ODD, ADHD, dyslexia, inability to sound out words, low comprehension, poor verbal expression, difficulty understanding

verbal and/or written instructions, bullying, disengagement, difficulty spelling, limited vocabulary, gaps in education, health issues (e.g. spent significant time in hospital), low stamina for writing and reading, illegible handwriting, low expectations of themselves due to failing every semester for YEARS, lack of early intervention, working at different year levels significantly below the grade they're in.

(Merga, 2019a, p. 380)

While I encourage you to read the whole paper for a fulsome explanation of the challenges facing these students as perceived by their teachers (Merga, 2019a), the coverage I've given here hopefully highlights that SLLs face complex and often collocated issues, and that supporting these learners should ideally involve teams of supportive educators, family members and community supports. However, in reality, these classroom-based educators working with these students often do so with very little support, as I explore further herein, and this is where a helping hand from the school library professional can make all the difference.

Where libraries and library professionals fit in

While this consideration has been neglected in the research for years, in recent times, more attention has been given to the role that library professionals may play in supporting SLLs in their schools (Huffman et al., 2020; Merga, 2019b). Given that the challenges of meeting the needs of SLLs are considerable, it is unsurprising that the SSSLL project found that many teachers lack adequate time and resourcing to support students facing diverse literacy challenges in mainstream classes (Merga et al., 2020a). Teachers may also lack confidence in their education and training, given the wide array of issues they need to be deeply knowledgeable in to meet these students' needs (Merga, Mat Roni & Mason, 2020c).

Furthermore, if you are reading this and you are working in a school where your leadership team is not strongly literacy supportive, you are not alone. The SSSLL project found that school leadership support may not always be forthcoming, where only '56.51% of respondents agreed that their school leader is strongly committed to ensuring that SLLs have their literacy skills developed across all learning areas in their school' (Merga et al., 2020b, p. 541). This leadership is important because 'the strongest relationship among the variables examined was between perceived leadership commitment and realization of a supportive whole-school culture for struggling literacy learners' (p. 546), suggesting that leaders who take responsibility for addressing the issues faced by SLLs are essential to the creation of school cultures that are committed to their support and improvement. We weren't surprised by these findings, given what teacher librarians had told us in our earlier research, which found that the success of literacy-supportive initiatives such as whole-school reading cultures may be reliant on strong leadership support (Merga & Mason, 2019). Any research-supported contribution that school library professionals can make in the lives of these students constitutes a very worthwhile investment that may be badly needed by educators and students alike, and winning the support of leadership might be the most important starting point.

School library professionals are already supporting SLLs as part of their regular practices. For example, I analysed data I collected from teacher librarians at 30 schools in the 2018 Teacher Librarians as Australian Literature Advocates in Schools (TLALAS) project, to begin to unpack what school library professionals may contribute to the learning of SLLs. I found that among numerous strategies, teacher librarians provided support by:

1. identifying struggling readers
2. providing them with age- and skill-appropriate materials
3. undertaking skill scaffolding supporting choice
4. supporting students with special needs
5. providing one-to-one matching
6. promoting access to books
7. enhancing the social position of books and reading
8. reading aloud to students
9. facilitating silent reading
10. preparing students for high-stakes literacy testing.

(Merga, 2019b)

Teacher librarians often also taught explicit reading skills, such as where Hannah explained that

> she worked with 'a young boy who is dyslexic, and I was reading to him and made a dyslexic error, and went back and explained what I'd done and he said, "Yeah, I do that, too"'. She then connected him with 'Paul Jennings' really easy books', which are humorous works, 'with about five words per page', and this led to him 'now reading an enormous amount'.

(Merga, 2019b, p. 151)

Despite the reality that school library professionals can have a lot to offer SLLs, this capability may not be widely understood within school communities and beyond.

It is also worth noting that many of these strategies are concerned with reading for pleasure (RfP), which confers benefits for literacy knowledge and skills as explained in detail in the previous chapter. RfP is also important when students are still learning foundational reading skills. Sanacore (2002) notes that

> Helping students develop the lifelong love of reading increases the chances that they will become literate and will use literacy as an important part of their lifestyles. Using school time to promote the habit of reading provides a number of benefits, especially when authentic literature dominates the literacy program. (p. 68)

Sanacore has criticised an 'isolated and reductionistic' independent reading skills focus that solely attempts to build foundational skills without taking into account the importance of fostering reading engagement (as explored in the previous chapter). Whenever we target students' reading skill gaps, we need to make sure that we are *also* considering how we will support the development of positive attitudes towards reading, which may be particularly challenging in SLLs as they have often experienced many years of failure in reading, which can harm their sense of self-efficacy as well as their enjoyment of reading. Thus, the issue of meeting the needs of SLLs must be seen as addressing both skill and will. As SLLs will typically be reading below expected levels for their age, the role of the school library professional in connecting these students with books that are accessible enough in terms of readability while being age-appropriate and interesting is key.

It's also interesting that many of the research-supported strategies that promote reading engagement have also been explicitly linked to improved literacy performance in struggling readers. For example, Westbrook et al.'s (2019) study of 20 English teachers in the south of England involved reading two whole challenging novels aloud. The struggling readers made nearly twice the level of progress when compared with the mean, making 16 months' progress on assessment of reading comprehension. In this study, all of the students benefited from exposure to listening to novels read aloud in an engaging and rapid way; however, the struggling readers made the most gains.

Three things really stand out about the process these researchers used. First, books were at a higher degree of difficulty than might be typically used for struggling learners, leading one respondent to reflect that 'Normally I would think this book [*Now is the Time for Running*] is a top set year 9 book so it will be interesting to see if I've been doing them [poorer readers] an injustice by assuming that certain books go with certain sets' (p. 63). Second, the reading was relatively uninterrupted, which could give struggling readers whose own independent reading skills do not allow for such fluidity a chance to be exposed to a flowing story that could build momentum and meaning without constant interruption. Finally, students seemed to really enjoy the experience, and this seemed to influence their ability to recall the text, a key component in reading comprehension. This research suggests that a dichotomy of reading that is for skill acquisition *or* pleasure is false, and it also shows the close relationship between enjoyment and learning. While we do need more research that looks closely at how school library professionals influence the literacy learning experiences of SLLs, as I've detailed in the previous chapter, school library professionals are the reading engagement experts in many schools.

Increasing visibility of school library professionals' role

However, the role of school library professionals in this regard may not typically be explored by researchers, and when I was looking for supporting research in my write-up of the role of teacher librarians in supporting SLLs, I really struggled to find material that extended beyond anecdotal accounts. While I love to read about the amazing things that school library professionals are doing in their schools, as I find these accounts inspiring, informative and illustrative, unfortunately they don't typically meet the standards required to act as the literature basis for peer-reviewed work.

I also found that many of the things that school library professionals do were being discussed primarily in the classroom educator space. For example, Gambrell's (2011) useful paper on reading motivation connects research and practice, suggesting that

> struggling readers often make poor choices about texts to read for pleasure, most often selecting books that are too difficult. These students need help in learning how to choose appropriate reading materials. During teacher–student conferences, teachers can support these students by selecting four or five books related to the students' interest that are at the appropriate reading level and letting these students select which of these books they want to read. This is called *bounded choice* because students still get to choose what they want to read; however, the range of materials is narrowed to text at the appropriate reading level. (p. 175)

I think most school library professionals would read this and recognise that they are the ones who are, in many cases, providing opportunities for bounded choice for struggling students. However, school library professionals are rarely named and given credit or recognition for this aspect of their role, and if the research links are limited, it is little surprise that many educators and school leaders also do not understand this connection.

I feel that if we want classroom-based educators and leaders to understand that school library professionals can play an important role in this regard, there are two key questions that we can ask ourselves within our unique schooling contexts:

1   Do they know what you have for these students in the way of material resources?
2   Do they know what you offer for these students in the way of support?

With regards to resourcing, this doesn't have to just be about direct library professional to student resourcing, which would cover things like a diverse selection of reading materials that are age, skill *and* interest appropriate.

Another gap that also jumped out at me through the course of my research was the potential for school library professionals to connect teachers with learning experiences that can help to upskill them in their readiness to meet the diverse needs of these struggling learners. We know there's a widespread need for this resourcing role, as findings from the SSSLL project suggest that in relation to initial teacher education (ITE) and ongoing professional development (PD),

> adequacy of ITE to support struggling literacy learners seems to have been perceived as low for the majority of Australian English teachers entering mainstream classrooms that include struggling literacy learners. This gap in preparation could influence students' learning attainment. The findings relating to current levels of satisfaction with PD indicate that nearly two-fifths of respondents disagree that there have been sufficient professional development opportunities to build capacity to support struggling literacy learners, and teachers' confidence and strong knowledge to support these students is relatively low.
>
> (Merga et al., 2020, p. 258)

In addition to their literacy expertise, another reason why I feel school library professionals may have a lot to offer in this space is because supporting PD for staff is *already* part of the role expectations of school library professionals in some contexts. For example, in Australia, it is often part of their expected role scope to 'provide ongoing professional development for staff in areas such as literacy, information literacy and literature', 'promote educational developments, disseminate curriculum information and facilitate the incorporation of new ideas', and 'support the establishment of a vibrant professional learning community' (Merga, 2020, p. 896). Therefore, if you are not already providing resourcing and support for teachers looking to upskill in this area, this could be an area in which your efforts can lead to valuable outcomes. Furthermore, while working closely with teachers to fill any skill gaps they may be experiencing, you will be well-positioned to address the second point: increasing their familiarity with what you offer for these students in the way of support.

How to implement and measure the efficacy of literacy-supportive interventions

There is a bit of a tonal shift in this section as I will look at what you can do to implement and measure the efficacy of literacy-supportive interventions. If you are working in a school, you are no doubt aware that many school leadership teams are heavily dependent on internal data sources to inform the numerous operational decisions they are making. With growing internal and external pressures towards quantification and accountability, you can consider how you can harness these forces in a positive manner to demonstrate improved outcomes for your students.

I believe that if you add to this corpus of internal data with your own measurements of literacy-supportive practices you have enacted, you will travel a long way towards enhancing your visibility and related value in the school. It is also a good idea to measure the efficacy of any literacy-supportive practices you implement within your school, so that you can check that your approach is working and make adjustments as needed. While time-consuming to undertake, such data and their related initiatives can additionally bolster your career prospects, making it easier for you to argue that you are a reflective and research-informed expert as a school library professional. While there are many reasons to do this, the 'how' of the process may not be well understood; this means that in a consultancy capacity I am often asked to provide information about how to practically go about this, and I'll give some brief illustrations in this chapter. I am not providing a great deal of detail, given that this approach can easily constitute a book on its own, but there should be enough here to inform and hopefully inspire you if you do not already have a strong background in this area.

I suggest that you focus on increasing student reading engagement, given that this aligns with your expertise, the unique offerings of the library, and, as explored earlier in this book, it is aligned with literacy skill development and maintenance. As such, I suggest focusing your efforts on increasing your students' attitudes towards reading, and their frequency of engagement in the practice. As I've discussed in the previous chapter, many factors can influence students' reading engagement. If you want to create a formal or informal intervention in your school to improve reading engagement to support SLLs as well as the broader school population, you need to focus on research-supported factors.

Identify research-supported factors that you're interested in focusing on to increase reading engagement in your school

When it comes to enhancing reading engagement in your school, the good news is that there has been a lot of research done in this space to identify which factors can make a difference. Research suggests that these factors include, but are not limited to the following:

- Friends' attitudes (Merga, 2014a)
- Students' understanding of the importance of reading (Merga & Mat Roni, 2018)
- Library visitation (Mat Roni & Merga, 2019)
- Access to books (Merga, 2015a)
- Access to devices (negative influence) (Merga & Mat Roni, 2017)
- Reading aloud beyond the early years (Merga, 2017a)
- Challenge seeking (Merga, 2017b)
- Preference for other recreational pursuits, time availability (Merga, 2014b)
- Physical and cognitive factors affecting capacity for sustained reading (Merga, 2014b)
- Book-choosing skills (Merga, 2016a)
- Parental modelling (Merga, 2014c)
- Opportunities to silently read for pleasure at school (Merga, 2013)
- Teacher modelling positive attitudes towards reading, and knowing individual student interests (Merga, 2015b)
- Early literacy experiences (Mat Roni & Merga, 2019)
- Focus on RfP as well as testing (Merga, 2016b)
- Encouragement to read, and exposure to social agents who exert indirect and direct influence (Merga, 2016a)
- Age and gender.

(Merga, 2014d)

Obviously, some of these factors cannot be influenced by you (e.g. age) unless you have magical powers. However, many others can.

Start by reading some peer-reviewed research literature in the factors that are of most interest to you and/or are most appropriate to the unique needs of your school community and resourcing. The reference list for this chapter will be a good starting point for this further reading. You can also read about specific interventions undertaken in schools and communities. You may want to set up a Google Scholar Alert to remain abreast of new research literature as it becomes available in your area of interest, given that the corpus of useful literature is constantly expanding.

You don't need to read every paper ever written on the subject, just enough information for you to:

1 Understand what the factor really is (e.g. age is obvious, but parental modelling is more complex)
2 Know what strategies have been successful in the past in improving student engagement in relation to that factor.

You might find my papers where I asked teenagers (Merga, 2016a) and children (2017b) what would make them read more an accessible starting point, but if you find reading peer-reviewed research difficult and time-consuming, don't worry, you are not alone.

You can also read books (e.g. Merga, 2018), but just make sure that they are solidly informed by recent, quality research (i.e. check that most of the works that they cite are peer-reviewed and current), not just opinions or individual experiences. While these anecdotal works can be rich and valuable sources of information, your decisions should be research-based, not opinion-based, if you want to improve your chances of success and argue for the credibility of your approach when interacting with your school leadership team. I've seen some terrible decisions made in this space that were not research-supported, such as decisions to remove all paper books in libraries and replace them with devices (see Merga & Mat Roni, 2017).

I'm going to be referring to the initiatives and strategies that you actively employ to promote these factors as an *intervention*, even though the approach employed in your school is unlikely to fit the more rigorous scientific definition of this term (e.g. typically involving comparison groups). With any intervention that seeks to change behaviours/attitudes, the first thing you want to ensure is that it does no harm.

Identify how you can initiate and sustain change, being realistic about what is achievable in your context

Drawing on the research, there are a lot of ways you can initiate and sustain change in school learning contexts. You can choose more than one factor to focus on. There is absolutely no reason why school-based interventions should not be multifaceted, as long as you are not trying to explore the effectiveness of a single factor, as once you've put multiple factors into play, you won't really be able to determine which factor(s) drove any changes that you see in your evaluation (which is only a problem if you are a researcher). The point of your intervention is to improve students' reading engagement, not adhere to research-dictated methodological fidelity, so feel free to pile on as many factors as you can realistically and fulsomely support. If you've adhered to the first step, you'll only be working with factors and strategies that already have at least some degree of research support, and if I were designing a school-based intervention to improve students' literacy performance, I'd include interventions with coverage of as many research-supported factors as feasible given time and resourcing constraints.

So what might this look like? For example, a school library professional might decide to focus on enhancing student exposure to positive modelling and reading aloud while improving student access to books. Here are three examples of how factors can be promoted within a school. I am not suggesting that these are the 'best' factors to focus on; they are just here as an example.

Enhancing exposure to modelling
- Social influences such as teachers and parents can positively influence children's reading engagement through clearly modelling personal enjoyment of the practice (e.g. Applegate & Applegate, 2004; Clavel & Mediavilla, 2020; Mancini & Pasqua, 2011; Mullan, 2010; Wollscheid, 2013).
- Some possible initiatives could include: implementing a staff reading programme, engaging staff to read from favourite books at whole-school assemblies, and engaging parents in modelling reading at home.

Regular exposure to reading aloud
- Reading aloud with students can help them to make significant literacy gains (e.g. Swanson et al., 2011; Westbrook et al., 2019; Xie et al., 2018), as well as promoting enjoyment for reading (e.g. Baker et al., 1997; Merga, 2017a; Sung, 2020).
- Some possible initiatives could include: creating a time for school-wide reading aloud daily; organising buddy-reading of older students reading to younger students; and engaging parents in reading aloud at home with children, even once they've learned to read independently.

Increasing access to books
- With books being the text type most strongly associated with literacy benefit at this stage (Jerrim & Moss, 2019; OECD, 2010), simply increasing student access to books can influence students' literacy performance.
- Some possible initiatives could include: revisiting timetabling so that all students have weekly access to the library during class time; daily opportunities to refresh books on completion; and engaging parents in supporting access to books at home, such as through parent time in your library where you help them choose books with their child/children.

Once you decide which factors you are going to address, and the initiatives you are going to use to promote them in your school, you need to find out what is currently happening in your school so that you know for sure that you will not be replicating strategies that are already in play.

For example, if you are looking to increase access to books in your school by giving all students weekly access to the library during class time, you need to find out what their current levels of access are so that you can demonstrate that what you did made a difference. As I've explained previously, just because a class has timetabled access to the library, this does not necessarily align with actual levels of access to the library, as school library professionals have reported that these timetabled sessions may be often interrupted due to other curricular demands (Merga, 2019c). As such, observing and recording access of each class over a period of months may be far more accurate than relying on what has been timetabled as a measure of current frequency of access prior to the intervention. This takes us to my next point.

Measure the baseline situation and choose your measures of success

Once you decide how you are going to intervene to enhance reading engagement, find out what is happening through quantitative (usually numbers) and qualitative (usually words) measures on student engagement before you start (and collect data on student achievement if you have decided to measure that too). You can't claim to have implemented a successful approach unless you can prove that there has been a shift in however you're measuring change at school level.

How you want to measure this is up to you. For example, you might want to see if initiatives you've implemented to increase access to books result in:

- Increased borrowing as determined by library borrowing records (volume of reading)

- Increased student reading frequency as determined by student reading logs and/or surveys (frequency of reading)
- Improved student attitudes towards reading as determined by student interviews and/or focus groups and/or surveys (attitudes towards reading).

When you mix it up and collect both quantitative and qualitative data, this makes for rich reading, and also sometimes the qualitative data will capture a change that is less apparent in the quantitative data and the reverse. For example, I might collect changes in students' attitudes towards reading on scales in a survey (quantitative), but I might also want to interview a random selection of students to collect some rich description around any changes to their attitudes, also to collect feedback on how I could improve the programme for the next iteration (qualitative).

You *may* also want to see if your interventions on reading engagement lead to improved student literacy results in student achievement. This will involve measuring student achievement on specific skills such as reading comprehension or vocabulary both before and after the intervention (and at mid-point if feasible). While measuring the impact of your intervention on student achievement as well as student engagement can be useful, it is *crucial* that you be aware that you need to allow several months to see movement in this regard; it is not something that will change in a few weeks or months. Engagement changes (concerned with reading attitudes and frequency) will typically be detected before you see changes in achievement. Therefore, you should be able to track changes in volume of reading, frequency of reading and attitudes towards reading before you see meaningful shifts in student performance, so you should not limit your measures to performance only. Setting realistic goals is so important. For example, you are almost certainly not going to see a significant improvement in student reading comprehension three weeks after rolling out an intervention.

There is also no need to limit your measurement of success to the few examples I briefly share here. Many factors can shape your choices, including but not limited to the age of the students, the key goals you hope to achieve, and what the leadership team will expect to see and receive from you in terms of reporting. This might involve qualitative, quantitative or mixed-methods approaches, and they may be fixed or longitudinal. You may include student self-report, or be reliant on the report of others. You need to weigh up the pros and cons for diverse methods and make the decisions that best fit what you need to deliver.

I am giving you a lot of options here, but feel free to keep it *very simple* for yourself, especially if you are still learning how to do this kind of thing. You could always just start with one factor and approach (such as increasing opportunities for silent reading for pleasure from *fortnightly* to *daily*, and for the same or longer time per session), and measure students' attitudes, reading frequency and volume on a survey before and after this intervention.

Consider the rights of your participants

As a further caution, I'd encourage you to be very careful about how you use these data in relation to whichever measures you choose to employ, and how the data are shared and reported. Sometimes I'm at conferences and I see what I would perceive as sensitive student data being shared with the whole auditorium, and I utter a silent hope that consent has been given at some point, and/or pseudonyms are being used.

Whenever I work with schools to develop interventions, I always very strongly stress that *even within the school community*, information about students' research contributions, attitudes and achievements need to be shared with close consideration given to its possible impact on how these students are seen within the school, by their peers and by their teachers. Even if you are not required to run your school-based interventions through any kind of ethics committee, consideration of how to conduct research that will not lead to untoward impacts on students still needs to be contemplated. This is why I think that school-based interventions should also get student consent to participate where possible, and that you should state up front how their data will be used and shared.

Discussions about the ethics of collecting data from or about children are almost solely concentrated on the data collected by external researchers (e.g. Homan, 2001). However, I believe that internal data collection has just as much potential to be damaging for young people if their wellbeing is not placed at the forefront of our considerations. I feel that this is particularly the case given that at least in Australia, institutional ethics approvals are contingent on students and their parents providing informed consent for participation with the opportunity to opt out of involvement in research, with the same provisions not required for internal research within schools unless there is an academic partner involved.

Simply, before you share data that either explicitly identifies a student by name, or where the student is not named, allows the identity to be surmised through deductive disclosure (where it is likely others will be able to guess who it is, such as where there is only one student from a certain background in your school, and the response references that background), you need to ask yourself the following questions:

- Has the student agreed to me sharing this data about them?
- Could sharing this data on this student lead to negative consequences for the student (such as stigmatisation by teachers or peers)?

Get everyone on board

You will need school community wide buy-in to promote and garner support for the intervention before you start. Mace and Lean (2020) described the efforts they made to get the school staff engaged in their whole-school silent reading intervention, stating that

> The existing teaching timetable needed to be completely overhauled to create a dedicated 20 minutes per day of sustained silent reading. It took many meetings with key stakeholders from the Executive, pastoral teams and heads of department to generate this time. This was a long, drawn-out process that presented many roadblocks to overcome. However, including of all these key stakeholders ensured open, honest and thorough communications and maximum buy-in from all the key areas of the school. (para. 4)

First and foremost, you need to get the unequivocal backing of your leadership team, and depending on whether or not they have form for being a bit flaky, you might need this backing in writing. Then you need to identify who is already on your team, and don't take any of this for granted. You need to know who will be in the car with you as co-drivers of this initiative.

Ideally brainstorming with your team if you have one, you need to identify who you need to win over to make it work, and how can you do this. For example, you may need to organise professional development for teachers. You may need to create a series of parent newsletters and seminars if home support is needed. While I don't go into much detail here, this stage is absolutely crucial to your success, so plan to get everyone on board early, and revisit the success of your buy-in strategies often. You need to get everyone on board as far as humanly possible, so it's better to slightly delay the start than to proceed without the core support you need. In reality, you may never get 100% base support, so don't get discouraged if there are a few dissenting agents, though listen to their feedback *if it is constructive/informed*. Try to identify the minimum buy-in (and from whom) that you will need to get things moving.

Roll out, measure and report

Now it's time to roll out your intervention. You've already decided on your formal measures of success across this period, but you should also keep informal notes as you go about things you might do differently/adjust for the future, but also things that seemed to be working well. You can use your reporting of progress to maintain buy-in and momentum going forward as long as it won't impact on the results of the intervention. The reporting process is really important, not only for showing how the intervention assisted reading engagement (assuming it was successful!), but also bear in mind that as with much work in schools, a lot of your labour in making this happen will be invisible to leadership, unless you make it clear. Therefore, don't just report on your findings; make sure you clearly report on your process as well so that they understand the level of effort and commitment that was involved.

Further thoughts

I hope that this chapter has given you some exciting ideas about how you might further support SLLs in your school, and how you might make visible this support so that leadership and educators understand and value what you do. Given that meeting the needs of SLLs is a growing priority in many contexts, this is an area where your support can make a powerful difference to students' opportunities. I hope that you also found the tips on interventions to be a handy starting point for your plans going forward. As a final note, I encourage you not to feel discouraged if you experience issues with your intervention as it progresses. Just keep doing your best for your students, drawing on the available knowledge base around best practice.

References

Applegate, A., & Applegate, M. (2004). The Peter effect: Reading habits and attitudes of preservice teachers. *The Reading Teacher, 57*(6), 554–563.

Australian Bureau of Statistics (ABS). (2013). *Programme for the International Assessment of Adult Competencies, Australia, 2011–2012 (4228.0)*. Australian Bureau of Statistics.

Baker, L., Scher, D., & Mackler, K. (1997). Home and family influences on motivations for reading. *Educational Psychologist, 32*(2), 69–82.

Clavel, J. G., & Mediavilla, M. (2020). The intergenerational effect of parental enthusiasm for reading. *Applied Economic Analysis, 28*(84), 239–259.

Cubillos Guzmán, M. (2021). *Reading analyses with Chilean children* [Doctoral thesis, University of Maryland].
https://drum.lib.umd.edu/bitstream/handle/1903/27271/CubillosGuzman_umd_0117E_21417.pdf?sequence=2&isAllowed=y

Daggett, W., & Hasselbring, T. (2007). *What we know about adolescent reading*. International Centre for Leadership in Education.

Gambrell, L. B. (2011). Seven rules of engagement: What's most important to know about motivation to read. *The Reading Teacher, 65*(3), 172–178.

Goss, P., & Sonnemann, J. (2016). *Widening gaps: What NAPLAN tells us about student progress*. Grattan Institute.

Homan, R. (2001). The principle of assumed consent: The ethics of gatekeeping. *Journal of Philosophy of Education, 35*(3), 329–343.

Huffman, S., Shaw, E., & Thompson, A. (2020). Meeting the needs of students with dyslexia: Librarians, teachers, and students working together hand-in-hand. *Reading Improvement, 57*(4), 161–172.

Jerrim, J., & Moss, G. (2019). The link between fiction and teenagers' reading skills: International evidence from the OECD PISA study. *British Educational Research Journal, 45*(1), 181–200.

Keslair, F. (2017). *How much will the literacy level of the working-age population change from now to 2022?* Organisation for Economic Co-operation and Development (OECD).

Kim, Y. S. G. (2020). Toward integrative reading science: The direct and indirect effects model of reading. *Journal of Learning Disabilities, 53*(6), 469–491.

Kirsch, I., De Jong, J., Lafontaine, D., McQueen, J., Mendelovits, J., & Monseur, C. (2002). *Reading for change: Performance and engagement across countries*. Organisation for Economic Co-operation and Development (OECD).

Lupo, S. M., Strong, J. Z., & Conradi Smith, K. (2019). Struggle is not a bad word: Misconceptions and recommendations about readers struggling with difficult texts. *Journal of Adolescent & Adult Literacy, 62*(5), 551–560.

Mace, G., & Lean, M. (2020). The time to read. *Schools Catalogue Information Service*. https://www.scisdata.com/connections/issue-117/the-time-to-read

Mancini, A. L., & Pasqua, S. (2011). *On the intergenerational transmission of time use patterns: Is a good example the best sermon?* IZA Discussion Paper No. 6038, October 2011.

Mat Roni, S., & Merga, M. K. (2019). Using an artificial neural network to explore the influence of extrinsic and intrinsic variables on children's reading frequency and attitudes. *Australian Journal of Education, 63*(3), 270–291.

McIntosh, S., & Vignoles, A. (2001). Measuring and assessing the impact of basic skills on labour market outcomes. *Oxford Economic Papers, 53*(3), 453–481.

Merga, M. K. (2013). Should Silent Reading feature in a secondary school English programme? West Australian students' perspectives on Silent Reading. *English in Education, 47*(3), 229–244.

Merga, M. K. (2014a). Peer group and friend influences on the social acceptability of adolescent book reading. *Journal of Adolescent and Adult Literacy, 57*(6), 472–482.

Merga, M. K. (2014b). Western Australian adolescents' reasons for infrequent engagement in recreational book reading. *Literacy Learning: the Middle Years*, *22*(2), 60–66.

Merga, M. K. (2014c). Exploring the role of parents in supporting recreational book reading beyond primary school. *English in Education, 48*(2), 149–163.

Merga, M. K. (2014d). Are Western Australian adolescents keen book readers? *Australian Journal of Language and Literacy*, *37*, 161–170.

Merga, M. K. (2015a). Access to books in the home and adolescent engagement in recreational book reading: Considerations for secondary school educators. *English in Education*, *49*(3), 197–214.

Merga, M. K. (2015b). 'She knows what I like': Student-generated best-practice statements for encouraging recreational reading in adolescents. *Australian Journal of Education 59*(1), 35–50.

Merga, M. K. (2016a). What would make them read more? Insights from Western Australian adolescents. *Asia Pacific Journal of Education*, *36*(3), 409–424.

Merga, M. K. (2016b). 'I don't know if she likes reading': Are teachers perceived to be keen readers, and how is this determined? *English in Education*, *50*(3), 255–269.

Merga, M. K. (2017a). Interactive reading opportunities beyond the early years: What educators need to consider. *Australian Journal of Education*, *61*(3), 328–343.

Merga, M. K. (2017b). What would make children read for pleasure more frequently? *English in Education*, *51*(2), 207–223.

Merga, M. K. (2018). *Reading engagement for tweens and teens: What would make them read more?* ABC-CLIO/Libraries Unlimited.

Merga, M. K. (2019a). 'Fallen through the cracks': Teachers' perceptions of barriers faced by struggling literacy learners in secondary school. *English in Education*, *54*(4), 371–395.

Merga, M. K. (2019b). How do librarians in schools support struggling readers? *English in Education*, *53*(2), 145–160.

Merga, M. K. (2019c). *Librarians in schools as literacy educators*. Palgrave Macmillan.

Merga, M. K. (2020). School librarians as literacy educators within a complex role. *Journal of Library Administration*, *60*(8), 889–908.

Merga, M. K., & Mason, S. (2019). Building a school reading culture: Teacher librarians' perceptions of enabling and constraining factors. *Australian Journal of Education*, *63*(2), 173–189.

Merga, M. K., & Mat Roni, S. (2017). The influence of access to eReaders, computers and mobile phones on children's book reading frequency. *Computers and Education*, *109*, 187–196.

Merga, M. K., & Mat Roni, S. (2018). Children's perceptions of the importance and value of reading. *Australian Journal of Education*, *62*(2), 135–153.

Merga, M. K., Mat Roni, S. & Malpique, A. (2020a). Do secondary English teachers have adequate time and resourcing to meet the needs of struggling literacy learners? *English in Education.* https://doi.org/10.1080/04250494.2020.1838897

Merga, M. K., Mat Roni, S. & Malpique, A. (2020b). School leadership and whole-school support of struggling literacy learners in secondary schools. *Educational Management Administration & Leadership.* https://doi.org/10.1177/1741143220905036

Merga, M. K., Mat Roni, S., & Mason, S. (2020c). Teachers' perceptions of their preparedness for supporting struggling literacy learners in secondary English classrooms. *English in Education, 54*(3), 265–284. https://doi.org/10.1080/04250494.2020.1775488

Mullan, K. (2010). Families that read: A time-diary analysis of young people's and parents' reading. *Journal of Research in Reading, 33*(4), 414–430.

Niyozov, S., & Hughes, W. (2019). Problems with PISA: Why Canadians should be sceptical of the global test. *The Conversation.* https://theconversation.com/problems-with-pisa-why-canadians-should-be-skeptical-of-the-global-test-118096

Organisation for Economic Co-operation and Development (OECD). (2010). *PISA 2009 results: Executive summary.* OECD Publishing.

Organisation for Economic Co-operation and Development (OECD) & Statistics Canada. (2000). *Literacy in the information age.* OECD Publishing.

Sanacore, J. (2002). Struggling literacy learners benefit from lifetime literacy efforts. *Reading Psychology, 23*(2), 67–86.

Schleicher, A. (2019). *PISA 2018: Insights and interpretations.* OECD Publishing.

Sizmur, J., Ager, R., Bradshaw, J., Classick, R., Galvis, M., Packer, J., Thomas, D., & Wheater, R. (2019). *Achievement of 15-year-olds in England: PISA 2018 results. Research report, December 2019.* Department for Education.

Stanovich, K. E. (2009). Matthew effects in reading: Some consequences of individual differences in the acquisition of literacy. *Journal of Education, 189*(1–2), 23–55.

Sung, H. Y. (2020). Togetherness: The benefits of a schoolwide reading aloud activity for elementary school children in rural areas. *The Library Quarterly, 90*(4), 475–492.

Swanson, E., Vaughn, S., Wanzek, J., Petscher, Y., Heckert, J., Cavanaugh, C., Kraft, G., & Tackett, K. (2011). A synthesis of read-aloud interventions on early reading outcomes among preschool through third graders at risk for reading difficulties. *Journal of Learning Disabilities, 44*(3), 258–275.

Thomson, S., De Bortoli, L., & Underwood, C. (2016). *PISA 2015: A first look at Australia's results.* Australian Council for Educational Research.

Thomson, S., De Bortoli, L., Underwood, C., & Schmid, M. (2019). *PISA 2018: Reporting Australia's Results: Volume I Student Performance.* Australian Council for Educational Research.

Westbrook, J., Sutherland, J., Oakhill, J., & Sullivan, S. (2019). 'Just reading': The impact of a faster pace of reading narratives on the comprehension of poorer adolescent readers in English classrooms. *Literacy, 53*(2), 60–68.

Wollscheid, S. (2013). Parents' cultural resources, gender and young people's reading habits: Findings from a secondary analysis with time-survey data in two-parent families. *International Journal About Parents in Education, 7*(1), 69–83.

Xie, Q. W., Chan, C. H., Ji, Q., & Chan, C. L. (2018). Psychosocial effects of parent–child book reading interventions: A meta-analysis. *Pediatrics, 141*(4), e20172675.

4

School Libraries and Reading Engagement for Student Wellbeing

How does the library enable reading for pleasure (RfP), and how does this relate to student wellbeing? It's time to start tying together the two key concerns of this book: wellbeing and literacy as facilitated through reading engagement.

In the Introduction to this book, I defined wellbeing as relating to more than just a lack of physical or mental illness, but rather a broader construct that includes diverse 'physical, social, emotional, intellectual, spiritual, and environmental aspects' (Bladek, 2021, p. 3). I have also demonstrated that reading engagement and student wellbeing have some interesting intersections, which I further explore in this chapter, with attention on how school libraries play a role in fostering wellbeing through reading engagement.

RfP can be associated with a positive emotional response in young people (e.g. Kartal & Bilhan, 2021). It is associated with reduced psychological distress in college students (Levine et al., 2020), and mental wellbeing in children (Clark & Teravainen-Goff, 2018). As I've briefly covered previously in this book, the regular reading of fiction is also associated with the development of prosocial characteristics (e.g. Mar et al., 2009), which readers can draw upon to facilitate smooth social interactions. Furthermore, recent research has experimented with reading-based interventions to support children who have experienced trauma, finding positive, short-term effects on emotion recognition, though further research is needed (Michalek et al., 2021). Recent research also suggests that reading can provide respite from the stressors of pandemic conditions, 'supporting children's mental wellbeing and enabling them to dream about the future', with 59.3% of young respondents affirming during lockdown 'that reading makes them feel better' (Clark & Picton, 2020, p. 2). As such, RfP can play an important role in meeting the social and emotional needs of young people, building a sense of optimism and hope in troubling times.

My own previous research has explored how reading can be used by avid readers to support mental health, noting that for some readers, 'the escape of reading was often used in order to regulate emotion' (Merga, 2017a, p. 152). Furthermore, more than one in five of the 1,022 adult respondents in this study used the word 'escape' when describing their reasons for reading books, suggesting that reading for this purpose may be common (Merga, 2017a). While there is limited research collecting data from school-aged children about their perceptions of how reading influences their wellbeing and related emotional states (Merga, 2020), I recently found that young TikTok users have used the escape of reading as part of their narrative around books in the #booktok community, with the videos they created around reader experience exploring 'reading as an escape and a deeply immersive and potentially surreal experience' (Merga, 2021, p. 5).

As argued by Clarke (2020), enhancing student academic achievement and wellbeing are not goals in opposition with each other, and in this vein, as explored in the previous chapters, children may experience gains in literacy skills and knowledge while *also* enhancing their wellbeing through educative practices such as RfP. Indeed, in general, improvements in student wellbeing should offer benefits for their academic achievement, with a recent meta-analysis finding a positive association between the two, leading the authors to conclude that 'schools and parents should focus not solely on cognitive abilities for better academic performance, but children's well-being as well' (Kaya & Erdem, 2021, p. 20). Similarly, Dix et al. (2020) found that programmes focusing on students' wellbeing can offer academic advantages. As such, when you seek to advocate for your role and your library as promoting student wellbeing, don't allow this role to be dismissed as somehow 'education lite' – research has found an unsurprising link between wellbeing and academic performance that you can share in your advocacy efforts.

School libraries fostering wellbeing through reading engagement

School libraries can play an important role in fostering wellbeing in students. However, while there is much anecdotal commentary in this area, as per my recent review (Merga, 2020), there is a paucity of current research that explores the role that school libraries can play. That noted, some attention has been given to the roles that other kinds of libraries may play, such as academic libraries (Cox & Brewster, 2020) and public libraries (Elia, 2019). In this chapter, I share research from the 2020 'School libraries promoting wellbeing in Australian primary and secondary schools' project (I'll refer to it in this chapter as the Project), making the connection between reading engagement and student wellbeing that has been explored in some previous research, but that certainly warrants further attention. For reference to how I have conceptualised the terms I use in this chapter, I've previously defined *reading engagement* in Chapter 2 and *wellbeing* in the Introduction.

On an anecdotal level, the sense of wellbeing that students can access through reading facilitated in their libraries is typically visible when you enter the library space and see young people absorbed in reading, their attention deeply and perhaps uniquely focused on a single task. However, very little research has been conducted that places these young people at the centre of inquiry, asking them directly about how reading engagement may influence their sense of wellbeing.

Given the need to start directly and explicitly asking young people about the perceived connection between reading engagement for student wellbeing, in the latter part of 2020 I visited three schools to interview students and library managers (LMs) about diverse issues relating to libraries and wellbeing. I wanted to include LMs as well as students, as they can offer insights into what they have observed, but also explain how some of the aspects described by the students were intentionally established by school library professionals to promote reading engagement, which I expected to be the case from my previous research with school library professionals.

I explain more about the general methods of the Project in Appendix 1, including the specific semi-structured interview questions I asked around reading engagement and wellbeing. In order to arrive at the findings I discuss in this chapter, I carefully analysed what both the students and their LMs said in relation to these questions. After having the interviews professionally transcribed, I identified recurring thematic codes by using a process of constant comparative analysis (Boeije, 2002; Kolb, 2012). It is important to remember that given the small sample and the deliberate sampling of students who made good use of the school library, broad generalisability of the findings I explore in this chapter cannot be inferred. Schools that had wellbeing strategies in place were deliberately selected, along with students who made good use of the library. However, what this chapter does do is show how children in upper primary and lower secondary schools and their LMs can perceive the relationship between reading and wellbeing. Information about the participants and their pseudonyms can also be found in Appendix 1 (Table 3). I found that reading was connected to wellbeing by the respondents in diverse and often interconnected ways, as I explore below.

Reading, emotions and escape

Like adult readers (Merga 2017a), the students in this study described using reading to regulate their emotions and escape, with these elements very closely entwined in the responses. Perhaps when we imagine young people escaping reality in present times, we might be more likely to envision them absconding into a world mediated by electronic devices such as in popular computer games, but young people are not a homogenous group, and that world is not necessarily preferred by *all* young people.

For example, Momo explained that 'I'm one of those people who cannot sit on a device for a long time, and it'd just be, like, "What do I do? What do I do? What do I do?"'. Instead, she found refuge in books and reading:

> I always feel like I can just escape while reading a book. And if I can't get to sleep, I'll read a book. Or even if I'm bored, I'll read a book. If I finish a task in class, I'll read a book. And, like, literally, I've got a book in the classroom right now . . . if you don't know what to do, or if you're sad, or if you're angry, or whatever the case is, you can just read, and it feels like you're just escaping the world. And you're going into the world of the book, and you're just there.

As such, for Momo, reading was a kind of self-directed bibliotherapy, and this is not a new use of literature. Heath et al. (2005) note that

> historically, ideas from literature have assisted individuals in coping with the world around them. Above the entrance of an ancient Greek library is inscribed, 'The Healing Place of the Soul'. Similar words are inscribed in Alexandria, Egypt: 'Medicine for the Mind'. (p. 562)

As such, books and reading can offer opportunities for regulating emotions and bringing peace, but the point can be the recourse for departing a difficult situation, with Piper explaining that 'sometimes you need to have your alone time, and you need to sometimes escape from reality. But because if there's, like, issues or something going on in your life, it's good to escape from reality for a little bit'. In this vein, Bob situates this escape as a kind of relocation:

> Because sometimes if you're feeling down or sad, you might not want to be where you actually are because you're all upset. But then if you're reading it then it takes you someplace where you're happy, where you can be you, where anything is possible . . . if I'm having a rough day, it just gives me an opportunity to escape from the real world.

Temporary alleviation of the pressures of realities can provide respite; similarly for Chris, reading books is 'something I do when I want to calm down . . . I start imagining what's happening in the book, which makes me not realise what's happening around me'.

However, students didn't always use books as an emotional comfort. Sometimes, they just wanted to *feel* and could even get pleasure out of books that evoked emotions more typically seen as negative, such as sadness. Skyla explained this point, noting that

> just if you feel like you are feeling sad sometimes, you could just be able to read a book and it would make you all calm and it would be really interesting to read . . . They also make me feel sad sometimes, because some stories are sad, and they don't always end up in a happy ending. And I just like to be able to get emotions and emotions can be read throughout books and stuff.

This reflects my recent research, which found that in an analysis of #Booktok data from TikTok, young people could 'connect with books primarily for the emotional response they will elicit, and millions of views are collectively accrued by CPs (content producers) promoting books to give a certain desired emotional reaction, including readers seeking books that will "destroy" them emotionally' (Merga, 2021, p. 8).

Young people seeking book experiences that will evoke emotions that are typically seen as negative may seem out of alignment with wellbeing; however, sadness is not necessarily a bad or harmful emotion. Lomas (2018) argues against the pathologising of sadness and conflation of this emotion with depression, asserting that 'for the majority of people, their experiences of sadness are not mild forms of disorder, but rather serve an important instrumental function in their lives, and may even be intrinsically valuable in their own right' (pp. 24–25). He details potential adaptive functions of sadness, which include but are not limited to 'compassion (sadness arising out of concern for the suffering of others)', and 'eliciting care (sadness evoking compassionate responses in other people)', as well as exploring the 'possibility of sadness being intrinsic to flourishing' (p. 24). There has also been research done on the pleasures that can be afforded in the reading of sad books, with findings suggesting that 'both eudaimonic motives ("insight" and "personal growth") and meta-emotions (liking to feel various emotions while reading) predict a preference for sad books' (Koopman, 2015, p. 27). Further research should look at the wellbeing effects of reading sad literature on young people, particularly given that we have evidence that some young people have described finding pleasure in reading this kind of literature.

Students could expressly use the escape of reading to deal with specific situational stressors, while at the same time enabling a learning experience. For example, Josh noted that

> it takes your mind off stress and, like, if you've got a test coming up, if you're stressing a lot about studying, you can read a book about something like it and you can take your mind not only off that, but you're also studying at the same time. So, I love to read books about the Indigenous culture and all of that, because we had an Indigenous test thing and I had to know everything about it. So, I started reading a few Indigenous books and it completely took my mind off it. But at the same time, I got a few questions in which I didn't know from that book. So that's also why I like to read.

Students' decisions to use books and reading in this manner may to some extent be the result of intentional interventions from school library professionals. For example, LM Anne explicitly encouraged students to use books to relieve stress, noting that 'the evidence is showing that you can reduce your anxiety and stress by just removing yourself from a situation and quietly reading a book'. This involved 'taking yourself into another space, being able to breathe, think about the situation, or just put that into perspective'. She explained that 'all of those things, we talk about that all the time'.

Connecting with characters

I was interested to note that the young respondents in this study also reported experiencing pleasure in finding characters like themselves in books, which was described almost as a kind of friendship or companionship with these characters. This is reflective of Chapple et al.'s (2021) work with autistic adult readers, which found a degree of character investment that was described as a relationship, with a respondent stating that 'I feel like I'm becoming friends with the characters . . . when I read it back, it's like meeting an old friend of mine' (p. 10), which the researchers refer to as 'simulated friendships with characters' (p. 11).

Similarly, Tribe et al.'s (2021) work on using the *Harry Potter* world for mental health recovery found that connecting with the characters and their experiences can instil hope in the reader, as 'closely following the fictional protagonist and his friends face and overcome challenges appeared to prompt hope and optimism about the future, and in the possibility of recovery' (p. 7). Furthermore, 'participants reported experiences of identification with the characters, of seeing themselves in them, in their mistakes and flaws and quirks' (p. 7), and the authors note that this kind of identification can offer a range of benefits for mental wellbeing. In relation to engagement with characters, Rain and Mar (2021) also made links with mental wellbeing, noting that readers may 'engage with characters in a myriad of ways, including feeling close to a character – having parasocial interactions or forming parasocial relationships – or coming to see the fictional world through the eyes of that character, identifying with that character' (p. 4). They also observed that 'parasocial interaction seems well-suited to aid the self-soothing strategy of anxious individuals, as the fictional character is perceived as "real" and a separate entity: someone who can form the other half of a close relationship' (p. 6).

This resonates with the discovery that for some of my respondents, connecting with characters was about more than enjoyment: it was also affirming and confidence-building. For example, one of Josh's favourite characters was 'Timmy from *Timmy Failure*, because he is just such a funny character'. He explained that

> obviously, he fails at stuff a lot. Especially when he was trying to do a few things around the house, he kept on knocking things over and then his mum got mad and then he had to sit in his room, and it's really funny how he did stuff when he was young . . . it's kinda like me when I'm clumsy, which is most of the time, but . . . yeah, it's just funny how he does stuff because I can relate to it most of the time.

The shared commonality with Timmy and his many failures seemed to give Josh permission to make mistakes and laugh them off rather than be hurt by them. As such, identification with characters has the potential to support resilience.

Similarly, Skyla drew strength from her favourite book character Violet from *Thea Stilton*. 'because she's a very kind and gentle . . . a loving person who likes to take care of her friends'. She explained her attachment to this character as follows.

> I find it makes me stronger in a way, because I sometimes find it hard to be resilient sometimes, and that character just makes me feel a bit stronger and happier . . . she's a very joyful and shy and sweet person, and I find that she's very similar to me in the outside world.

As such, while humour was commonly cited as a source of connection with a character, there was also a sense of a reflected self that gives the reader confidence that qualities that they already possess can serve them well.

Role models

Connecting with characters was closely related to the aspirational role model; though there is a noteworthy distinction, in some instances the respondents blurred the two. Rather than the relatable previous connecting with characters theme, the role model was not so much like them as what they wanted to become. Other researchers have explored how children forge connections between themselves and story characters to derive inspiration for facing difficulties (Suvilehto et al., 2019). For example, Kai's favourite character was 'a strong empowering woman, so I just enjoy that about her. She doesn't take anything from no one'. Bob explained that he idolised his favourite character, Harry Potter:

> Because he's very cool. He's, like, very brave and heroic, and then he does all these wild things, and he protects his friends at all costs. He doesn't want them to get into danger. He stands up for what he believes is right. He doesn't let anyone tell him different. He's just a really brave and heroic character and I like to idolise him.

In some instances, the role model was a real person, with Lacey describing her experience of 'reading the autobiography of Malala':

> I thought it was incredible how no matter what happened to her, even after her horrific injury, she just came back and kept fighting for what she believed in. And I think being . . . thinking very strongly about feminism myself, I think she did so incredible, and she just didn't stop, even after that, and she just could have decided, 'Nuh, I'm done, this is causing too much harm to myself'. But she's continued, and she's changed the world. It's incredible.

Again, behind the scenes, school library professionals supported students to make these connections. LM Anne specifically built her collection to make sure that there were role model characters available for her students. For example, to support a student who had 'a bit of an unfortunate home life' she noted that 'we have created for her . . . a safe world, become an avid reader'; 'for her . . . I recommend quite a number of books where we've got a very strong female character, main character, who's sort of, in a number of adverse situations and where she navigates her way through those'. In this instance, Anne is explicitly connecting this student with a troubled home life with resources found in fiction to build her resilience, and this aligns with a definition of bibliotherapeutic practice as 'a projective indirect intervention that uses carefully selected thematic books or reading materials of any kind, such as biographies, novels, poems, short stories, to help children cope with changes, emotional or mental problems' (Lucas & Soares, 2013, p. 139). This is a great example of the many activities that school library professionals undertake to enhance student wellbeing, and how reading engagement can become integral to this mission.

Perspective-taking and personal development

Reading fiction, in particular, can support the reader to view the world from others' perspectives and foster their capacity for empathy (Mar et al., 2009), and recent research suggests that 'fiction reading experience is related to emotion recognition abilities and that statistical properties of language experience may contribute to emotion knowledge' (Schwering et al., 2021, p. 7). My related research suggests that some 'readers read for insight into other perspectives, to develop their capacity for empathy. These readers enjoyed the opportunity to "see the world through other peoples' eyes", with another respondent describing this as "the merging of myself and the characters"' (Merga, 2017a, p. 150). In a closely related purpose, readers can draw on what they read to facilitate their own personal development (Merga, 2017a). In the adult context, I described these readers as 'interested in learning about the human condition', often 'strongly motivated by a desire for self-improvement and personal development', reading 'in order "to be spiritually enlightened"; "to be humbled"; "to develop my understanding of the world, to learn how to deal with situations"; for "self-improvement"; "personal growth"; and "lessons in living"' (p. 151). Some of the young people in this study described embracing the alternative perspectives afforded to them through fiction reading experiences, framing them as growth opportunities.

For example, Felix enjoyed learning through perspective-taking, adopting a philosophical perspective on the subjectivity of values, explaining that

> you get to see in their input, and then you go, 'Well, actually, they're not the bad guy. Really, the other guy is, it's just their point of view makes it seem like the other guy's the bad guy'. Yet, if you see what the other person actually thought and saw, you actually see he's kind of right, and then you get to make your choice of who's the real villain in the story.

Similarly, Sophia enjoyed reading to change the way she thought, and to understand possible alternative viewpoints:

> I like knowing the way other people, like, think and interpret information that I would interpret normally very, very differently. I just like knowing how people would interpret information and comparing it to how I would interpret that

same information. I just like to know how I could . . . not necessarily improve, but, like, change my thinking to maybe be better for what I'm trying to accomplish by that mode of thinking. I read to make myself more creative, to change my thinking, normally, just on certain matters.

Lacey's perspectives were also shaped by her reading, as she noted that 'it just makes me think, "Wow, I take so many of these things for granted, all these things that people just can't do anymore, or are so difficult to them"'. She felt that this led to her better appreciating her own circumstances and privilege.

Pleasure in being read to

Being read to can be more than enjoyable; it can also have a positive impact on students' wellbeing, though this facet of the experience has been under-researched, and limited attention has been given to the role of librarians reading aloud in the library. Students described the benefits of being read to and the related activity of listening to audiobooks. My previous research noted that

> listening to books being read seemed to have a regulatory emotional impact on the children in this sample. This was perhaps best explained by Marco, who found opportunities to be read to at school or home ideal, as 'I like how like sometimes I don't have to be the one that actually reads it, sometimes I like having someone else read to me . . . 'cos it's also very relaxing when someone else reads to you'. Relaxation was also sometimes related to suspension of physical discomfort experienced during sustained independent reading. For example, Tyrone enjoyed being read to by his teachers, 'because sometimes when you're reading a big book for a long time it hurts your eyes'.
>
> (Merga, 2017b, p. 336)

In this vein, recent Indonesian research has found that where students were read to in the school library, this potentially improved their mood, increased their interest in visiting the library and enhanced their interest in reading and their communicative skills (Fadhli et al., 2020).

In this study, Lacey described being read to by her teacher librarian as a great opportunity for enjoyment and a common social practice.

> There's story time often in the [name of] area of the library, over there with the red chairs. And every now and then Mr [Name] or some other teacher-librarian, in lunchtime, they will read a chapter of a book, a few chapters of a particular

book. And I think that's really good . . . it's difficult to describe, but it's a kind of different sensation when you're hearing it out loud, and in your head yourself. And I think it's just a good way to bring people together as well, people that enjoy reading. You can also socialise and make friends, because if people are there, they obviously like the same things as you, and you've got similar likes and interests.

As such, being read to by the teacher librarian was seen to create a shared social experience, which is particularly interesting given that reading is an independent practice. Gambrell (2011) has noted that 'students are more motivated to read when they have opportunities to socially interact with others about the text they are reading' (p. 175), and these read-aloud opportunities can thus further enhance young people's attitudes towards books and reading.

For Piper, her librarian was the preferred person for reading aloud, because 'she puts on the voices':

> One time she read us this book. I think it was one of the Roald Dahl books of, like, the *Twisted Tales* or something, and it was something to do with the Big Bad Wolf. She put on a big scary Big Bad Wolf voice. And when she did, like, when we were younger, she read us The Three Little Pigs, she put on, like, little high-pitched voices with all the pigs and a deep voice for the wolf.

The potential for relaxation was noted, along with the chance to be influenced by the perspectives of a reader other than themselves in the interpretation of the text, with Kai explaining that 'you can just sit back, relax, and fine . . . it's good to see how other people read the book as well, again more perspectives'. Rose echoed this perspective in relation to interpretation, explaining that 'someone might say it a different way. Like, they might say it in a really boring, dull tune, but someone else might say in a really exciting tune'.

It's also important to explore how students found themselves freed from the cognitive load of independent reading. For Chris, the pleasure of being read to allowed him to 'get relaxed and imagine what's happening in the story if there's no pictures', expressing pleasure in opportunities to activate the visual imagination (Pearson, 2020). Being read to could support reading comprehension, with Josh explaining that 'it's just easier to understand sometimes, like, some books are definitely easier to read to yourself because you need to get all the pages in. But sometimes when someone else reads to you, you just easily can catch on'.

Similarly, listening to audiobooks helped to keep the experience of reading fluidity, with Sophia explaining that

I don't have to, like, turn the pages myself, because that's always just annoying. Like, you're in the middle of a thought . . . as part of the end of the page, and then you have to turn the page and you lose that thought. And then you keep reading and you're, like, what was that interesting thought I had before? So, since I don't have to turn the pages myself, I can remember my thoughts.

On a humorous note, it was also inconvenient to turn the pages when she was trying to secretly read when her parents expected her to be sleeping, as 'I have to rustle them all whenever I'm trying to hide them whenever my parents come into my room . . . I like listening to audiobooks because there's none of that, like, holding up the books that I have to do'. It was easier to be a secret reader of audiobooks. Sophia's perspective was not unique, given that this secret reader identity resonated with the findings from my analysis of #Booktok content on TikTok, where CPs posted videos about the challenges of being a 'reader in the family', 'concerned with feeling disconnected with and criticized by parents and family for avid reading behaviors', which included 'reading when CP should be sleeping according to parents' (Merga, 2021, 7).

Resourcing for inclusion

The last theme relates to practices reported by LMs that relate to reading and wellbeing. Resourcing for inclusion demonstrates how library staff accommodate student diversity in the library. My previous research has also captured examples of these kinds of practices, though far more research is needed in this space. I gave examples of teacher librarian reported strategies for 'providing age and skill-appropriate materials for struggling readers', which included 'liaising with a local bookstore to source easier books with "secondary topics, but written at not quite pre-reader . . . almost . . . at the year 1 level, so they're actually getting the content at the right reading level"', and making sure there were books with dyslexia-friendly formats for these students (Merga, 2019, p. 150).

LM Jane gave many examples of resourcing for inclusion, including use of texts with a 'read-aloud facility', and other supports for the vision-impaired students in her school. Anne described how she accommodates difference while consciously avoiding stigma being attached to students with dyslexia:

In the past, we've had children with certain disabilities, and we have certainly accommodated it, whether it's a wheelchair or a specific seat or a weighted blanket, or those kinds of things, those physical things. And then, of course, you know, within the content, then there's the differentiation, which is across all classrooms . . . I work closely with the enrichment teachers when they're talking

> about wanting specific material for the children who are struggling. So you know, I will suggest, rather than it being a very obvious dyslexia format, then we go to ... a publisher like Barrington Stoke, who provides great stories, run-of-the-mill stories, but in a different format so that the children don't feel so different. But I don't actually keep them aside just for the children who have dyslexia. I like them to be in the general collection so that it doesn't matter who's reading it.

Resourcing for inclusion may be done in close consultation with the student's other educators, and it is about more than intervention to enhance learning outcomes. LMs may also take into account the social needs of students to avoid drawing attention to their difference from peers.

LM Veronica used a story dog (who has been given the pseudonym Katie) as a resource to build students' confidence in reading in a non-threatening way. She explained that 'the story dog works with Year 1s and 2s mostly who don't have parents reading with them at home, or who are just a bit nervous, and it's amazing':

> The child without the dog will pick up a book or not say a word. Katie comes in, and they lay on the mat, one hand on Katie, and just read, they'll read out loud to you. Because all of a sudden, it's just taken away ... like, it seems like that part of their brain that worries about what's going on is taken up with this tactile, beautiful ... the smell of the dog, the touch of the dog, and so ... She's a retriever. Oh my gosh, she's beautiful.

While further research is needed, the available research suggests that reading to dogs can enhance young people's perception of their wellbeing (Henderson et al., 2020). These can be valuable opportunities for children to develop their reading skills and enjoy reading aloud without judgement, with a small recent sample of children experiencing an 'increase in self-confidence, self-esteem and concentration and a reduction in anxiety and stress' (Canelo, 2020, p. 106).

Further thoughts

This research articulates what school library professionals already know; some young people need libraries as wellbeing supportive spaces where they can read for enjoyment and experience respite from the challenges of daily life. The connections that young people make with books and characters are not arbitrary, and school library professionals have often put strategies, pedagogy and resources into play to support students to get the most out of books and reading.

Given recent world events, future research should also look at how individuals may turn to RfP when facing significant psychological stressors. For example, recent research has looked at the influence of the COVID-19 lockdown on reading frequency, with a Nigerian study finding that there was a significant increase in reading during lockdown (Adeyemi, 2021). A recent study of the effect of COVID-19 school closure on students' reading in Singapore included a qualitative component that can begin to account for students' self-prescribed reasons for changes in their reading patterns, and this study found that during school closure,

> reading provided enjoyment and relaxation and became a preferred leisure activity. Students . . . who expressed that they liked reading felt that reading was a viable alternative for coping with the boredom of staying at home during the school closure. In other words, they saw reading in a more positive light during the school closure . . . participants used words and phrases such as *'relaxing'*, *'exciting'* and *'I love reading more'* repeatedly to describe their reading experience during the school closure.
>
> (Sun et al., 2021, p. 7)

This led the authors to suggest that their results indicate that there may be a relationship between leisure reading and benefits for children's mental wellbeing.

This chapter draws on the voices of students and LMs to explore potential links between school libraries, reading engagement and student wellbeing. School libraries are spaces that facilitate RfP, allowing opportunities for escape and respite from stressors. RfP enables young people to connect with relatable characters to build confidence and source role models for inspiration. Students also read for perspective-taking and personal development, and found pleasure in being read to, notably by their school library professionals. LMs illustrated some of the many ways they worked behind the scenes to enhance young people's reading experiences and provide resourcing for inclusion to ensure that the library is a safe space that co-facilitates RfP and student wellbeing. Sullivan and Strang (2002) note that 'in attempting to help students with socio-emotional difficulties, school professionals are searching for ways to promote the skills and cognitive strengths necessary for successful adjustment, both inside and outside the classroom'. This chapter illustrates how providing time and opportunity for students to enjoy RfP in the library can help them to achieve this goal.

References

Adeyemi, I. O. (2021). Influence of COVID-19 lockdown on reading habit of Nigerians: A case study of Lagos state inhabitants. *Reading & Writing Quarterly, 37*(2), 157–168.

Bladek, M. (2021). Student well-being matters: Academic library support for the whole student. *The Journal of Academic Librarianship, 47*(3), e102349.

Boeije, H. (2002). A purposeful approach to the constant comparative method in the analysis of qualitative interviews. *Quality and Quantity, 36*, 391–409.

Canelo, E. (2020). Perceptions of animal assisted reading and its results reported by involved children, parents and teachers of a Portuguese elementary school. *Human-Animal Interaction Bulletin, 8*(3), 92–110.

Chapple, M., Williams, S., Billington, J., Davis, P., & Corcoran, R. (2021). An analysis of the reading habits of autistic adults compared to neurotypical adults and implications for future interventions. *Research in Developmental Disabilities, 115*, e104003.

Clark, C., & Picton, I. (2020). *Children and young people's reading in 2020 before and during the COVID-19 lockdown*. National Literacy Trust research report. https://files.eric.ed.gov/fulltext/ED607776.pdf

Clark, C., & Teravainen-Goff, A. (2018). *Mental wellbeing, reading and writing: How children and young people's mental wellbeing is related to their reading and writing experiences*. National Literacy Trust.

Clarke, T. (2020). Children's wellbeing and their academic achievement: The dangerous discourse of 'trade-offs' in education. *Theory and Research in Education*. https://doi.org/10.1177/1477878520980197

Cox, A., & Brewster, L. (2020). Library support for student mental health and wellbeing in the UK: Before and during the COVID-19 pandemic. *Journal of Academic Librarianship, 46*(6), e102256.

Dix, K., Ahmed, S., Carslake, T., Gregory, S., O'Grady, E., & Trevitt, J. (2020). *Student health & wellbeing: Systematic review*. Australian Council for Educational Research.

Elia, H. (2019). Public libraries supporting health and wellness: A literature review. *School of Information Student Research Journal, 9*(2), 1–11.

Fadhli, R., Indah, R. N., Widya, N., & Oktaviani, W. (2020). Strategi perpustakaan sekolah dasar dalam mengembangkan emotional branding melalui storytelling. *JMIE (Journal of Madrasah Ibtidaiyah Education), 4*(1), 68–85.

Gambrell, L. B. (2011). Seven rules of engagement: What's most important to know about motivation to read. *The Reading Teacher, 65*(3), 172–178.

Heath, M. A., Sheen, D., Leavy, D., Young, E., & Money, K. (2005). Bibliotherapy: A resource to facilitate emotional healing and growth. *School Psychology International, 26*(5), 563–580.

Henderson, L., Grové, C., Lee, F., Trainer, L., Schena, H., & Prentice, M. (2020). An evaluation of a dog-assisted reading program to support student wellbeing in primary school. *Children and Youth Services Review, 118*, e105449.

Kartal, H., & Bilhan, D. (2021). Okuma üzerine sanat temelli boylamsal bir araştırma: Çocuklar okurken nasıl hissediyor? *Türk Kütüphaneciliği, 35*(2), 274–312.

Kaya, M., & Erdem, C. (2021). Students' well-being and academic achievement: A meta-analysis study. *Child Indicators Research*. https://doi.org/10.1007/s12187-021-09821-4

Kolb, S. M. (2012). Grounded theory and the constant comparative method: Valid research strategies for educators. *Journal of Emerging Trends in Educational Research and Policy Studies, 3*(1), 83–86.

Koopman, E. M. E. (2015). Why do we read sad books? Eudaimonic motives and meta-emotions. *Poetics, 52*, 18–31.

Levine, S. L., Cherrier, S., Holding, A. C., & Koestner, R. (2020). For the love of reading: Recreational reading reduces psychological distress in college students and autonomous motivation is the key. *Journal of American College Health* https://doi.org/10.1080/07448481.2020.1728280

Lomas, T. (2018). The quiet virtues of sadness: A selective theoretical and interpretative appreciation of its potential contribution to wellbeing. *New Ideas in Psychology, 49*, 18–26.

Lucas, C. V., & Soares, L. (2013). Bibliotherapy: A tool to promote children's psychological well-being. *Journal of Poetry Therapy, 26*(3), 137–147.

Mar, R. A., Oatley, K., & Peterson, J. B. (2009). Exploring the link between reading fiction and empathy: Ruling out individual differences and examining outcomes. *Communications, 34*(4), 407–428.

Merga, M. K. (2017a). What motivates avid readers to maintain a regular reading habit in adulthood? *Australian Journal of Language and Literacy, 40*(2), 146–156.

Merga, M. K. (2017b). Interactive reading opportunities beyond the early years: What educators need to consider. *Australian Journal of Education, 61*(3), 328–343.

Merga, M. K. (2019). How do librarians in schools support struggling readers? *English in Education, 53*(2), 145–160.

Merga, M. K. (2020). How can school libraries support student wellbeing? Evidence and implications for further research. *Journal of Library Administration, 60*(6), 660–673.

Merga, M. K. (2021). How can TikTok inform readers' advisory services for young people? *Library & Information Science Research*. https://doi.org/10.1016/j.lisr.2021.101091

Michalek, J. E., Lisi, M., Awad, D., Hadfield, K., Mareschal, I., & Dajani, R. (2021). The effects of a reading-based intervention on emotion processing in children who have suffered early adversity and war related trauma. *Frontiers in Psychology, 12*, e613754.

Pearson, J. (2020). The visual imagination. In A. Abraham (Ed.), *The Cambridge handbook of the imagination* (pp. 175–186). Cambridge University Press.

Rain, M., & Mar, R. A. (2021). Adult attachment and engagement with fictional characters. *Journal of Social and Personal Relationships*. https://doi.org/10.1177%2F02654075211018513

Schwering, S. C., Ghaffari-Nikou, N. M., Zhao, F., Niedenthal, P. M., & MacDonald, M. C. (2021). Exploring the relationship between fiction reading and emotion recognition. *Affective Science*. https://doi.org/10.1007/s42761-021-00034-0

Sullivan, A. K., & Strang, H. R. (2002). Bibliotherapy in the classroom using literature to promote the development of emotional intelligence. *Childhood Education*, *79*(2), 74–80.

Sun, B., Loh, C. E., & Nie, Y. (2021). The COVID-19 school closure effect on students' print and digital leisure reading. *Computers and Education Open*, e100033.

Suvilehto, P., Kerry-Moran, K. J., & Aerila, J. A. (2019). Supporting children's social and emotional growth through developmental bibliotherapy. In K. J. Kerry-Moran, & J. A. Aerila (Eds.), *Story in children's lives: Contributions of the narrative mode to early childhood development, literacy, and learning* (Vol. 16, pp. 299–314). Springer International.

Tribe, K. V., Papps, F. A., & Calvert, F. (2021). 'It just gives people hope': A qualitative inquiry into the lived experience of the Harry Potter world in mental health recovery. *The Arts in Psychotherapy*. https://doi.org/10.1016/j.aip.2021.101802

5
School Libraries, Health Resourcing and Information Literacy

When we think about school libraries fostering young people's wellbeing, we should take into account the fact that library professionals, regardless of the setting, are passionate about connecting their clients to current and important information. Some of that information will be health information that supports students' capacity to understand and be responsive to issues impacting on their wellbeing, such as information about health conditions in themselves and others. Providing young people with access to current health information and teaching them the skills they need to individually source it and determine its credibility are key affordances of the contemporary school library that may be lost if we do not value them, given the diverse roles that our libraries play in students' lives. However, given schools' increasing interests in fostering digital and information literacy in their students to the extent that, in some cases, such instruction has been mandated as an educational requirement (Phillips & Lee, 2019), this may perhaps be an aspect of the school library professionals' roles likely to garner increasing attention.

While information literacy is conceptualised in various ways, as noted by McKeever et al. (2017), these definitions 'revolve around the same ideas of being able to access, use and communicate information effectively' (p. 51), and Fadhli (2021) links information literacy skills to an individual's capacity for lifelong learning. For at least the past 50 years, library professionals have taken responsibility for connecting their clients with the largest body of information possible (Thomas et al., 2011). It is part of the core role of school library professionals to support information skills in both staff and students. In the US, the school library is expected to increasingly adopt 'a proactive role in student learning as today's information and technology environment becomes an integral and natural part of life' (American Association of School

Librarians (AASL), 2013, p. 1), and the AASL's National School Library Standards (2018) detail the role of the school librarian and library in supporting information literacy, primarily in relation to inquiry-based learning. In the UK, job description documents (JDFs) commonly expected school librarians to facilitate information literacy (Merga, 2020a), and in 2011, Streatfield et al. noted that school librarians in the UK had been involved in information literacy for over 30 years.

As I previously explored in Chapter 1, in Australia and the UK, information literacy is also an important part of the expected role of school library professionals. In Australia, in order to demonstrate proficiency, teacher librarians are expected to 'work with students to develop learning goals incorporating information literacy, inquiry and literacy skills', and 'embed the elements of information literacy into learning and teaching programs' (Australian School Library Association (ASLA), 2014, p. 9). This expectation is also regularly articulated in JDFs for Australian teacher librarians, with 90% of documents analysed promoting this role (Merga, 2020b). The available research suggests that the information literacy role of the school library has been perceived by Australian school students, with high levels of agreement with the statements 'the information in the school library has helped me work out the questions for the topics I am working on' (96.3%), 'the school library has helped me know the different steps in finding and using information' (95.7%), and 'the school library has helped me find different sources of information (such as books, magazines, CDs, websites, videos) for my topics' (94.8%) (Hay, 2005, p. 23).

Health literacy and information literacy

While developing information literacy skills in students and teachers is a core component of the role of school library professionals, relatively little is known about the role of the school library in the provision of health and wellbeing resources, and the fostering of *health literacy*. Health literacy is a specific kind of information literacy that relates to consumers being able to understand health or medical information and obtain information through a variety of sources. It also includes the capacity to use the health information selected 'to make good decisions about their own course of care' (Schardt, 2011, p. 1). Attention needs to be given to fostering health literacy in young people, as it can impact upon their health outcomes, and dealing with voluminous and often contradictory health information can pose a real challenge:

> The ubiquitous nature of health information is both a benefit and burden for health consumers; freely available health information on the Internet and a wide

variety of media platforms allow access to multitudes of information. However, that wealth of information can be questionable, inaccurate, and overwhelming, particularly for those with low health literacy or fluency.

(Ottosen et al., 2019, p. 208)

The school has an important role to play in this regard, with Elmer et al. (2020) noting that 'schools provide a critical nexus between the teacher (as service provider), the student (as learner) and their family (carers and wider community) to support the development of children's health literacy' (p. 1). With the school library professional resourcing information literacy and scaffolding the skills needed, this can and should also encompass related health literacy.

In current times in particular, there may be a complex interplay between the news literacy component of information literacy and health information literacy, with health advice about COVID-19 commonly disseminated through mainstream media. As noted by Farmer (2019),

> mass media play an increasingly significant role in today's society. Even when one is not searching for information, mass media permeate everyone's environment, influencing individual world views and decision-making. Therefore, people need to consciously and critically analyze and evaluate mass media messages and, only then, decide how to respond. Otherwise, they will not make reasoned decisions, and they will suffer the consequences of their assumptions or ignorance. They must be news literate. (p. 2)

Where such media stand to influence the health decisions of all of their consumers, including students, a plurality of literacies needs to be drawn upon for important health messages to be accessed, understood and acted upon in potentially life-saving ways. We can't take for granted that just because health messages are communicated they reach their intended audience, and that they are accessible to them. Fake news has proliferated around life-threating conditions such as COVID-19, with recent research concluding that 'misinformation fuelled by rumours, stigma, and conspiracy theories can have potentially severe implications on public health if prioritized over scientific guidelines' (Islam et al., 2020, p. 1627).

School librarians can play an important health literacy role. They may act as 'health information gatekeepers' (Lukenbill & Immroth, 2009, p. 3), supporting students to access resources in mental health and wellbeing (St. Jean et al., 2017). They can also help students to identify the reliability of the information they find, as supporting students' critical and digital literacy is part of their role, teaching 'students critical information literacy skills such as evaluating information and sources' (Merga, 2020a, p. 895). While there is limited research that explores the role of school libraries in disseminating health information and fostering health literacy for student wellbeing, this is an accepted part of the role of public libraries, with Elia's (2019) review finding that 'public libraries have been contributing to the wellness of their communities for some time, and opportunities to offer these kinds of health-based services have increased in recent years', and 'some of the most frequent offerings include consumer health information provision' (p. 8).

As in the previous chapter, this chapter reports on previously unpublished data from my research project on school libraries and wellbeing, the 2020 'School libraries promoting wellbeing in Australian primary and secondary schools' project (I'll refer to it in this chapter as the Project). View Appendix 1 for details about respondents, and the method, but I'll reiterate here that the Project reports on a small qualitative sample of 12 students and three library managers (LMs) at three schools that presented themselves as effective at using school libraries to promote wellbeing. Due to this deliberate sampling of schools and students who made good use of the school library, broad generalisability of the findings cannot be implied. Instead, this chapter gives insights into how children in upper primary and lower secondary schools and their LMs can draw on their libraries for health information resourcing. As mentioned in the previous chapter, interviews were professionally transcribed, and then I identified recurring themes using a process of constant comparative analysis (Boeije, 2002; Kolb, 2012). You can find the specific questions I asked in Appendix 1, as well as more detail around ethics considerations for opening a line of questioning with minors, which could be seen as potentially leading to their disclosures around personal health issues as an unintended tangent.

In relation to provision of health and wellbeing resources, I summarise the main findings around the key themes of searching in the library, checking information is correct (from LM and student perspectives), resourcing for teachers and parents, and non-fiction books.

Searching in the library

First, most students interviewed in this Project had a clear understanding of how to locate health and wellbeing resources in their library. For example, Jennie described using the online library catalogue to search for keywords and then locating resources in the library as a reference. Similarly, Momo detailed online, personal advice and book options for information, explaining that you could probably search something about that up or could just ask someone . . . if it's something to do with your body or something, you could check a book all about, like, the human body and see a book about medicines, or whatever. And you could see if it has anything to help you in it.

Rose explained how she could search for health and wellbeing resources without having to worry about accessing inappropriate material:

I would go into the library to get a book and if I can't find it there, I'd normally go on the library web page and look at a few things on that . . . there's lots of sort of apps, like, *Safe Search* and all those, like, they help with, like, if any inappropriate things come up on the internet, they don't have it. So, I normally go on *Safe Search*.

Skyla explained that her library was well-resourced around her specific condition, noting that 'I can get a book about [specific health condition], because there's loads of those books and stuff in the library. And I also might just search it up on, like, online books and stuff'. As such, there was confidence in using varying resources in the library to locate health information.

Checking information is correct from library manager perspectives

Confirming the veracity of health information sourced in the library was something that LMs focused their instruction on. For example, LM Veronica ostensibly drew on the 'Be SMART online rules' (Childnet International, 2018) that she used to underpin her information literacy instruction, explaining that

we've been doing a digital program for some years, and I have taught research for a long time. Part of teaching research has always involved being SMART, having SMART searching skills, and that includes explaining about the high percentage of information that's available online that's unedited, and what editing means, and talking about the olden days when we used to have books that were published and fact-checked and everything like that and the differences. We used to teach about, obviously, finding multiple sources, sources that can't be altered by anyone else, such as Wikipedia and such.

Veronica constantly updated the affordances of this programme so that it remained abreast of students' evolving information needs:

Now we've now moved into a more advanced digital literacy program. So again, yes, we have talked about safely navigating their way through the web and through using online resources, ways to avoid falling into phishing traps and looking at URLs for validity . . . So, (there are) lots of specific things that they can do to try and make sure that they're looking at safe sites, and sites where they're going to get reliable information. So, looking at big providers, looking at companies where all their information is streamlined and put out through appropriate channels rather than just doing a random Google search and finding an article, So, like, backing up your fact checks. Clickbait . . . the curiosity gap, teaching kids about what to look for, what people are going to prey on in order to get them to go in a direction that maybe is not a real and valid one.

So, at the moment, the focus is on evaluating how we live online and how we find information online and exploring some websites, and just basically looking at how we kind of judge and gauge the validity of a site, what we can look for, so that we know that it's at least, possibly, going to provide us with some safe and reliable information.

She had also specifically created a library portal due to COVID-19 related school closures, on which she provided 'some safe, reputable links that I had checked out myself on there, and including some good science, because it was a period where wellbeing was quite in the forefront'. In this vein, LM Jane described accessing online courses in order to upskill herself in web resource evaluation, so that 'looking at who's behind it, not just . . . natural reading, not just vertical reading. So, checking other websites, and all that sort of stuff'.

Anne highlighted how the shift to heavier student device use in her primary school was coupled with increased support from her in checking information is correct as well as ensuring student safety. She explained that she worked

very closely with the teachers that are beginning with the one-to-one device. We use the eSafety website a lot. They've got some fantastic scenarios that we run through with the kids. And that's why we enforce the use of the dedicated library webpage as a starting point, using safe search. And then going on all the different skills, all the different things to look out for if you're going to be a responsible digital citizen.

She also encouraged students to adopt regular processes to evaluate the veracity of information, noting that 'any resource that we go through', 'we look at all of the little things, do we know who wrote it? Can we identify any part of the URL? Is it familiar to us? Have you heard of these people before?' As such, LMs described comprehensive and highly responsive strategies for equipping students with the plurality of literacies needed to be competent and confident health information consumers in their libraries.

Checking information is correct from student perspectives

I was interested to see if LM knowledge and instruction on this area was trickling down to student knowledge, and while not all students indicated knowledge, others could confidently articulate the processes they used.

For example, Piper was taught the following by her teacher librarian in digital media lessons, showing understanding of how to evaluate text but also how to avoid reacting to clickbait:

> You look for the way things are written, if there are spelling mistakes, or grammar mistakes, not proper use of, like, introduction and greetings. And if it's, like, a notification or something, if they do, like, they make it seem really urgent, even though it might not be urgent.

Skyla also primarily learned about how to identify whether information is correct or not in 'digital media' instruction from her 'librarian teacher'; 'she teaches our class, and we get to do a lot of fun activities learning about digital media'. She explained that the way her school library professional did this was particularly engaging, as it used humour:

> There's things like if it's you wouldn't believe what happened, like, a guy kissed a Cobra or something, that would probably be fake, because you could probably die from doing that . . . she (has) done more things, like . . . you don't have to listen to what other people say on online things.

Furthermore, students did not confine their information checking to information from websites. Sophia explained that she would normally check information from a book 'against other books', and checking multiple sources for information to determine veracity was common, reflecting recent findings from Croatia that suggest adolescents often use multiple sources when seeking information about health (Martinović et al., 2021).

Many students in the Project mentioned Wikipedia when describing unreliable websites. For example, Momo advised, 'don't use websites where you can literally go in it, and press a button, just type in whatever you want', and Lacey explained that 'some websites really tell lies . . . I think a lot of things, for example, Wikipedia, anyone can just go on and put their information on, which doesn't mean it's reliable'. Bob explained why Wikipedia is not a reliable source of information, noting that 'they can just say wild stuff, like, they could say Australia isn't real, dogs are actually cats, or something like that'. Sometimes he took information from Wikipedia and cross-referenced it with other websites, leading him to conclude that 'sometimes the information can be true. I know that because I've checked more websites and then I'm, like, "that's true". Well, most of the time; it hasn't been very reliable for me, personally'. While he often checked with reliable influences in his life about whether information was correct, such as parents or teachers, he was confident in his information literacy skills, noting that 'my class teacher's had to tell me if the information was real or not. But I can kind of determine what it is because [of] the skills I've been taught'.

Some students positioned their teachers or parents as more trustworthy resources of information than online sources, reflecting a recent Chinese study that suggested that cultural reasons could have been behind 'children's trust in the teacher', 'rather than a genuine belief that the teacher was more likely to be accurate' (Wang et al., 2019, p. 257). While further research is needed with a much larger Australian sample, the findings here suggest that Australian children may also have more confidence in their teachers than in online sources of information. However, the reason for greater trust in the teacher may very well be due to information literacy training students receive from their school library professionals, rather than cultural conditionings, so this possibility should be explored if such studies are undertaken.

Resourcing for teachers and parents

LMs didn't only provide health information resources for students; they also made it available for teachers and parents. For example, Anne worked closely with teachers to ensure that she could meet their health resourcing needs:

> They have a bulk load at the beginning of every term where I actually ask them to tell me what areas they're covering in each curriculum area, to be fairly specific, what skills they're covering, what general capabilities. How do we work together on that? Are there any specific texts? And they'll often be very literal, and then I'll try and tease that out.
>
> So, if they're looking at health, then I will throw in some of these books, and I will actually say to them, 'Have a look in this chapter, this covers this. Here are some ethical questions you might need to, you know, be discussing'. You know, they'll be touching on various . . . very lightly on elements of sexuality. So that will come into it. We've got a lot about Protective Behaviours. So that comes in as well, addressing a lot of that.

This example shows how the task of curation, 'a mainstay of school library practice' (Spiering & Lechtenberg, 2020, p. 83), is applied to health information resourcing in schools. It is a common facet of the role, as 'very few days go by in a school library when the librarian is not asked to pull books on a topic, locate digital resources to support research, or select a set of resources to display and promote' (p. 83).

However, as an information literacy expert, Anne also encouraged teachers to think about health and wellbeing resourcing holistically, also encouraging them to address complex wellbeing themes with students through the medium of fiction:

> But also, when they're looking at their health about, you know, looking after your body, it will be what about considering a bit of meditation, what about the benefits of music, think about your diet, think about, you know, this book addresses bullying, however, have a look at the techniques or the skills that have been sort of implemented during the story, and then that will run through.
>
> So, whenever there's an issue in a classroom, I'll go, 'Read this book. How about this one?' You know, it's friendships, all of those kinds of things.

UK research has suggested that classroom teachers may lack strong knowledge in information literacy (McKeever et al., 2017), highlighting the importance of the role of school library professionals in building classroom teachers' capacity in this regard. Anne managed this intervention by being closely responsive to teachers' specific health information needs, but also broadened the scope of typical resources that would be drawn upon. This also illustrates how school library professionals actively engage classroom teachers in the curation process (Spiering & Lechtenberg, 2020).

Parents also came into Anne's library at various times to resource information about various issues. Similarly, Veronica provided parents with health information. As she explains below, in some cases, parents were referred to the LM for information by their own children. Veronica explained that

> Parents come in quite often asking for, you know, 'My child wants to know about puberty. What do you recommend? What's a good one?' You know, what's this? What's that?
>
> I had one child once who said to his mum, 'I'm feeling really sad. Go and ask Mrs [Librarian's Name] if there's a book about boys who are sad'.
>
> After she asked me, we both cried, first of all, and then I gave her a whole stack of books. Because he didn't want to say (it) in front of his friends, but his mum ... and I said to him later, 'You know you can come and ask me',

He went, 'I know, but she's just bugging me about why I'm so sad'. And so, he said, 'I thought I'll give her something to do and come and get books from you'.

This example demonstrates that LMs can be viewed as compassionate health literacy supporters who are able to support and provide resources to meet the needs of parents and their children in ways that are respectful and discreet.

Non-fiction books

Non-fiction books certainly appeared to be the resource of choice in this small sample, suggesting that it is worth maintaining the currency of these resources in school libraries. Non-fiction books were a valued source of health information that students indicate competence and confidence in accessing. For example, Kai explained that in 'one of the rows of non-fiction they've got a specific section for that, even the issues section in the library for non-fiction', and Josh noted that 'they would have stuff on your health and about the body and how you can grow up to be a really healthy and good person'. Non-fiction books were described by Momo as 'very reliable', 'not like a computer or anything like that where it runs out of batteries. And it means that if you need to check something, and you can always just look through the index and just find what you need'.

While Lacey saw online searches as the easy option, her concerns with the veracity of this material meant that non-fiction books were still worth consideration, in her view:

> because I'm lazy I would probably begin to go to one of the computers over there and look it up. However, if there happened to be nothing, and again there's lots of false information out there, but there are lots of fun fact books as well, and there are lots of books that teach you methods of controlling anxiety and depression here. And I do think that's a good source.

This finding that some students prefer to access health information in books rather than online is interesting in light of recent research which has found that 'participants' comprehension of health-relevant information was (marginally) greater when the information was presented in a printed format than a digital format' (Haddock et al., 2020, p. 455). This means that health information could potentially be more accessible to students in paper form rather than on screen. While future research should explore this more closely, it is possible that this is one of the underlying reasons for the unanticipated student preference that seemed to be present in the respondents of this study.

LM Jane curated her non-fiction section in order to be responsive to student needs, but also evolving issues:

> there's a lot of mental health stuff in there . . . there's some really good books about dealing with stress and resources there. So, we had a display at the end of one of these bay ends, just saying 'feeling stressed out', especially towards the end of last term because . . . of COVID, 'try one of these'.

However, it is not a given that a substantial and current range of non-fiction materials can be easily maintained in school libraries. Anne talked about the challenges of maintaining non-fiction resources for her students, explaining that in terms of her collection,

> nonfiction is dropping down more and more. Even though I'm a firm believer that the junior grades need the books and those children who are struggling definitely benefit from a text. Unfortunately, they are quite expensive, and I often find they are way too text heavy. So, finding good, age-appropriate content, you know, driven and connected to the curriculum, takes a lot of time.

It would be useful for further research to look closely at whether school resources in non-fiction books are compatible with student demand for these materials, and whether the finding here that students view non-fiction books as a preferred resource for health information holds broader generalisability.

However, it is important to note that while students were more likely to mention using non-fiction for health and wellbeing resourcing, some students and LMs also described using fiction in this manner. For example, Kai explained as follows:

> There are (non-fiction) books in the library about it, so you can go check that out yourself, and then in the fiction area you have, like, different people's perspective of it, because it's not non-fiction, but yeah . . . You can definitely take it from different point of views, so it's great to see how someone else can view it, whereas you're viewing it from a different angle and it can really open your mind.

LM Anne also explained that 'we've got some wonderful picture books, novels, young adult books that address those issues. Just as a theme running through, rather than, you know, here's a text on how to manage your mental health'.

Further thoughts

School libraries foster students' information literacy, and therefore directly or indirectly foster the subset of health literacy that falls within it. They also provide access to current resources on health issues which are absolutely crucial, given the pervasive misinformation around issues such as the global COVID-19 pandemic. School library professionals can upskill students in a plurality of literacies, including but not limited to related information, health and media literacies, and are constantly responsive to changing training needs for both their own professional learning as well as their instruction.

As noted by Barr-Walker (2016) in her review of the literature on health literacy and libraries, 'school librarians have a unique opportunity to improve the health literacy of children and teachers, but these libraries are underrepresented in the literature' (p. 200). Furthermore, the potential of school libraries as well as libraries more broadly may be relatively untapped (Ottosen et al., 2019), with a Croatian study finding that adolescents 'desire for schools to provide them with more health-related knowledge' (Martinović et al., 2021, p. 15). Given that school library professionals continue to look for ways to better serve their communities, and to be responsive to their students' needs, improving school libraries' health literacy affordances and resourcing may benefit students while also playing to the already existing strengths of school library professionals as information literacy experts. Future research that explores the impact of library-based training and resourcing in health literacy, particularly in relation to students' health literacy and health outcomes, could be a powerful basis for advocacy going forward, and such research should be undertaken as a priority, given the global pandemic that we are currently living through.

If we are going to enhance this aspect of the school library professional role, it is inevitable that attention must be given to resourcing. Libraries need adequate funding to be effective and appealing; however, many libraries worldwide are poorly funded, and there are wide disparities in the extent to which governments invest in their libraries (Krolak, 2005). For example, in Bangladesh, 'only a minority of schools have well-stocked functional school libraries and qualified librarians' (Hossain, 2019, p. 7). However, even school libraries in more economically privileged nations may be severely under-resourced. When it comes to information literacy skills, budget does matter, and school libraries may more typically sustain declines rather than receiving gains in terms of budget over time (Softlink, 2021). As noted in the Great School Libraries report (2019), underfunding of school libraries can lead to restricting access to credible and current resources:

teaching research skills in a modern context requires digital search (information retrieval) techniques. Without supplying access to published online resources we risk re-enforcing the idea that all information is free online, and an over-reliance on free information sites such as Wikipedia and BBC Bitesize (p. 13)

While the students in this study knew better than to unequivocally trust the information provided in Wikipedia, a broader range of information sources must be available so that students are not forced to 'make do' with potentially problematic information.

In relation to health resourcing, provision of adequate and current resourcing is particularly pertinent, as information in this area is constantly evolving. While the research in this area is sparse, I see it as a highly promising space for future inquiry, the findings of which could lead to better health outcomes for students but also to a strengthening of the contribution of school library professionals to student wellbeing. However, research will need to explore the role of adequate resourcing in this regard. Furthermore, if future research supports the possibility raised here that some young people prefer to read books to source health information rather than source it online, and if the varying affordances in relation to reading comprehension are implicated, it will be essential to ensure that non-fiction book resources are maintained and updated. This is only viable where budgets are sufficient to allow it, and it is concerning to imagine that health information availability may be yet another area where privileged, well-resourced schools can provide superior outcomes for their students, and therefore equity implications will need to be considered in parallel with evolving findings in this area.

Furthermore, additional training may be needed for school library professionals seeking to build their capacity in fostering students' health literacy. For example, a study of rural school librarians in Missouri found that the 'school librarians want more training on mental health support, which can be accomplished in professional development modules or in pre-service instruction', but also that 'the areas where school librarians indicate the greatest confidence are the areas that correspond to their domain – providing informational and recreational resources to students, providing a safe space for those students, and providing a caring listener for those students' (Adkins et al., 2019, p. 433).

I suggest that the role of the school library professional in regard to health literacy be clearly and comprehensively defined at national and international levels, so that school library professionals do not find themselves expected to take on roles that are far outside their scope, and more appropriate to the training of school nurses and psychologists. Health information provision and evaluation need to remain the focus, as arguably this already aligns with current information literacy expectations of school library professionals. It is also worth noting that school library professionals may find that the credible information they present contradicts the health information being provided by some parents, so school library professionals may 'need to think more about mediating appropriate health information obtained from personal and non-personal sources' (Martinović et al., 2021, p. 15). This is certainly an important area that deserves greater attention from both the research and the school library professional communities moving forward.

References

AASL. (2013). *Implementing the Common Core State Standards: The role of the school librarian.* http://www.ala.org/aasl/sites/ala.org.aasl/files/content/externalrelations/CCSSLibrariansBrief_FINAL.pdf

AASL. (2018). National School Library Standards crosswalk with Future Ready Librarians. http://standards.aasl.org/wp-content/uploads/2018/08/180828-aasl-standards-crosswalk-future-ready.pdf

Adkins, D., Brendler, B., Townsend, K., & Maras, M. (2019). Rural school libraries anchoring community mental health literacy. *Qualitative and Quantitative Methods in Libraries, 8*(4), 425–435.

ASLA. (2014). Evidence Guide for teacher librarians in the proficient career stage. https://www.asla.org.au/resources/Documents/Website%20Documents/evidence_guide_prof.pdf

Barr-Walker, J. (2016). Health literacy and libraries: a literature review. *Reference Services Review, 44*(2), 191–205.

Boeije, H. (2002). A purposeful approach to the constant comparative method in the analysis of qualitative interviews. *Quality and Quantity, 36*, 391–409.

Childnet International. (2018). SMART rules poster. https://www.childnet.com/ufiles/SMART-rules-poster-A3-Free.pdf

Elia, H. (2019). Public libraries supporting health and wellness: A literature review. *School of Information Student Research Journal, 9*(2), 1–11.

Elmer, S., Nash, R., Kemp, N., Coleman, C., Wyss, M., & Roach, J. (2020). HealthLit4Kids: Supporting schools to be health literacy responsive organisations. *Health Promotion Journal of Australia.* https://doi.org/10.1002/hpja.412.

Fadhli, R. (2021). Implementasi kompetensi pembelajaran sepanjang hayat melalui program literasi di perpustakaan sekolah. *Jurnal Kajian Informasi & Perpustakaan, 9*(1), 19–38.

Farmer, L. (2019). News literacy and fake news curriculum: School librarians' perceptions of pedagogical practices. *Journal of Media Literacy Education, 11*(3), 1–11.

Great School Libraries. (2019). *Great School Libraries survey findings and update on phase 1*. https://d824397c-0ce2-4fc6-b5c4-8d2e4de5b242.filesusr.com/ugd/8d6dfb_a1949ea011cd415fbd57a7a0c4471469.pdf

Haddock, G., Foad, C., Saul, V., Brown, W., & Thompson, R. (2020). The medium can influence the message: Print-based versus digital reading influences how people process different types of written information. *British Journal of Psychology, 111*(3), 443–459.

Hay, L. (2005). Student learning through Australian school libraries Part 1: A statistical analysis of student perceptions. *Synergy, 3*(2), 17–30.

Hossain, Z. (2019). Status of non-government secondary school libraries in Bangladesh: A survey. In J. L. Branch-Mueller (Ed.) *Proceedings of the 48th Annual Conference of the International Association of School Librarianship and the 23rd International Forum on Research in School Librarianship*. IASL. https://journals.library.ualberta.ca/slw/index.php/iasl/article/download/7437/4328

Islam, M. S., Sarkar, T., Khan, S. H., Kamal, A. H. M., Hasan, S. M., Kabir, A., & Seale, H. (2020). COVID-19–related infodemic and its impact on public health: A global social media analysis. *American Journal of Tropical Medicine and Hygiene, 103*(4), 1621–1629.

Kolb, S. M. (2012). Grounded theory and the constant comparative method: Valid research strategies for educators. *Journal of Emerging Trends in Educational Research and Policy Studies, 1*, 83–86.

Krolak, L. (2005). *The role of libraries in the creation of literate environments*. UNESCO Institute for Education.

Lukenbill, B., & Immroth, B. (2009). School and public youth librarians as health information gatekeepers: Research from the Lower Rio Grande Valley of Texas. *School Library Media Research, 12*, 1–35.

Martinović, I., Kim, S. U., & Katavić, S. (2021). Study of health information needs among adolescents in Croatia shows distinct gender differences in information seeking behaviour. *Health Information & Libraries Journal*. https://doi.org/10.1111/hir.12369

McKeever, C., Bates, J., & Reilly, J. (2017). School library staff perspectives on teacher information literacy and collaboration. *Journal of Information Literacy, 11*(2), 51–68.

Merga, M. K. (2020a). What is the literacy supportive role of the school librarian in the United Kingdom? *Journal of Librarianship & Information Science*. https://doi.org/10.1177/0961000620964569

Merga, M. K. (2020b). School librarians as literacy educators within a complex role. *Journal of Library Administration, 60*(8), 889–908.

Ottosen, T., Mani, N. S., & Fratta, M. N. (2019). Health information literacy awareness and capacity building: Present and future. *IFLA Journal, 45*(3), 207–215.

Phillips, A. L., & Lee, V. R. (2019). Whose responsibility is it? A statewide survey of school librarians on responsibilities and resources for teaching digital citizenship. *School Library Research*, 22. https://files.eric.ed.gov/fulltext/EJ1218561.pdf

Schardt, C. (2011). Health information literacy meets evidence-based practice. *Journal of the Medical Library Association*, 99(1), 1–2.

Softlink. (2021). *2020 School Library Survey*. https://www.softlinkint.com/assets/img/content/2020_School_Library_Survey_United_Kingdom_-_Report.pdf

Spiering, J., & Lechtenberg, K. (2020). Rethinking curation in school libraries and school library education: Critical, conceptual, collaborative. *School Libraries Worldwide*, 26(1), 83–98.

St. Jean, B., Greene Taylor, N., Kodama, C., & Subramaniam, M. (2017). Assessing the digital health literacy skills of tween participants in a school-library-based after-school program. *Journal of Consumer Health on the Internet*, 21(1), 40–61.

Streatfield, D., Shaper, S., Markless, S., & Rae-Scott, S. (2011). Information literacy in United Kingdom schools. *Journal of information literacy*, 5(2), 5–25.

Thomas, N. P., Crow, S. R., & Franklin, L. L. (2011). *Information literacy and information skills instruction: Applying research to practice in the 21st century school library*. ABC-CLIO.

Wang, F., Tong, Y., & Danovitch, J. (2019). Who do I believe? Children's epistemic trust in internet, teacher, and peer informants. *Cognitive Development*, 50, 248–260.

6
Librarians Creating Environments for Reading and Wellbeing

When our children and students head off to school in the morning, we want them to have safe and supportive experiences during their day that allow them to develop their academic and social skills. A key factor that may impact on their wellbeing within schools is the social climate of the school. Lenzi et al. (2017) define this broadly as 'the physical and social features of the school context', 'represented by the aggregation of students', teachers', and other staff members' perceptions and behaviors' (p. 527). School libraries can make a positive contribution to the school climate, and they are also subclimates themselves, as inviting spaces that are intentionally constructed, often on meagre budgets, to foster a sense of belonging in students.

While school libraries are adaptive spaces used for many purposes (BMG Research, 2019), school library professionals may purposefully create environments that support reading for pleasure (RfP) and related student wellbeing. As I have explored in detail in the earlier chapters of this book, research suggests that RfP can be related to student wellbeing (Levine et al., 2020) and that regular reading of fiction can support development of empathy and prosocial characteristics (e.g. Mar et al., 2009). Books and reading can be used to provide respite from challenges in readers' lives (Merga, 2017a). For more on the relationship between RfP and student wellbeing, please refer to Chapter 4 of this book, as the focus of this chapter will be specific to the role of library environments and spaces and how they contribute to student wellbeing.

Given the challenges we face in our everyday lives, both children and adults alike may crave safe spaces where they can relax, let down their guards, and be themselves. Safe spaces are environments where students feel comfortable and secure (Butler et al., 2017), and research suggests that school libraries can be learning environments that are also supportive of student wellbeing (Willis et al., 2019). Recent research with children from low socio-economic contexts found that the most commonly selected reason for visiting the school library was because it was a 'friendly space' (Wood et al., 2020, p. 14), and 'this impression was reinforced by the open-ended responses', where 'the most-frequently mentioned reasons for using the school library were: *school curriculum, quiet place, safe haven, book access, equipment access,* and *self-improvement*' (p. 13). Responses included statements such as: 'A good place to get away from all bad things'; 'Because I have literally no friends. And I stay by myself'; 'Because it is the only safe place in the school'; and 'It's a safe haven from bullies' (pp. 14–15). Earlier work by Hay (2006) found that 'a positive learning environment that supports student learning, where students feel comfortable and can pursue their own information, ICT and recreational interests, was central to students' view of the school library' (p. 30).

We know that libraries can be positioned as valued safe spaces within the school due to the diligent work of their staff, and 'school librarians can shape an environment that beckons to children and inspires them to become partners in protecting the unique space where everyone is welcome' (Wittmann & Fisher-Allison, 2020, p. 42). Comfortable furnishings can play a key role in creating a pleasant environment in interaction with numerous other factors such as staff attitudes, ambient noise, and perceived atmosphere, which can influence students' sense of belonging (Shenton, 2007). Libraries also continually revisit and reimagine their role in supporting student wellbeing. For example, as noted in reference to academic libraries, 'library spaces figure prominently in discussions about the library's contribution to student wellness. As they consider their role in fostering student well-being, libraries have been rethinking how their spaces are designed and used' (Bladek, 2021, p. 5).

Safe spaces may also be reading spaces; as noted by Sung (2020), 'not only does the school library offer equal access to books and space, but it also provides a shared, relaxing, and informal reading experience, supporting the creation of a community of readers' (p. 489). It cannot be assumed that young people have spaces conducive to RfP at home or in other schooling environments, and even avid readers may struggle to read for enjoyment in environments that are not conducive (Merga, 2017b). However, in the context of academic libraries, the competing demand of the library as a social learning space has been weighted against the more traditional affordance of the library as a silent learning space (Layton & Love, 2021). As school libraries seek to meet growing purposes and needs, these kinds of discussions and trade-offs will increasingly be undertaken, as a balance between often competing needs is sought.

This chapter will report on my research on reading and wellbeing in relation to space from two different data sources: the 2020 'School libraries promoting wellbeing in Australian primary and secondary schools' project (hereafter the Project in this chapter) and my recent analysis of job description documents (JDFs) for teacher librarians.

Insights from the Project on how students value the library environment

I collected data on libraries as wellbeing supportive spaces in contemporary schools based on the data from the Project, some of which was presented in my recent journal article (Merga, 2021a). In this chapter, I make use of these data to pay closer attention to which students may most benefit from the library being a safe space.

As I've explained earlier in this book, the Project included consideration of how school libraries may operate as safe spaces for young people, as well as how they promote and resource mental health and wellbeing initiatives in schools and their communities, and foster reading as a practice associated with enhanced wellbeing in young people. I collected interview data from three library managers (LMs) and 12 students at three schools in relation to these focus areas (see Appendix 1 for details on participants and method). Schools were selected because they felt they were effective in promoting student wellbeing, and the students who were invited to participate were identified as avid users of the library. As such, the Project findings are not broadly generalisable; rather they offer insights into how school libraries can foster wellbeing in young people. To view the specific questions I asked these respondents, please refer to Appendix 1. Themes were then identified using a constant comparative approach (Boeije, 2002). The young respondents on this project were able to clearly articulate how it feels to occupy a safe library space, and the LMs revealed the behind-the-scenes considerations and investments they made to create safe and supportive environments for student wellbeing.

My recent research analysis concluded that

> school libraries can be highly valued safe spaces for avid users in the middle years of schooling, and that they may be valued for their capacity to foster belonging and sanctuary, allow exposure to books and opportunities for reading, and provide a space for relaxing and recharging. There was recognition of the role of their supportive staff, whose contribution to student pastoral care may not be fully recognised by school leadership. Library staff created inviting and supportive environments with careful selection of furnishings and decorations, and the school libraries in this study sought to cater for highly diverse purposes, supporting both lively and social activities as well as quietude.
>
> (Merga, 2021a)

However, in this chapter, I diverge from this previous work in that I adapt my analysis to focus on the *kinds of students* that may benefit from the library as a safe space, with consideration too of how reading may relate to this. As school library professionals read this chapter, I expect that they will recall certain students whom they have worked with over the years and how they found a haven for themselves within their libraries, and I created the student profiles herein based on students' own representations of themselves and their feelings towards their library environment.

Students seeking sanctuary from weather conditions

First, the library can be a sanctuary for students who are seeking respite from unfavourable weather conditions, and temperature is one of the facets of schooling that can influence student learning as well as their comfort (e.g. Porras-Salazar et al., 2018). Given the very hot summers and cold rainy winters in Western Australia where this research was conducted, the period of the year that students may seek sanctuary from unfavourable outdoor conditions is typically quite lengthy.

For example, Josh explained how hot weather led him to use the library during his free time and potentially influenced how he used his time:

> Well, there are games in the cupboards, but I like to read and just relax. Especially if it's a really hot day, like, the other day on Friday or Thursday, I was really hot. So, I just relaxed and had a chill day because it was boiling. So, I came in here and read one book and then I went out on Thursday, yeah.

For some students experiencing sensory issues, even very slight changes in the weather can pose issues. LM Veronica described how one such student made use of her library:

> I've got one child who is very sensitive to wind and external outdoors . . . so she'll just come in, she doesn't say anything at recess, or lunchtime, she'll just come in and start drawing or . . . whatever day it is, and we don't have to say anything, I just know that she's feeling that way. She doesn't need to be embarrassed about it.

As such, the library can be a place where students can escape environmental stressors to achieve physical comfort that may have a flow-on impact on their overall sense of wellbeing.

Students with developing social skills, anxiety and introversion

Research has established that 'childhood and adolescence is the core risk phase for the development of symptoms and syndromes of anxiety that may range from transient mild symptoms to full-blown anxiety disorders' (Beesdo et al., 2009, p. 483). School libraries can provide spaces where students with developing social skills, anxiety and introversion can begin to form social connections in controlled and low-risk contexts.

LMs observed students with developing social skills, anxiety and introversion using the library as a space in which they could feel secure and not overwhelmed. When asked about who benefits most from the library being a safe space, Anne explained the benefits for 'introverts' and 'anxious children', noting that in her school,

> We do have a lot of anxiety. Children who are struggling with friendships, Bookworms, children who thrive in small groups who are not sporty . . . I'm not saying that they don't play sport and things but . . . they don't want to be out there in a full-on soccer game, and those that are just the daydreamers.

Similarly, Veronica explained how tentative social relationships can be carefully cultivated in the library space:

> I think the library provides positive interactions, positive social interactions for children who might struggle with making friendships and socialisation . . . the playground's scary for kids, and sometimes a small amount of space with a familiar and safe environment allows them to just make friends gently.
>
> (Merga, 2021a)

The nurturing and safe space of the library allows for a gentle process of forging meaningful social connections to be enacted by vulnerable students.

Students seeking mentor and mentee relationships

Mentor and mentee relationships within schools hold the potential to 'have a direct effect on mentees' social skills, behavioural self-management, and self-esteem' (Karcher, 2005, p. 74). Young people may seek meaningful mentor or mentee relationships with peers in order to give or receive support, and the library is a space where this can be possible. Veronica explained how mentorships evolved in her library:

> I think there's a really lovely mentorship that exists in the library because the older students, and many of them who had challenges in their own past, are able

to achieve success by kind of mentoring and helping these little kids . . . They kind of role model and make a safe friendship and encourage the little ones to actually make these friendships. But in return, the little ones kind of look up to the older ones, and often that's the first time that's ever happened for them. Often, the children who choose to be library monitors are ones who've seen others do that and thought that 'I'd like that for me'. And so, they receive that positive reinforcement.

As such, the library monitor position was a formalisation of the mentor role and allowed young people to establish themselves in a leadership role that was suited to their interests and dispositions. Veronica explained that

I've got a little library monitor at the moment who's amazing . . . she is very rare . . . I was very surprised when she said she wanted to (do it) . . . she's kind of a bit closed in her daily life. She does amazing illustrations, amazing, dealing with lots of tough stuff. But they're beautiful. And we've spoken about it a lot.

But I've noticed this year being a library monitor, she's actually opened up and she talks to the little kids, and she loves the fact that they speak to her. And little kids don't care, they'll just say anything to you. And so, she actually has relaxed a lot into herself, and I've really noticed her coming out of herself. And I've known her since she was three years old, but this is this blooming and blossoming of her talking to younger kids and answering their questions.

This is a great illustration of benefits for mentors, with a relatively introverted student able to develop leadership capacity in a safe space, experiencing visible personal growth while supporting the growth of others. This is also interesting because when we think about school leadership opportunities within the school, we might more typically think of sports leadership, academic leadership or whole-cohort leadership. It is very positive that the library monitor role opens up leadership possibilities for those who may have leadership qualities but who are not extroverted personalities, academic achievers or highly proficient in sports.

Students seeking to reset

In this regard, the library really is there for every student. Even the most confident of students may experience challenging days where they fall out with their friendship groups or need time to process troubles at home. For some students, the library can be a place to reset in order to deal with external challenges and enhance their mood.

In Chapter 4, I explored how reading can be one way that students work through challenging emotions, but the library also offers other affordances beyond books for this purpose. For example, Jennie explained that 'I quite often like to look around for books, and quite often I'll go on the computer, just to make me feel good about myself before the day ahead' (Merga, 2021a). When I asked how this helped her, Jennie explained that

> By bringing positive energy from people on social media that personally I like to listen to as well, and it just makes me feel good about myself since I'm listening to something positive to help me get through the day, instead of being all moody.
>
> (Merga, 2021a)

LM Veronica also observed students using the library for this purpose, noting that

> I think that coming into the library is like a bit of a new slate for some kids. So, some of the ones that don't come regularly, it's like they need a reset. They just need to come and breathe and be someone else just for one day.
>
> And that's the other group of kids that I love to see because you'll see them and you'll think, 'Yep, you're having a tough day, or something's happened, you've fallen out with your friend, and you don't know what to do, and you don't know where you can go', and I like that they come, and they'll find someone in there. There's always someone who wants to play a game with you, or, you know, wants to watch what you're doing.

Both the resources and social opportunities available in the library supported students seeking to regulate their mood or escape social conflict, and even students who very rarely visited the library of their own volition could draw upon it as a supportive resource in periods of need. This finding resonated with previous research in Japan which found that while school libraries can meet social needs for some high school students, others may use school library shelves as 'an informal place to spend time alone', and 'browsing behavior among the bookshelves allowed students to narrow their visual field and to avoid other students' eyes', 'providing students with a more informal place where he or she could browse or spend time alone, despite being in a public place where every student could visit' (Arai, 2017, p. 38)

Students who love to read

The library can be an engaging space for students who enjoy RfP, and creating a school reading culture may be contingent on the library environment being 'an attractive space for students' and 'a reading and learning hub' (Loh et al., 2017, p. 179). The library can also celebrate keen readers in a similar way to how students who are successful in sports are rewarded in physical education contexts. This can make students feel that their interest in reading is valued and valuable.

For example, Kai talked about some of the many exciting activities and competitions that took place in her library, noting that

> we do a competition where we read (for) a certain amount of time, we record that time in minutes, and then we put that time into the library and they'll give it into points, and whoever has the most points wins at the end. We have it every year, and it's so much fun. And every day you get a sheet to fill it in, and it's so good . . . I'm so prepared.
>
> Our class got first place out of the whole school for the first week, so we've got three very strong readers in the class, so that's not really a surprise.

Kai's sense of pride was clearly apparent, and avid participants in the reading competition that Kai described had the opportunity to enjoy being valued for bringing points and maybe even victory to their classes, potentially also increasing the social value of books and reading by linking it with extrinsic recognition not normally given to readers. As I also found in earlier research with teenagers, while there is debate about the value of extrinsic motivators to encourage reading (e.g. McQuillan, 1997), prizes and reward systems appear to motivate some students (Merga, 2015).

Furthermore, previous research has suggested that some adolescents would read more if they perceived greater encouragement to read (Merga, 2016), and these kinds of social activities that have a competitive element may also heighten the social positioning of books and reading. Given that my earlier research found that 'adolescents who deemed books to be socially unacceptable were less likely to read books in their free time, and to enjoy recreational book reading', 'the importance of raising the social capital of books in the classroom' is clear (Merga, 2014, p. 479), and libraries can do this through involving young people in activities where success in reading can mean something beyond the individual, conferring benefit for the broader social group, bringing with it its own kind of glory.

Students who are creative

The school library is a space where students can enjoy expressing themselves creatively, and while more research is needed on how makerspaces may function as a wellbeing resource, wellbeing benefits have been anecdotally reported in the literature (e.g. Henrich, 2020).

Students such as Kai described enjoyment in using the makerspace as a creative and social activity that she looked forward to, and it is also important to note that makerspaces could also have a tangible influence on the environment where students' artistic creations are subsequently incorporated into the library decor. As such, makerspaces provide opportunities for students to change their learning spaces, making material contributions to the library space that they can recognise and 'own' every time they see them on display. For example, Kai described her recent art project as an enjoyable social activity, where 'we literally get to glue and paint them together, and then, oh, it's just awesome! . . . All the decorations over there, they were all made in the makerspace, especially the ones hanging from the ceiling'.

LMs also described how creative students had a chance to have their needs met in the library, with Veronica describing how it brought children together across the years of schooling:

> I think in our library, particularly, the students have got a big ownership in this space. I like to let the library monitors really drive the lunchtime crew, and they do things like 'off their own bat' without any encouragement from me. They organised a craft club on Friday and the big kids show the little kids how to do things in beading, and it's lovely, and they make these little cute kind of family groups of the big ones, the middle ones, you know, younger ones all working together.

This evocative image of the library fostering supportive and creative 'families' of students of varying ages through shared interests and activities illustrates how libraries can build social connections. In this instance, the makerspace is able to meet the needs of students with creative interests, while increasing student ownership of and contribution to the library space. While not all libraries will be able to afford to resource a makerspace due to budgetary constraints (e.g. Cao et al., 2020), when mounting a case for a makerspace within a school library, potential contribution to student wellbeing as well as provision of a creative outlet should be kept in mind.

These findings suggest that the unique affordances of the library may be particularly tailored to meet the needs of students who are: seeking sanctuary from weather conditions; experiencing developing social skills, anxiety and introversion; seeking mentor and mentee relationships; seeking to reset; avid readers; and, seeking creative social outlets. Students and LMs describe the library as a supportive space, with LMs providing some insights into how this was intentional, but also how it has naturally evolved given the unique affordances of the space. While more research is needed to explore the broader generalisability of these findings, they provide valuable insights into what school libraries can mean for young people.

What library environments are Australian teacher librarians expected to foster?

While the previous section focused on the *kinds* of students that may benefit from the library as a safe space, this section switches attention to another data source and related purpose. In this section, I explore how expectations that teacher librarians create a supportive space are articulated in their JDFs. This shows the reader what school leaders who ostensibly sign off on these JDFs are looking for in relation to school library environments, but also how they see the creation of supportive environments as intentionally fostered by school library professionals, rather than as something that is incidental.

My analysis of JDFs of Australian teacher librarians found that influencing the library and learning environment was a highly common aspect of their role (Merga, 2020). While in this prior article, I provided some brief insights into what was expected from teacher librarians in relation to environment, in this chapter, I revisit the data to pay more intensive attention to this facet of the role and give the reader a fulsome sense of these expectations.

As per this previous work, this is a key and common aspect of the teacher librarian role in Australia, and the scope of the library and learning environment role related to the following:

> Create and maintain a library learning environment that is friendly, well-ordered, welcoming, flexible, productive, vibrant, stimulating, inclusive, positive and safe. Provide displays that make the space a showcase for students' learning achievements. Provide a space that accommodates students with diverse needs and interests.
>
> (Merga, 2020, p. 895)

I have revisited these data to focus on aspects of this role, and how they are expressed in the documents, to give the readers a sense of how broad and considered this concern is within the role. I found that school library professionals are expected by their future employers to create spaces that are warm and welcoming; flexible and supportive of learning; and, vibrant and stimulating.

Warm and welcoming

School library professionals were expected to create library spaces that were warm and welcoming, safe and friendly. This reflects the recent research of Dix et al. (2020), who noted that 'as part of their role, 91% of library staff ensure that the library is a safe place for students' (p. 6), and as such, influencing the library environment to promote a warm and welcoming space may be a common aspect of school library professionals' role.

Teacher librarians were expected to 'create a warm, welcoming learner-centred environment' (S29), and to 'provide a learning environment that is safe, positive, caring and respectful, in which students feel confident that their information needs will be addressed . . . a welcoming and friendly learning environment in which students feel confident (S14)'. As such, the teacher librarian is tasked with the responsibility to create a space that will promote student confidence as well as safety. Interestingly, this positive environment was not only described in relation to benefits for students; teacher librarians were also tasked with 'creating a work environment for library staff that facilitates high levels of engagement, teamwork and development (S2)'. As such, the warm and welcoming library should benefit both students and the staff members who work within it or access it.

Flexible and supportive of learning

Teacher librarians were also expected to create a space that was flexible to support varied learning needs, and also to meet the needs of students with diverse needs. I have touched on this flexibility requirement in my previous research, as it sometimes manifests in unexpected ways, such as the requirement that school library professionals have a furniture movement and removal role. For example, a teacher librarian previously explained that

> we have to move furniture. So, we've got a moveable space, our shelving is on wheels. But that enables you to move it, for flexibility . . . So, this furniture gets moved sometimes quite a bit. We've had two meetings in here this week. We've had to shift furniture and move tables and stuff to set up for them after hours. So, when we come in the next day, we have to put everything back . . . And even like, I'll say choreographing it. Even logistically working out how it's going to work. And how we're going to shuffle the areas takes a lot of time. Those sorts of things can definitely take away from other things that we do.
>
> (Merga, 2019, p. 155)

As such, when JDFs note that they need their school library professional to create a flexible and supportive space, this can have both figurative and literal implications, some of which may not be visible at the very general level of description typically found in these documents.

Within the documents, the library space was expected to be conducive to the key learning purposes enacted within the library context, such as inquiry-based learning, but it was also expected to be reflective of best practice in inclusivity and design:

> As part of a team ensure the provision of a welcoming library environment that promotes inquiry, creativity, collaboration and community . . . Ensure the library layout and equipment /furniture promotes equal access for school members and reflects current research on the design and use of contemporary learning spaces. (S36)

Organisation was often positioned as key to creation of a flexible environment that was supportive of learning, with teacher librarians needing to ensure 'the organisation of library spaces is conducive to the smooth operation of the Library as a learning space (S28)', and 'establish structures and processes to achieve a productive learning environment while responding to learners needs (S30)'.

The space needed to be able to transform to meet diverse requirements. To this end, teacher librarians were expected to 'provide and develop flexible learning spaces that accommodate different uses and needs: class presentations, group work, teaching areas, (and) leisure reading (S27)', and this was related to ensuring regular use of the library resource, and 'to create and maintain a learning environment that is accountable and supportive, and which encourages active use by students and staff (S34)'. Meeting the needs of students with specific learning needs was also referenced as 'maintaining a positive environment in the library which is respectful of all present and fosters student learning, and understanding and accommodating the learning needs of all students, including those with a disability or special learning needs (S32)'. The purpose of this 'positive and disciplined learning environment' was to ensure that 'each student is challenged to grow in knowledge and maturity, according to their potential, in all aspects of their life (S4)'.

Vibrant and stimulating

Often positioned directly alongside the notion of the library as a safe and welcoming space was the expectation that it also be vibrant and stimulating, and include 'showcasing of student learning achievements (S27)'. For example, teacher librarians were tasked with 'creation and maintenance of safe and challenging learning environments (S23)', and providing 'a stimulating and friendly learning environment for the College community (S16)'. That these two elements of safety and stimulation need to be balanced was recognised, with S15 noting that there was a need for 'a stimulating but well-ordered learning climate which nurtures each student and encourages co-operation' with the teacher librarian creating 'a learning environment which stimulates learning and promotes excellence, where students are both challenged and supported'.

Given that safe spaces are not typically situated as also challenging for students, the need for the space to be vibrant and stimulating holds the potential to cause a departure from it being warm and welcoming. That these facets were often positioned in the same documents shows that we need high-quality school library professionals who can foster these kinds of spaces which may appear to be contradictory, maintaining a careful balance between these aspects to support student needs at both group and individual levels.

Adaptive, safe and stimulating spaces

As such, the teacher librarian was required to foster an environment that was warm and welcoming, flexible and supportive of learning, and vibrant and stimulating, while potentially grappling with a far more diverse range of activities than typically enacted within a classroom. There should be greater research in, and recognition of, how school library professionals sustain safe spaces while catering to these diverse needs, and what it means on a practical level to create spaces that are simultaneously challenging and safe, as little is known in the research about how school library professionals achieve these potentially contradictory goals.

Further thoughts

This chapter provides research support for what many school library professionals already know and do, hopefully providing insight into the benefits of what they offer for the creation of safe and supportive library spaces. It explores the kinds of students that may most benefit from the library being a safe space, and what school leaders are looking for in relation to the role of school library professionals as influencers on their school library environments. I hope that you can draw on these illustrations to argue for the importance of your library to meet diverse student needs, and the valuable role you play in building uniquely supportive spaces within the school.

Our libraries are clearly being positioned as spaces that are expected to be warm and welcoming, flexible and supportive of learning, and vibrant and stimulating, and the role of library spaces as supports of student wellbeing and related reading engagement deserves greater attention. It is particularly important that greater research attention be given to how school libraries meet the needs of their culturally diverse school communities; to support intercultural education, 'learning environments that are non-discriminatory, safe and peaceful should be provided' (Boelens et al., 2012, p. 7), and future research drawing on the perspectives of students from diverse cultural backgrounds could help school library professionals in the important task of creating library spaces that reflect the expectations and interests of students from widely varying backgrounds.

It is also important to make school leadership and policymakers aware that by restricting students' access to libraries, 'we are not just limiting the academic potential of pupils from low-income backgrounds', 'we are also potentially putting their wellbeing at risk' (Wood et al., 2020, p. 18). School libraries have the potential to both support student achievement and provide respite from the challenges that young people face in their daily lives, and while the focus in advocacy on the relationship between libraries and educative attainment is important, libraries can also make other meaningful contributions to young people's lives.

The challenge of meeting the diverse needs and demands of libraries is more commonly explored in the context of public or academic libraries (e.g. Layton & Love, 2021); however, school libraries deserve greater attention as the demands placed on them can be equally diverse and significant. It is also important to note that some readers may work in libraries facing major barriers around resourcing and space; for example, the most recent Softlink (2021) report from the UK suggests that '86% of respondents reported that they have a designated library in a separate room/classroom/floor/ building' (p. 6), which means that 14% may lack the luxury of a space that is uniquely the domain of the library. As such, space and influence over how it will be used are not necessarily a given, and future research needs to look at the implications of shared spaces and how they might impact on school library professionals' capacity to shape their space to meet student wellbeing needs.

This is a research interest where there will continue to be new ideas that can be drawn from diverse sources, such as #Booktok on TikTok (Merga, 2021b), to make us more effective at supporting young people, and responsive to their evolving needs over time. In addition, future research will also need to give attention to the potential wellbeing and literacy affordances of the 'virtual' environments created by libraries, particularly given the recent school closures relating to COVID-19. For example, Hall (2020) explained that her school implemented a range of strategies and activities to foster a positive remote learning experience at home. For instance, she noted that 'as part of our visible well-being program, we promoted our collection of digital resources for recreation and relaxation', and she implemented '"Horizon Reads" which became our online campus Book Club with blogs, discussion groups and activities to share and foster literacy and literature for our students and staff', further noting that 'we had 100 students enrol for "Horizon Reads" the first time it was offered, which was fantastic' (p. 5). It would be good to evaluate student and staff experiences of these affordances, to capture their perceived benefits for end-users. While anecdotal insights into experiences of the role of school libraries during COVID-19 related disruption are interesting and can provide directions in which to focus research (e.g. Ahlfeld, 2020), the research also is needed.

References

Ahlfeld, K. (2020). Poised to Transform: Lessons learned from COVID-19 in a school library. *Journal of Library Administration, 60*(8), 958–965.

Arai, C. (2017). How junior high school students spend time in a Japanese school library during their lunch breaks: A focus on the role of bookshelves. In L. Farmer (Ed.) *IASL Conference Proceedings (Long Beach, California, US): Learning Without Borders* (pp. 34–38). IASL. https://journals.library.ualberta.ca/slw/index.php/iasl/article/download/7150/4150

Beesdo, K., Knappe, S., & Pine, D. S. (2009). Anxiety and anxiety disorders in children and adolescents: Developmental issues and implications for DSM-V. *Psychiatric Clinics, 32*(3), 483–524.

Bladek, M. (2021). Student well-being matters: Academic library support for the whole student. *The Journal of Academic Librarianship, 47*(3), e102349.

BMG Research. (2019). *National survey to scope school library provision in England, Northern Ireland, and Wales.* https://d824397c-0ce2-4fc6-b5c4-8d2e4de5b242.filesusr.com/ugd/8d6dfb_8b81a7c94c2c4c4a970265496f42307a.pdf

Boeije, H. (2002). A purposeful approach to the constant comparative method in the analysis of qualitative interviews. *Quality and Quantity, 36*(4), 391–409.

Boelens, H., van Dam, H., & Tilke, A. (2012). School Libraries across cultures. In *IASL Conference Proceedings (Doha, Qatar): The Shifting Sands of School Librarianship.* https://doi.org/10.29173/iasl7799

Butler, J. K., Kane, R. G., & Morshead, C. E. (2017). 'It's my safe space': Student voice, teacher education, and the relational space of an urban high school. *Urban Education, 52*(7), 889–916.

Cao, F., Wu, S., & Stvilia, B. (2020). Library makerspaces in China: A comparison of public, academic, and school libraries. *Journal of Librarianship and Information Science, 52*(4), 1209–1223.

Dix, K., Felgate, R., Ahmed, S. K., Carslake, T., & Sniedze-Gregory, S. (2020). *School libraries in South Australia: 2019 Census*. Australian Council for Educational Research. https://doi.org/10.37517/978-1-74286-583-6

Hall, J. (2020). Thriving in the new normal: Changing perceptions and leading change. *Synergy*. https://www.slav.vic.edu.au/index.php/Synergy/article/view/370/365

Hay, L. (2006). Student learning through Australian school libraries. Part 2: What students define and value as school library support. *Synergy, 4*(2), 28–38.

Henrich, K. (2020). Supporting student wellbeing and holistic success: A public services approach. *International Information & Library Review, 52*(3), 235–243.

Karcher, M. J. (2005). The effects of developmental mentoring and high school mentors' attendance on their younger mentees' self-esteem, social skills, and connectedness. *Psychology in the Schools, 42*(1), 65–77.

Layton, E., & Love, M. (2021). A happy medium: Academic library noise from the perspectives of students and librarians. *Codex, 6*(1), 32–53.

Lenzi, M., Sharkey, J., Furlong, M. J., Mayworm, A., Hunnicutt, K., & Vieno, A. (2017). School sense of community, teacher support, and students' school safety perceptions. *American Journal of Community Psychology, 60*(3–4), 527–537.

Levine, S. L., Cherrier, S., Holding, A. C., & Koestner, R. (2020). For the love of reading: Recreational reading reduces psychological distress in college students and autonomous motivation is the key. *Journal of American College Health*. https://doi.org/10.1080/07448481.2020.1728280

Loh, C. E., Ellis, M., Paculdar, A. A., & Wan, Z. H. (2017). Building a successful reading culture through the school library: A case study of a Singapore secondary school. In L. Farmer (Ed.) *IASL Conference Proceedings (Long Beach, California, US): Learning Without Borders* (pp. 168–182). IASL. https://journals.library.ualberta.ca/slw/index.php/iasl/article/view/7162

Mar, R. A., Oatley, K., & Peterson, J. B. (2009). Exploring the link between reading fiction and empathy: Ruling out individual differences and examining outcomes. *Communications, 34*(4), 407–428.

McQuillan, J. (1997). The effects of incentives on reading. *Reading Research and Instruction, 36*(2), 111–125.

Merga, M. K. (2014). Peer group and friend influences on the social acceptability of adolescent book reading. *Journal of Adolescent & Adult Literacy, 57*(6), 472–482.

Merga, M. K. (2015). 'She knows what I like': Student-generated best-practice statements for encouraging recreational book reading in adolescents. *Australian Journal of Education, 59*(1), 35–50.

Merga, M. K. (2016). What would make them read more? Insights from Western Australian adolescents. *Asia Pacific Journal of Education, 36*(3), 409–424.

Merga, M. K. (2017a). What motivates avid readers to maintain a regular reading habit in adulthood? *Australian Journal of Language and Literacy, 40*(2), 146–156.

Merga, M. K. (2017b). Meeting the needs of avid book readers: Access, space, concentration support and barrier mitigation. *Journal of Library Administration, 57*(1), 49–68.

Merga, M. K. (2019). *Librarians in schools as literacy educators*. Palgrave Macmillan.

Merga, M. K. (2020). School librarians as literacy educators within a complex role. *Journal of Library Administration, 60*(8), 889–908.

Merga, M. K. (2021a). Libraries as well-being supportive spaces in contemporary schools. *Journal of Library Administration, 61*(6), 659–675.

Merga, M. K. (2021b). How can TikTok inform readers' advisory services for young people? *Library & Information Science Research*. https://doi.org/10.1016/j.lisr.2021.101091

Porras-Salazar, J. A., Wyon, D. P., Piderit-Moreno, B., Contreras-Espinoza, S., & Wargocki, P. (2018). Reducing classroom temperature in a tropical climate improved the thermal comfort and the performance of elementary school pupils. *Indoor Air, 28*(6), 892–904.

Shenton, A. K. (2007). Attitudes to books and school libraries among teenagers in an English high school. *New Review of Children's Literature and Librarianship, 13*(1), 31–57.

Softlink. (2021). *2020 School Library Survey*. https://www.softlinkint.com/assets/img/content/2020_School_Library_Survey_United_Kingdom_-_Report.pdf

Sung, H. Y. (2020). Togetherness: The benefits of a schoolwide reading aloud activity for elementary school children in rural areas. *Library Quarterly, 90*(4), 475–492.

Willis, J., Hughes, H., & Bland, D. (2019). Students reimagining school libraries as spaces of learning and wellbeing. In H. Hughes, J. Franz, & J. Willis (Eds.) *School spaces for student wellbeing and learning: Insights from research and practice* (pp. 121–137). Springer.

Wittmann, P., & Fisher-Allison, N. (2020). Intentionally creating a safe space for all: The school library as refuge. *Knowledge Quest, 48*(3), 40–49.

Wood, C., Clark, C., Teravainen-Goff, A., Rudkin, G., & Vardy, E. (2020). Exploring the literacy-related behaviors and feelings of pupils eligible for free school meals in relation to their use of and access to school libraries. *School Library Research, 23*, 1–22.

7
Challenges to Visibility and Advocacy for School Libraries and Staff

For school libraries to survive and thrive in current times, and therefore be in a position to deliver the literacy and wellbeing benefits outlined in this book, they must be willing to shout about what they do from the rooftops and actively and consistently market the benefits they bring to students' schooling lives. To compete with the other diverse demands for resourcing within schools, school libraries and their staff need to be able to clearly and comprehensively articulate the specific benefits they offer for students and their learning.

This comes down to effective advocacy, but there are a number of challenges to visibility and advocacy for school libraries and staff that need to be considered, and this is a problem across many nations. For example, Loh et al. (2019) found that the invisibility of the school library professional's work remains a problem across Singapore, Hong Kong and Japan. My own research 'calls for increasing teacher librarian advocacy and awareness raising of their role as educators', contending that

> staffing vulnerability, their status as educators outside the classroom, patchy teacher support, low administrator regard and understanding, and decline in regard for the profession over time could potentially be addressed if there was greater understanding in the school community of the educational role that teacher librarians deliver.
>
> (Merga, 2019a, p. 34)

When I started to plan and then write this chapter on challenges to visibility and advocacy for school libraries and staff, it was clear that this chapter could constitute a book in itself. As such, the challenges that I have decided to focus on here are just a small subsample of considerations.

Challenges of the professional role and burgeoning workload

First, as I have clearly illustrated in Chapter 1, the complexity of the role of school library professionals can be immense, and therefore there is an ongoing risk that literacy and wellbeing related aspects of the role will be crowded out. I include the challenge of the professional role and burgeoning workload here because I feel that you may have sensed them as the elephant in the room as you read Chapter 1, which presented an incredibly diverse and presumably continually diversifying role expected in job description documents (JDFs), which might also be reasonably expected to be even more diverse in practice, given the aforementioned applied salience criteria which limited the role scope and the unspecified 'other duties' commonly alluded to.

While research with longitudinal reach is needed to capture how the school library professionals' role changes over time in varying contexts, I am concerned that expectations placed on school library professionals will continue to burgeon, putting more and more pressure on school library professionals to be everything to everyone. As previously discussed in Chapter 1, this also relates to exploiting your organisational citizenship behaviours – that tendency that many of you have to work overtime for free and do a lot of invisible labour that extends way beyond your defined professional role. The concerns articulated by Combes (2006) earlier still hold currency, and she described the ongoing challenges of remaining abreast of technological innovations relating to information, but also how to support others to attain practical knowledge in these new areas.

There is also a need for school library professionals to emerge from their training as work-ready graduates, and the Australian Library and Information Association (ALIA) (2020) discussion paper cites specific concerns around poor engagement between educators and employers and a 'lack of work-ready graduates' (p. 5). My recent research has made progress in this area by providing insights into how employers specifically characterise the role of school library professionals in their JDFs (Merga, 2020a, 2020b). I hope that institutions providing training for school library professionals consider potentially auditing what these employers want against what their training offers future and current school library professionals in order to fill any gaps. Clearly, this work has the potential to ensure that training better reflects employers' needs, so this work can be viewed as serving a needs analysis role. However, this work will need to be ongoing, so that training offerings continue to be adjusted to remain relevant to a role that may be subject to constant change.

It is undeniable that moving forward, to meet the challenges of the professional role and burgeoning workload, and to prevent unmitigated job creep that might result in the burnout of school library professionals, school library associations may need to play an important and protective role in (re)defining the scope of the role. This is not to suggest that the role must stay the same; it is inevitable that it will evolve to meet the changing needs of schools and students. However, simply adding to workloads without subtracting any tasks and roles is not sustainable, and school library professionals may need support to overcome organisational citizenship behaviours and gently but firmly adopt protective strategies that can enable them to continue to do their jobs without working large volumes of unpaid overtime. Future research should begin to quantify the extent to which school library professionals are working beyond the scope of their role, and beyond their working hours without remuneration, as we already know from my previous research that this is happening (Merga, 2019b), and the commonality of unspecified other duties in JDFs suggests that job creep may be a norm. We need to think seriously about sustainability and how we can be responsive to schools' and students' while still maintaining viability. This research also needs to look at how vital aspects of the role, such as fostering literacy and wellbeing, are influenced by changes to the role.

Issues with training, morale and the greying workforce

We cannot take for granted that school library professionals will always be available to schools and students, so issues with morale and greying workforce warrant attention. The reality is that concerns have been expressed about the greying of librarianship (Franks, 2012; Steffen & Lietzau, 2009), and the population of teachers in a library role in nations such as Australia appears to be ageing (Weldon, 2016), though further data are needed. We need to find ways to engage young people in the professional pathways that lead to this vocation and raising recognition of the importance of school library professionals is inextricably related to this goal.

When we lose a school library professional to retirement, we may also lose that role for good. Anecdotally, when I collected the sample for the Teacher Librarians as Australian Literature Advocates in Schools (TLALAS) project, I found that where the teacher librarian no longer worked at the school, in numerous cases, no replacement had been appointed. Similarly, in the US, Kachel (2018) found that library positions are often discontinued when school library professionals retire without a replacement, further suggesting that the ageing of the school library profession is a contributing factor. Perhaps if the professional training pathways for school library professionals increase their use of preceptorship models, where the next generation has more sustained periods of training in schools with current, experienced staff, this could play a role in arresting this unfortunate trend.

Furthermore, if we are to find replacement staff for these retiring workers, assuming that their positions still remain available, prospective school library professionals also need to be able to readily access high-quality training. This may be an issue in some contexts; at the time of writing this chapter, there is only one university in all of Australia that offers a preparatory course in teacher librarianship, and this has led to 'a realisation that, with only one university providing this qualification, it would be increasingly difficult to replace retiring professionals at this level' (ALIA, 2020).

However, in order to ensure the continuance of the profession, it is also paramount that issues around morale be considered. Weldon (2016) found that teachers who work in school libraries had lower levels of satisfaction than teachers generally, and Steffen and Lietzau (2009) have found that in general, 'librarianship is frequently misunderstood by those outside of the profession and undervalued, including monetarily' (p. 191). My own research conducted with teacher librarians across 30 schools in the TLALAS project found that the lack of understanding and valuing perceived by a number of my respondents could have an influence on morale and job satisfaction (Merga, 2019a). Therefore, any efforts to support the library workforce into the future need to take into account measures to enhance school leaders' understanding of what these school library professionals have to offer their schools and communities. Overall awareness of the role also needs to be promoted, due to the 'library profession's persistent problem of the public not even being aware of librarianship as a possible occupation' (Jones, 2010, p. 184).

Challenges of deprofessionalisation

There is no subject more likely to lead to open conflict at the conferences at which I present than the topic of deprofessionalisation. I cannot exclude it from consideration in this chapter, even as I prepare for my inbox to be filled with many missives of frustrated school library professionals and paraprofessionals either supportive of or furiously opposed to what I present here. I am a researcher primarily interested in what the data say (while acknowledging that data are often sparse and invariably come laden with many limitations), so please bear in mind that I do not approach this section with a personal agenda. Feel free to educate me by presenting contrary empirical data: I need everything I can get, particularly given that there is so little empirical data in this area.

Deprofessionalisation is causing a lot of anxiety in the Australian context from which I write, though I know that it is also an issue elsewhere. My research found that the replacement of qualified library professionals in schools with unqualified staff, such as library officers, has led to considerable concern in current school libraries (Merga, 2019b). It's something that we tend to approach cautiously to avoid disrespecting the hard-working paraprofessionals in libraries. Litwin (2009) suggests that the trade-off towards unqualified staff in libraries who are cheaper to employ can have consequences that we should not ignore, as he contends that these libraries 'are able to operate with greater economic efficiency but are less helpful to the people who encounter them' (p. 54). We know that qualifications are likely to matter in relation to the benefits of libraries, with Lance and Kachel (2018) finding a 'positive relationship between full-time, *qualified* school librarians and scores on standards-based language arts, reading, and writing tests, regardless of student demographics and school characteristics' (p. 16, my emphasis). However, more research is needed to establish a causal relationship between school library professional characteristics such as qualifications and student learning outcomes (Kimmel et al., 2019).

Unfortunately, if we avoid addressing the growing issue of deprofessionalisation in school libraries to avoid giving offence, we are actually tacitly supporting the devaluing of qualified staff, and potentially supporting the exploitation of paraprofessionals expected to act beyond the scope of their qualifications. At present, there is a limited challenge put forward as unqualified staff continue to occupy leadership positions in Australian school libraries (Dix et al., 2020) to the detriment of qualified staff. This is a zero-sum game, and to ignore this fact seems negligent.

These unqualified individuals no doubt in many cases have valuable experience and creative ideas to contribute, and many are worth their weight in gold. However, is the professional learning of the qualified school library staff so worthless that it can be readily dismissed? Furthermore, there is the potential for unqualified staff to face being pushed to work outside the scope of their expertise, as raised in the ALIA (2020) discussion paper:

> People raised the issue of positions being downgraded from Teacher Librarian to Librarian to Library Technician in schools; from Librarian to Library Technician in other libraries, for the purposes of cost-cutting. In some schools, where staff numbers had shrunk, Library Technicians were tasked with running the library single-handed. This was also the case in some special libraries. While some Library Technicians saw this as recognition of their skills and experience, others felt it bordered on exploitation. (p. 10)

Rather than fearing offence, wherever deprofessionalisation is occurring, library advocates worldwide need to put their weight (however strong or limited it may be) behind their qualified staff so that their roles do not continue to be replaced by unqualified staff with impunity. We also need to create stronger and more effective pathways for unqualified staff to progress towards qualifications if they wish to advance their skills. I believe that the ALIA is currently taking a close look at this, and that they have a strong creative team that is up to the challenge, so I am cautiously optimistic about how things may change in the Australian context moving forward.

That said, I am aware that I am writing this from a position of relative privilege. Due to the capacity in Australia to defer higher education costs, even when I have lived below the poverty line, as I have unfortunately done at a number of periods during my life due to diverse life events, I was still able to afford to study as upfront fees were minimal. In countries where higher education is costly, and costs cannot be deferred, professional qualifications may only be affordable for the wealthy or those willing and able to accrue substantial debt, and where wages for school library professionals are also not high, this may be a very risky investment. As such, any pathways to promote professionalisation need to consider affordability and alternative revenue sources (such as local government or school sponsorship of training places), and professional associations may need to be proactive in exploring these possibilities.

Challenges of inconsistent nomenclature and shrinking staffing

The next challenge I raise is in part self-serving, as inconsistent nomenclature makes my job a lot harder. This is because researchers and advocates try to keep tabs on contractions and growth in the school library workforce over time, so that the alarm can be sounded if we find ourselves facing unacceptable losses. Sources of reliable information about numbers of school library professionals are sparse; for example, in Australian census data on professions, teacher librarians are aggregated with other forms of librarian, and therefore 'census data are not able to distinguish teacher librarian' (Mitchell & Weldon, 2016, p. 2).

However, one of the biggest barriers to getting the numbers right is the diverse nomenclature used for school library professionals, particularly in the US and the UK. When trying to account for perceived losses in the numbers of school librarians, Lance (2018) speculated about the impact of nomenclature on these figures, wondering

> are school librarian jobs simply evolving into other ones with different names – digital learning specialist, digital media content specialist, technology integrator, and information literacy teacher, for example? Are those now calling themselves curriculum specialists, educational technology specialists, and instructional design specialists more likely to be counted as instructional coordinators? As in

the case of California, are librarians now called 'teacher librarians' and being reported only as teachers?

(Lance, 2018)

While there has been speculation about the role of nomenclature, just how diverse it is across nations has not been known, but my recent research on current JDFs has shed some light onto this issue. As per Table 1, the variety in nomenclature within and between nations is notable, with the US and the UK particularly implicated.

Table 1 *Names for school library professionals in the US, Australia and the UK*

Role title and location	% in sample
Role title (US, N= 126)*	
Library Media Specialist	51.6
Librarian	14.3
Media Specialist	11.9
School Librarian	9.5
Teacher Librarian	2.4
Library and Digital Media Specialist	1.6
Library Media Teacher	1.6
Teacher Media Specialist	0.8
Library Media Specialist Teacher	0.8
Media Specialist Librarian	0.8
Library Media Education Teacher	0.8
Teaching/Library Media Specialist	0.8
Lead Media Specialist	0.8
Librarian School Media	0.8
Library Media	0.8
School Library Media Coordinator	0.8
Coordinator Media	0.8
Library Media Technology Specialist	0.8
Instructional Technology Information Specialist	0.8
Role title (AU, N= 61)*	
Teacher Librarian	82.0
Library Coordinator	3.3
Head of Library and Information Services	3.3

Continued

Table 1 Continued

Role title and location	% in sample
Teacher Librarian Literacy Specialist	1.6
Lead Librarian	1.6
Library Manager	1.6
Library Resource Centre Leader	1.6
Librarian	1.6
Information Literacy Teacher Librarian	1.6
Information Specialist	1.6
Leader of Information Resources	1.6
Digital Innovation Specialist	1.6
Resource Centre Manager	1.6
School Librarian	1.6
Role title (UK, N=40)	
School Librarian	35.0
Librarian	32.5
Senior School Librarian	2.5
Deputy School Librarian (E-Librarian)	2.5
Deputy Librarian	2.5
Reading Champion	2.5
Librarian/Learning Resources Centre Manager	2.5
Learning Resource Centre Manager	2.5
Information Centre Manager	2.5
Library Coordinator	2.5
School Librarian and Archivist	2.5
Library Manager	2.5
Library/Resources Manager	2.5
School Senior Librarian	2.5
Library Supervisor	2.5

* Where multiple possible titles were presented, both titles were used and therefore the full number of titles exceeds the N.

(Adapted from Merga, 2020b and Merga & Ferguson, 2021)

Bear in mind that the total list of titles was actually even more diverse, with very similar titles rolled in together.

There are certainly cases where there are good reasons for differences in titles; for example, the title of Head of Library and Information Services may imply leadership within a team of teacher librarians, and therefore could be a useful distinguishing feature of seniority and accountability. However, where distinctions do not serve a *practical purpose*, for the sake of supportive advocacy and the sanity of the researchers who try to keep across workforce fluctuations, it would be really good if a greater degree of uniformity in naming could be achieved if possible, particularly in the US.

I have already discussed the greying workforce as one reason for the shrinking pool of school library professionals, but clearly that is not the only issue at play. Budget cuts reduce the school library workforce, and in order to prevent school libraries falling to the bottom of the pile of school priorities, school library professional associations need to strengthen their relationships with influential stakeholders so that the concerns of the school library community are more widely heard and understood. An answer may lie partly in upskilling of library professionals (Kachel & Lance, 2020). However, school library professionals already have valuable roles and skills; where these are currently being poorly understood or ignored, I'm not confident that it is realistic to expect that any new suite of skills will fare any better, so upskilling alone is unlikely to be a sufficient solution.

My experiences with school library professionals and my previous research projects in this space, including the TLALAS project (Merga, 2019a) and the recent job description analysis I report on in Chapter 1 (Merga 2020a, 2020b), suggest that school library professionals in the UK and Australia may *already* be showing and be expected to show a diverse and adaptative skill set, as well as a chameleon-like tendency to adapt to meet the diverse needs of schools. If this is not yielding the hoped-for professional security, it could be more useful, given the demonstrated alignment of library offerings with one of the most important preoccupations in schooling, student literacy, and the emerging concern of student wellbeing, to focus on raising awareness and explicitly connecting what school libraries *already* offer that aligns with what schools need.

Perhaps we just need to become more effective at making our preoccupations and concerns resonate with those of the key stakeholders who make staffing and resourcing decisions, and to demonstrate the power of what school libraries do. School library professionals may need to undertake needs analysis, whereby they look at what schools' current and projected needs are (and related accountabilities and measures required), and show how what they contribute sits within the scope of their role. They may also want to amplify some of the things they already do, or adopt interventions that fit within the scope of their role. I explored one way of doing this in Chapter 3 in my discussion on how to implement and measure the efficacy of literacy-supportive interventions, so I have provided some practical details on how you can make this happen in your school.

Challenge of conducting research and dissemination of a credible research base

According to a member survey of the American Library Association (2018), remaining abreast of current trends in the field is a key professional challenge, and researchers play a vital role in driving these developments. Furthermore, we need an ongoing pipeline of credible research to inform advocacy in schools, and promote student literacy and wellbeing. It is the hope that my work can make a difference that has kept me motivated through the various challenges I have encountered as a researcher. There are many barriers to conducting school library research (Merga et al., 2021; Stefl-Mabry & Radlick, 2017), and the challenges of conducting research currently in schools have grown significantly in the COVID-19 pandemic, so these barriers are not expected to subside in the near future. As we've noted elsewhere, 'methods such as randomized controlled trials in schools are simply not realistic in the current uncertain climate. At present what are needed are research approaches that can yield quality findings while being optimally responsive and resilient' (Merga et al., 2021, p. 339). Drawing on sound research-informed methodologies, researchers will need to continue to do the best they can, given the challenging circumstances we face in conducting research, which can include poor support from our own institutions (Branch-Mueller, 2017).

I understand why many in the school library profession are concerned that research is failing to permeate in ways that are accessible and supportive. In the US, Johnston and Green (2018) observed that 'although the roles of the school librarian have been investigated from various perspectives (including those of the principal, the teacher, and the student)', it remains the case that 'teachers and administrators still demonstrate a lack of understanding of the school librarian's five roles, signifying a need for better dissemination of the results of this school library research strand to the broader field of education' (p. 23). In the Australian ALIA discussion paper (2020), I was interested to read that less than a fifth of respondents agreed that 'there is an active exchange between academics, researchers and employers to expand the reach and impact of LIS research, and maximise the return from the available funding'.

Personally, I have worked really hard to share my research as broadly as possible, and I have actively worked on expanding the body of research on libraries, literacy and wellbeing. However, school library professionals should know that while there are excellent researchers in the library space, researchers may really struggle to secure financial support for their research. For example, the situation with competitive grants in Australia is not good, with an ever-shrinking pot of funding being sought by a growing pool of researchers, many of whom have greater face-value to their research propositions when compared with library and literacy-related research, such as curing cancer.

Furthermore, I have often been asked why I do not always have open access licensing on my articles so that school library professionals can easily access them, as though this is a choice I am making on a whim. The unfortunate reality is that researchers are not permitted by their academic employers to publish findings just anywhere. First, it needs to be a peer-reviewed outlet to typically 'count' towards our workload (which I am relatively comfortable with, as I value the credibility conferred). Second, journal esteem is a big factor. Publishing in journals that are ranked lower than quartile 1 (or at a stretch, quartile 2) in impact ranking (as determined by Scimago) is frowned upon for complex reasons related to institutional rankings. This means that when I am employed by an Australian university, almost every journal that I am permitted to publish in that meets the criteria of being peer-reviewed and in the upper two quartiles charges a hefty open access fee typically between three and six thousand dollars when converted to Australian currency. To get the money for this, I have been lucky to have funder support in some cases, or win small pots of money from internal grant processes that I also have to apply for; otherwise, there is no option for open access.

To get around this, I post pre-prints where I am permitted to do this, given the licensing constraints of the journals, and share access to the free sources of my research through my Twitter feed. However, I have also had it suggested that I must be making a lot of money out of promoting my journal articles. I need to clarify that researchers working for universities do not get paid for writing journal articles (other than that it falls within the scope of their jobs), and we certainly do not receive anything when our articles are read; there is no royalties system. When I share my articles, I am not trying to save up for a new bicycle; beyond increasing the chance of citations, there is nothing in it for me other than the satisfaction of knowing that my research has a far higher chance of being useful if I share it outside academia, which is why I devote so much time to research dissemination. As I've explored in my previous work in research communications, this engagement work is often very poorly valued by our academic employers, so it can be hard to undertake within the competing demands of our roles (Merga, 2021; Merga & Mason, 2020b).

It is not just access that is an issue; we actually need more researchers in this field conducting quality research using rigorous methods. One way that we can increase the volume and reach of research is by increasing the volume of research students undertaking Masters and PhD by research rather than course-work. Mentoring these students is time-consuming, so academics have limitations on the number that we can realistically take on among our other commitments, but reassuringly in recent times I've seen a slight increase in interest in enrolment.

Professional organisations might want to consider initiatives like joint PhD scholarships so that they can invest in some future research while having influence over its focus and scope. They could also establish a regular research newsletter with abstracts from current work and/or Plain English explanations of the work and its importance for professionals, researchers and employers to ensure that research findings achieve broad dissemination. Simply, as Mitchell and Weldon (2016) put it,

> what we really need to do is to get together a plan for a sustainable informing research trajectory. The library profession needs data. Without data there is limited basis from which to plan, to measure improvement, declare success or to explain the impact of one's work. Librarianship is not alone as a profession in need of data, but as a profession with information in its DNA there is no excuse for a lack of information. (p. 2)

Professional organisations and school library researchers need to 'put a ring on it' and start making some concrete supportive commitments to each other.

Research funding is incredibly limited. All of the 2020 Library Workforce Project findings that appeared in this book came from unfunded research, with in-kind support from my university employer at that time, but the research was also substantially completed in my own time due to the organisational citizenship behaviours I talked about earlier in this book (and which I too clearly suffer from!).

It would be really good to develop a cohesive and ongoing research plan that might include some funding, but where that is not feasible, researchers and professional organisations could join forces to approach prospective external funders to secure their investment in school library research. Arguing the case as a united front could make all the difference. Both Australia and the UK need a sustainable informing research trajectory for the credibility of advocacy going forward, and we cannot afford to continue to be dependent on recent US research in this area as there are a number of areas where school library professionals between nations *significantly* diverge (e.g. Merga & Ferguson, 2021).

When it comes to research translation, as I have already mentioned, I work very hard in this space. One of my higher education research interests is actually in knowledge mobilisation: making sure that the research findings reach end-users beyond academia in forms that are accessible and appealing to these audiences, and engaging with these end-users for identification of future research directions (Merga & Mason, 2020a). I should also add that our Japanese and Australian research suggests that while sharing research outside academia is something that universities increasingly expect, it's not something that they are good at supporting (Merga & Mason, 2020b), so when researchers get involved in this, it is not usually counted as part of their workload. This means that anything school library professional organisations can do to promote our findings will usually be very gratefully received. School library researchers want their work to make a difference, and even just sharing links to our work on Twitter can be a great way of showing support for our work.

Another thing I do to try to close the scholarly/accessible research communication divide is to use an academic voice that is readable. So far I've been publishing in high-quality peer-reviewed journals or books, and then sharing via Twitter, ResearchGate and the media. For example, Appendix 2 is a recent Plain English piece I did on libraries and wellbeing. Even when I am writing specifically for academic audiences, I use a relatively accessible style and tone. For example, my article on how school librarians provide support for struggling readers has been viewed more than 16,000 times (Merga, 2019c). This article reports on data from the TLALAS project. This high readership indicates that my pragmatic findings about how librarians can play a valuable support role for underperforming and often vulnerable literacy learners has reached a vast audience beyond academia. This is supported by the fact that at the time of writing this chapter, it was the most read article in this highly regarded peer-reviewed UK literacy journal, even though it is relatively recent and based on Australian data. In the past, I have led research on research communication to expand my own personal capacity in sharing research so that findings could have high impact beyond academia (e.g. Merga & Mason, 2020a; 2020b; 2020c); to sell my research plans I literally set out to make myself an expert in research communication and how universities can build academics' capacity in this (Merga & Mason, 2021), all the while learning how to more effectively share my research with the school library community.

Clearly, I could write more about the challenges of conducting research and dissemination of a credible research base to support school libraries, and next I will focus on the closely related issue of challenges facing school library researchers. On a final note, it's clear that to maintain visibility and advocacy for school libraries and staff, current and credible research is needed. However, the ongoing support of researchers is not a given, as in addition to the research communications challenges that I have already raised, we also face a number of additional challenges that may grow over time. For example,

> With the increasingly casualised higher education workforce, academics are increasingly contracted for short term teaching only with no research imperative or capacity. ALIA has recognised and recently reinforced its role in research, and it seems important to ensure that school libraries are part of that research agenda. Partnering with industry is becoming a priority and ALIA could ensure it is in a position to advance this.
>
> (Mitchell & Weldon, 2016, pp. 10–11)

In the same way that school library professionals may lack recognition for their contributions in schools (Merga, 2019a), school library researchers may struggle to attract support and funding in academic contexts that may not see their purpose.

Challenges to the existence of a physical library

Will there always be school libraries? I would argue yes, but with the additional caveat of only as long as they continue to serve a purpose not elsewhere replicated. Among its multiple other affordances, school libraries are homes for paper books. It can be argued that this is a key (though not the only) point distinguishing them from other learning spaces and facilities within contemporary schools.

Will there always be school library professionals? Again, this is likely to be the case as long as what school library professionals offer is unique, valuable and valued. What it means to be a school library professional can vary drastically depending on a range of factors, and as noted by Farmer and Safer (2019) in their US study, 'school level, poverty status, and governmental spending decisions on school library program staffing, resources, and activities' are just some of the factors at play:

> The school librarian's activities also correlate with library resources and their usage. The findings paint a bifurcated picture: the idea of a school library being a warehouse of resources when no school librarian is present versus a cross-curricular learning environment managed by a school librarian who provides instruction and works with the teaching staff. At the least, one can state with assurance that school library programs vary widely across regions, which raises the issue of equity. (p. 508)

These two examples juxtapose a library featuring a valued school library professional with a 'a warehouse of resources', suggesting a link between how the library is positioned within a school, and the related value of the school library professional.

This brings me to my point: I believe that in constructing and promoting the idea of the futuristic (bookless or book-lite) library, some library professionals may be courting their own obsolescence, particularly where the roles they ascribe to themselves, and the facility they offer can be duplicated by other staff.

I understand that books, literacy and reading are not the only things that school library professionals are involved with by a long shot, as per my research in Chapter 1. I also recognise that it is easy for me to raise concerns about the promotion of the 'future-ready library' or the library 'beyond books'; I am not working in a school with a technophile Principal that proudly announces that he hasn't read a book since his own school days, so I don't have to 'sell' my library to someone who has a poor understanding of the connection between libraries and literacy. I am also certainly not going to suggest that the role of the library as a vital source of information and technological literacy should be marginalised, as this is a very valuable affordance.

However, I would like to suggest that this 'future framing' can go too far, most obviously in the example of the bookless school library, which I would argue is not a library at all. This phenomenon has occurred in schools in Australia and the US, where all paper books are removed (see Merga, 2014 for a detailed exploration of this). Even where a full culling of paper books does not take place, books may be relegated to an undesirable and poorly designed nook in the corner of the library, with the technological affordances of the library given the prime real estate, almost as though books are an outdated embarrassment to be stashed away out of sight. I have already covered the research on the importance of books as the text most consistently associated with literacy benefit in Chapter 2 (e.g. Jerrim et al., 2020), so whenever we threaten their availability, we need to consider what this can mean for student literacy.

Fuelling these resourcing decisions is a mistaken belief that modern students have no need for paper books, bringing into question the value of the library in filling this role. This trend has been more visible in Australia and the US than in the UK, where uptake of e-books is limited, with three in five schools with none stocked in their library (BMG Research, 2019). However, research does not support this popular positioning. If we want students to experience optimal literacy benefits from reading, at this stage research suggests that continuing to provide access to paper books is essential. There are two key reasons for this.

First, despite what others may intuit, the reality is that at this point in time, according to the available research, most young people prefer to read books in paper form, rather than on a device. Loh and Sun (2019) found that 'contrary to popular belief that today's adolescents are digital natives who are completely immersed in technology, we found that adolescents in Singapore still preferred print books', reflective of earlier findings from Australian children (Merga & Mat Roni, 2017) and teenagers (Merga, 2014). Removing all books in the preferred mode could easily have a negative impact on young people's reading frequency, and therefore on their literacy skill development and maintenance, given the relationship between reading frequency and literacy gains that I outline in Chapter 2.

Second, reading books in paper form is not equal to reading on a device when it comes to literacy skills around reading comprehension and attention-related elements of reading. Recent research compared screen-based reading to paper-based reading, finding that screen-based reading was associated with comparatively shallow information processing when reading under pressure, which may lead to lower reading comprehension (Delgado & Salmerón, 2021). Similarly, Haddock et al. (2020) found that 'comprehension of story material was enhanced when participants read their short story in the printed format compared to a digital format' (p. 454). Indeed, meta-analyses on reading media influence on reading comprehension typically find that there are advantages for paper-based reading over screen-based reading (e.g. Clinton, 2019; Delgado et al., 2018; Kong et al., 2018). With the evidence base now available, this is not an issue that we can afford to ignore, given that school libraries are situated in educational contexts, and therefore the resourcing decisions we make *must* be reflective of research knowledge around optimisation of young people's educational outcomes.

Furthermore, a study of dyslexic readers found that 'reading from e-books reduces the sensory-motor interaction and leads to lesser literal comprehension, at least in dyslexic readers' (Cavalli et al., 2019, p. 256). This suggests that removing access to paper books in favour of e-books has equity implications, in that it has the potential to compound disadvantage for dyslexic students.

Third, this book looks at intersections between libraries, literacy and wellbeing, so it would be remiss of me to avoid pointing out that encouraging students to migrate their reading preferences from paper to screen-based form could have unintentional consequences for student wellbeing. I have published previous literature reviews about the numerous health and wellbeing related issues in increasing student screen time for educational purposes (Merga, 2015; Merga & Williams, 2016), and newer research in this field has found digital media use can have harmful wellbeing impacts on adolescents (Twenge & Martin, 2020).

We need physical libraries because we need to provide access to paper books to meet student preferences, optimise literacy outcomes and support student wellbeing. We need school library professionals because among the diverse and valuable facets of their role, they are the experts on literature and reading engagement, enabling schools to make the most of their school library resource. Any future framing of libraries needs to be undertaken with caution, with the research knowledge guiding rather than contradicting decisions made about library resourcing and staffing.

Further thoughts

While this chapter focuses on just some of the key challenges I perceive, it is by no means conclusive. Most of these challenges seem to have the same issue at the root. Challenges of the professional role and burgeoning workload; issues with morale and greying workforce; and challenges of deprofessionalisation and future framing revolve around respect for, valuing of, and related advocacy associated with the school library profession. Perhaps if this respect and valuing were felt, we wouldn't be facing the challenges of inconsistent nomenclature, whereby school library professionals may be at least partly motivated to rebrand themselves and their libraries in order to demonstrate continued relevance within their schools. The issues I describe around conducting research and dissemination of a credible research base, and the other challenges facing school library researchers, are more to raise awareness of the threats to an ongoing supply of high-quality and credible research to inform advocacy and protect the profession.

Without research-active academics in this space, the next generation of higher degree by research students lack academic supervisors, potentially threatening the creation of new scholars who can lead school library research. Furthermore, hopefully my illustration of the complexities of academic research in this space and the barriers to research dissemination have given some further food for thought, as I would love to see stronger relationships between school library professional associations and the school library researchers going forward.

References

American Library Association. (2018). *ALA executive board fall board meeting*. http://www.ala.org/aboutala/sites/ala.org.aboutala/files/content/ebd12_12_ALA_survey_results_AvenueM_presentation.pdf

Australian Library and Information Association (ALIA). (2020). *The future of library and information science education in Australia: Discussion paper*. https://read.alia.org.au/file/1408/download?token=xLacWPzf

BMG Research. (2019). *National survey to scope school library provision in England, Northern Ireland, and Wales*. https://d824397c-0ce2-4fc6-b5c4-8d2e4de5b242.filesusr.com/ugd/8d6dfb_8b81a7c94c2c4c4a970265496f42307a.pdf

Branch-Mueller, J. L. (2017). School library researchers in the digital age: Understanding teaching, research and service in the academy. In L. Farmer (Ed.) *IASL Conference Proceedings (Long Beach, California, US): Learning Without Borders* (pp. 224–236). IASL. https://journals.library.ualberta.ca/slw/index.php/iasl/article/download/7169/4169

Cavalli, E., Colé, P., Brèthes, H., Lefevre, E., Lascombe, S., & Velay, J. L. (2019). E-book reading hinders aspects of long-text comprehension for adults with dyslexia. *Annals of Dyslexia, 69*(2), 243–259.

Clinton, V. (2019). Reading from paper compared to screens: A systematic review and meta-analysis. *Journal of Research in Reading, 42*(2), 288–325.

Combes, B. (2006). *Opening Pandora's box: Teacher librarianship in the twenty-first century*. Proceedings of Transforming Information and Learning Conference. (pp. 48–60). Mount Lawley, Western Australia. Edith Cowan University.

Delgado, P., & Salmerón, L. (2021). The inattentive on-screen reading: Reading medium affects attention and reading comprehension under time pressure. *Learning and instruction, 71*, e101396.

Delgado, P., Vargas, C., Ackerman, R., & Salmerón, L. (2018) Don't throw away your printed books: A meta-analysis on the effects of reading media on reading comprehension. *Educational Research Review, 25*, 23–38.

Dix, K., Felgate, R., Ahmed, S. K., Carslake, T., & Sniedze-Gregory, S. (2020). *School libraries in South Australia. 2019 Census*. Australian Council for Educational Research. https://doi.org/10.37517/978-1-74286-583-6

Farmer, L. S., & Safer, A. M. (2019). Trends in school library programs 2007–2012: Analysis of AASL's School Libraries Count! data sets. *Journal of Librarianship and Information Science, 51*(2), 497–510.

Franks, R. (2012). Grey matter: The ageing librarian workforce, with a focus on public and academic libraries in Australia and the United States. *Australasian Public Libraries and Information Services, 25*(3), 104–110.

Haddock, G., Foad, C., Saul, V., Brown, W., & Thompson, R. (2020). The medium can influence the message: Print-based versus digital reading influences how people process different types of written information. *British Journal of Psychology, 111*(3), 443–459.

Jerrim, J., Lopez-Agudo, L. A., & Marcenaro-Gutierrez, O. D. (2020). Does it matter what children read? New evidence using longitudinal census data from Spain. *Oxford Review of Education, 46*(5), 515–533.

Johnston, M. P., & Green, L. S. (2018). Still polishing the diamond: School library research over the last decade. *School Library Research, 21*. https://files.eric.ed.gov/fulltext/EJ1173132.pdf

Jones, S. A. (2010). The occupational choice of school librarians. *Library Trends, 59*(1), 166–187.

Kachel, D. (2018). A perfect storm impacts school librarian numbers. *School Library Journal*. https://www.slj.com/?detailStory=perfect-storm-impacts-school-librarian-numbers

Kachel, D. E., & Lance, K. C. (2020). The role of school library organizations in developing advocacy capacity. *Teacher Librarian, 47*(5), 16–63.

Kimmel, S. C., Mardis, M. A., Pribesh, S., Pasquini, L. A., Schulz-Jones, B., Jones, F. R., Wine, L., & Colson, L. M. (2019). The preparation and certification of school librarians: Using causal educational research about teacher characteristics to probe facets of effectiveness. *School Library Research, 22*. https://files.eric.ed.gov/fulltext/EJ1232279.pdf

Kong, Y., Seo, Y. S., & Zhai, L. (2018). Comparison of reading performance on screen and on paper: A meta-analysis. *Computers & Education, 123*, 138–149.

Lance, K. C. (2018). School librarian, where art thou? *School Library Journal*. https://www.slj.com/?detailStory=school-librarian-art-thou

Lance, K. C., & Kachel, D. E. (2018). Why school librarians matter: What years of research tell us. *Phi Delta Kappan, 99*(7), 15–20.

Litwin, R. (2009). The library paraprofessional movement and the deprofessionalization of librarianship. *Progressive Librarian, 33*(Summer/Fall), 43–60.

Loh, C. E., & Sun, B. (2019). 'I'd still prefer to read the hard copy': Adolescents' print and digital reading habits. *Journal of Adolescent & Adult Literacy, 62*(6), 663–672.

Loh, C. E., Tam, A., & Okada, D. (2019). School library perspectives from Asia: Trends, innovations and challenges in Singapore, Hong Kong and Japan. In J. L. Branch-Mueller (Ed.) *Proceedings of the 48th Annual Conference of the International Association of School Librarianship and the 23rd International Forum on Research in School Librarianship*. IASL. https://journals.library.ualberta.ca/slw/index.php/iasl/article/download/7258/4286

Merga, M. K. (2014). Are teenagers really keen digital readers? Adolescent engagement in eBook reading and the relevance of paper books today. *English in Australia, 49*(1), 27–37.

Merga, M. K. (2015). 'Bring Your Own Device': Considering potential risks to student health. *Health Education Journal, 75*(4), 464–473.

Merga, M. K. (2019a). Do librarians feel that their profession is valued in contemporary schools? *Journal of the Australian Library and Information Association, 68*(1), 18–37.

Merga, M. K. (2019b). *Librarians in schools as literacy educators*. Palgrave Macmillan.

Merga, M. K. (2019c). How do librarians in schools support struggling readers? *English in Education, 53*(2), 145–160.

Merga, M. K. (2020a). School librarians as literacy educators within a complex role. *Journal of Library Administration*. https://doi.org/10.1080/01930826.2020.1820278

Merga, M. K. (2020b). What is the literacy supportive role of the school librarian in the United Kingdom? *Journal of Librarianship & Information Science*. https://doi.org/10.1177/0961000620964569

Merga, M. K. (2021). The academic labour of knowledge mobilisation: What scholarly publishers need to know. *Learned Publishing*. https://doi.org/10.1002/leap.1416

Merga, M. K., & Ferguson, C. (2021). School librarians supporting students' reading for pleasure: a job description analysis. *Australian Journal of Education*. https://doi.org/10.1177/0004944121991275

Merga M. K., & Mason, S. (2020a). Early career researchers' perceptions of the benefits and challenges of sharing research with academic and non-academic end-users. *Higher Education Research & Development*. https://doi.org/10.1080/07294360.2020.1815662

Merga, M. K., & Mason, S. (2020b). Perspectives on institutional valuing and support for academic and translational outputs in Japan and Australia. *Learned Publishing*. https://doi.org/10.1002/leap.1365

Merga, M., & Mason, S. (2020c). Sharing research with academia and beyond: Insights from early career researchers in Australia and Japan. *Learned Publishing*, *33*(3), 277–286.

Merga, M. K., & Mason, S. (2021). Mentor and peer support for early career researchers sharing research with academia and beyond. *Heliyon*, *7*(2), e06172.

Merga, M. K., & Mat Roni, S. (2017). The influence of access to eReaders, computers and mobile phones on children's book reading frequency. *Computers and Education*, *109*, 187–196.

Merga, M. K., & Williams, R. (2016). The role of health educators in mitigating health risk from increasing screen time in schools and at home. *Asia-Pacific Journal of Health, Sport & Physical Education*, *7*(2), 157–172.

Merga, M. K., Roni, S. M., Loh, C. E., & Malpique, A. (2021). Revisiting collaboration within and beyond the school library: New ways of measuring effectiveness. *Journal of Library Administration*, *61*(3), 332–346.

Mitchell, P., & Weldon, P. (2016). *The school library workforce in Australia*. Australian Library and Information Association National 2016 Conference, Adelaide. https://read.alia.org.au/sites/default/files/documents/the_school_library_workforce_in_australia.pdf

Steffen, N., & Lietzau, Z. (2009). Retirement, retention, and recruitment in Colorado libraries: The 3Rs study revisited. *Library Trends*, *58*(2), 179–191.

Stefl-Mabry, J., & Radlick, M. S. (2017). School library research in the real world: What does it really take? In L. Farmer (Ed.) *IASL Conference Proceedings (Long Beach, California, US): Learning Without Borders* (pp. 266–284). IASL. https://journals.library.ualberta.ca/slw/index.php/iasl/article/download/7174/4174

Twenge, J. M., & Martin, G. N. (2020). Gender differences in associations between digital media use and psychological well-being: Evidence from three large datasets. *Journal of Adolescence*, *79*, 91–102.

Weldon, P. R. (2016). What the Staff in Australia's Schools surveys tell us about teachers working in school libraries. http://works.bepress.com/paul_weldon/33

Conclusions and Directions for Future Research

If you have read the whole book through from beginning to end, I hope that you have encountered some new ideas that can help you going forward, as well as research insights that you already intuitively knew through your practice, but that you can now more confidently expound upon with supporting research at your back. I don't want to waste word-count by summarising what you have already read; I would like to use this conclusion as a springboard for what we need to look at next. The researcher could be you; if you are thinking about taking up the challenge of a higher degree by research such as a masters or a doctorate, this conclusion might hopefully spark some inspiration that you can then shape to fit your own unique innovation.

Even if you are a school library professional who is not interested in conducting school library research, you would be a welcome adviser if there are key areas that should be focused on that I miss out on in this short list. I encourage you to connect with library researchers in your areas of interest as your real-world insights can give us good ideas to pursue in future research.

School libraries and COVID-19

Given the immediacy of this issue, we need a research programme right now that can comprehensively explore the role that school libraries can play in mitigating the impact of COVID-19 on student literacy and wellbeing, including the role of school libraries as a health information resource on the ongoing issues in this area. Some of the respondents in my project began to touch upon this as reported on in this book. However, that project was designed before the outbreak of COVID-19, so it was not tailored to capture the unique circumstances which unfolded, and are still unfolding. Literacy impacts also deserve close consideration, particularly given that libraries may often have developed programmes for ensuring that reading was enabled within homes during periods of school closures.

However, interrupted opportunities to attend school do more than just interrupt learning, and more needs to be learned about the role of libraries as wellbeing supports during pandemic conditions, particularly to make the most of these affordances should such or similar conditions recur in the future. For vulnerable students with challenging home lives, this can also constitute interruption of access to a safe place, and loss of access to food and social supports (Drane et al., 2020). While research has begun to explore how academic libraries have adapted their wellness efforts to meet unique needs instigated by COVID-19 (e.g. Bladek, 2021), we need research to also look at school libraries, as findings from academic library contexts are not automatically applicable to the younger age groups and learning contexts within primary and secondary schools.

Collaboration for learning

We have research on school libraries and collaboration with partners within the school, but what we lack is 'recent research that captures what it means to collaborate in contemporary school libraries, the factors relevant to effective collaboration from current and diverse contexts, and how these factors can contribute to measures of effectiveness for school libraries' (Merga et al., 2021, p. 343). We need research on collaboration that shows *how* it can benefit schools leading to tangible advantages that are meaningfully aligned with the needs of school leaders, who we need to actively engage in order to get collaboration happening within schools.

We also need our collaboration research to be drawn from school libraries rather than extrapolated from other contexts. My recent research found that good collaborations may be supported by 11 characteristics:

1. Respectful communication
2. Goal setting
3. Timely and regular planning
4. Open and flexible mind-sets
5. Student-centred approaches with student benefit as the shared goal
6. Valuing of the expertise and perspectives of others
7. Advocacy for what each member can offer the collaboration
8. Generosity
9. Commitment to meeting both the group and individual needs of students

10 Willingness to evaluate the collaboration and provide supportive critical feedback
11 Safety to articulate concerns and issues without irrevocably damaging the collaborative relationship.

(Merga, 2019a, p. 71)

However, we do not know if these characteristics hold broader generalisability and are applicable across contexts. Current understandings of what it can mean to collaborate effectively in the school library need to be further interrogated, with one of the outcomes potentially being stronger preparation for library staff to facilitate collaboration.

Saunders and Corning (2020) contend that given the expectation that librarians be experts in collaboration: 'LIS faculty and professional associations might address these topics in a more systematic way to ensure that practitioners and emerging professionals understand the process and are developing the skills and qualities necessary for successful collaboration' (p. 468). However, before this can be done, we need research to revisit the research foundations that our collaborative strategies are built upon in order to increase their strength and currency (Merga et al., 2021). Given the themes of this book, it could be useful to look at how different elements of collaboration relate to measures of effectiveness in literacy performance, reading engagement and/or student wellbeing.

Wellbeing research that has broader generalisability and applicability

One limitation of this book is that it is heavily reliant on findings from the 2020 'School libraries promoting wellbeing in Australian primary and secondary schools' project (referred to in this chapter as the Project). While I have published findings from this project in a well-regarded peer-reviewed journal, suggesting that the method employed was credible and rigorous (Merga, 2021a), the nature of the Project means that I need to do more research (with a large sample and a quantitative method) before I can claim that the findings have generalisability. Findings detailed in this book could be used to drum up interest in a large-scale project that can achieve this goal, potentially following the model that I have outlined in my previous research (Merga, 2020). I also think that it is important that this research has the capacity to give close attention to the experiences of our most vulnerable clientele and take into account how students from diverse backgrounds are supported within the library. While there has been increasing interest in using texts in schools that are appropriately representative of the rich cultural diversity in our schools (e.g. Adam & Barratt-Pugh, 2020), looking at how school library professionals can promote student wellbeing by drawing on diverse resources needs further attention. A recent Penguin-commissioned report on diversity in literature in English schools further raises this issue:

> What does it say about our education system if the literature deemed most worthy of study disproportionately represents a whiteness in a multiracial society? Considering the huge potential for emotional, intellectual and imaginative growth offered, how can we accept such an imbalanced provision? How terribly sad that children of colour are unlikely to see people who look like them, who come from their backgrounds, represented in the books they are given to read in school, while white children are denied access to immersing themselves in Black and Asian characters, stories, perspectives and poems.
> (Elliot et al., 2021, p. 4)

Given that this study also found that the most substantial obstacles to teaching diverse texts in schools include subject knowledge and teacher confidence, it seems logical that the next direction for research would be to focus on how the school library professionals as literature experts within the school can play a key role in increasing the use of diverse texts. This research should also capture the wellbeing implications of this provision.

Workload realities

While analysis of job description documents (JDFs) I outline in Chapter 1 was the best I could do, given the research limitations imposed on collecting data from schools during the COVID-19 pandemic, I understand that these documents cannot capture workload realities. Beyond job descriptions and professional frameworks, more research is needed that captures what school library professionals actually do, and how this is responsive to factors such as unique school needs and the socio-economic context in which the school is situated. For example, in the US context, Farmer and Safer (2019) have noted that 'one can state with assurance that school library programs vary widely across regions, which raises the issue of equity' (p. 508).

We need research that shows:

- Who does what: Defining the role in reality, perhaps juxtaposing it with the role as identified in JDFs, or expectations of professional associations.
- Where they do it: Relating the role to content-specific factors where applicable (e.g. influence of low socio-economic context, rural versus urban contexts, as well as differences between states and nations).

- Why they do it: Exploring the other factors that may shape the nature of the role (e.g. professional qualifications, organisational citizenship behaviours).

It may be ideal to focus this inquiry on specific facets of the role, such as reading engagement. This research needs to be done to promote the wellbeing of the school library professional workforce into the future.

Establishing library and researcher partnerships

In recent times, I have begun to work more closely with schools in Australia on reading engagement and library-related interventions. For example, I recently worked in a consultancy capacity as a specialist mentor with Queenwood School (see Appendix 1 for details on project and funder). This school did an excellent job of implementing a whole-school silent reading programme driven by Gabrielle Mace, a creative and energetic leader in the library, and her team, as outlined in Appendix 1.

With some minor guidance from me, they developed and implemented the successful Building Readers for Life: A Sustained Silent Reading Program (hereafter the Program) which was reported on in the media and gained national attention. Watching the team of highly motivated educators achieve their goals was inspiring, and has increased my interest in establishing school library professional and researcher partnerships going forward. Even though I was the mentor, I learned a lot from the process, and I definitely need to get better at moving outside my researcher conditionings to more closely meet the needs of schools around how they might share their research findings. I feel like these partnerships may offer the best potential for researcher contributions that have pragmatic and real-world value.

I also think it would be great if some research attention could be applied to how school and public libraries might collaborate to address specific wellbeing needs relevant to their communities. Collaborations between school and public libraries can be highly fruitful (e.g. Leung et al., 2020), so it would be very interesting to undertake joint initiatives in the area of wellbeing using research-informed methods, and to evaluate their effectiveness with a view to sharing what works in this space.

Capturing the evolving interests of young people: #Booktok on TikTok

My recent (2021b) research has sought to draw on modern technological affordances to inform reader's advisory for young people. The reason this paper exists is that because during university closures in 2020, and COVID-19 related suspensions and delays of some of my research projects, I found myself with more time on my hands than usual. With many friends and family overseas in vulnerable places that were experiencing high levels of deaths and infections, I looked for ways to distract myself during my non-working hours that were high-immersion and positive, so that I could avoid focusing on things I couldn't control. As a result, I spent a fair bit of time on TikTok, learning about the community in general, and gradually developing a tentative research plan focused on the #Booktok community within TikTok.

For those of you who aren't on TikTok or who are unfamiliar with the app, I apologise in advance if this chapter acts as a gateway and lures you into many hours of watching TikTok videos of book recommendations, cats selecting which mineral water they prefer to drink, and songs about broccoli casserole recipes that are based on Facebook fights. TikTok will get to know you pretty quickly when you set up your account, and it will curate the videos you are exposed to, based on what you 'like' and view. TikTok will steer you towards different communities by controlling what you see on your For You Page (FYP). TikTok might decide that you should be a KPop stan or an avid Chinese drama viewer based on your other interests, and you may find yourself developing new interests and finding a sense of community.

As I spent more time in the #Booktok community on TikTok, I became increasingly interested in how young people were 'selling' books and reading to each other using humorous and compelling short videos that took both familiar and novel positions on encouraging reading. I designed and conducted a rigorous research project that you can read more about in Appendix 1 if you are interested in the method. If you're not that interested in method, all you really need to know is that I analysed 116 TikTok videos from a new account to try to capture the key themes or selling points that young people were using in this community. Young people gave really valuable insights into

1. Recommendations: Recommends books using a variety of angles and hooks.
2. Reader experience: Focuses on the performed action of reading.
3. Emotional reader response: Explores the range of emotions that reading may evoke in the reader.
4. Reader community and identity: Draws on commonalities and build a sense of reader community and reader identities.
5. Characters and places: Celebrates the characters and places in books.
6. Writer: Promotes the writing of CPs, either directly or indirectly.
7. Personal library management: Describes factors related to management of a personal library.

8   Reader in the family: Depicts tensions between avid reader behaviours and expectations of family members (primarily parents).

(Merga, 2021b)

As school library professionals, this might generate many ideas about how these data can be used to connect young people with books, drawing on strategies currently being used by young people. Here are just a few of the ideas I came up with.

1   As per *recommendations*, many school libraries already show book trailers. You could also make a loop of TikTok book videos to recommend books to young people. This should be relatively easy to do, as many TikToks are saveable.
2   Draw on the *reader experiences* videos to resource your reader spaces. For example, the bean bags, the blankets and the lighting could all be replicable, resourcing permitting. If you go for an exact match, you could even put a poster of a screenshot from something like the 'plans for you and me' video as a background, highlighting that you've created a TikTok endorsed, reader-responsive space.
3   As explored in *emotional reader response*, some young people specifically gravitate towards books that will cause them to live through challenging times alongside the protagonist. In the comments section of these videos, young readers were often asking for more recommendations of books that would 'destroy them' or produce other specific emotional responses. In this vein, you could display books by mood rather than theme. You could have a 'books to cheer you up' section alongside a 'books to kick you right back down' again section.

I'd love to hear how this looks/plays out in your library if you try it. I introduce this research here as I feel school library professionals and researchers should keep an eye on what is happening in these and other emergent online social spaces to gather ideas that can translate into real-world implications for the school library. It has been great to see some school library professionals already using this research to inform their displays and activities in their libraries. We need further research that continues to capture how evolving technological affordances can inform our approaches to readers' advisory, so I see this work as a starting point for future research with a pragmatic goal.

Final thoughts

At the end of the day, I'm just a researcher, and therefore I lack your current, lived experience as school library professionals. You know your library, your school community and your students, so you will know better than I which aspects of this book can be most useful in your context.

What I admire most about the school library professional community is that as information literacy experts, the vast majority of you respect research, while understanding its limitations. This has meant that even where I have presented research-supported findings that have challenged your existing views, most of you have shown a willingness to consider what I share. All research has limitations, and my own is certainly no exception; if you refer to my research papers, you will note that I address these limitations in some detail.

However, as a researcher, I do not have the luxury of being an unqualified advocate. I can't just tell you what I think you want to hear; I need to tell you what the current research suggests, while acknowledging that the knowledge base is not static, and therefore I might be telling you something different next week if we begin to develop a credible research base that contradicts the knowledge I am currently working with.

As a committed lifelong learner, I enjoy having my expectations confounded and challenged by research every day; that's why I like to do exploratory research. However, I know that sometimes my research can make some people uncomfortable. For example, the current research suggests that boys *can* enjoy reading fiction (Scholes et al., 2021), and they even typically prefer fiction over non-fiction (e.g. Merga, 2017), and that young people still prefer to read paper books (e.g. Merga, 2014c; Merga & Mat Roni, 2017). I know that this flies in the face of some people's assumptions and can even provoke their ire.

Nonetheless, I still need to share findings that make some people uncomfortable. For example, if we believe that all boys universally prefer non-fiction and encourage them to primarily read non-fiction, we can be inadvertently limiting their literacy attainment, given the associations between the reading of fiction and literacy benefit which do not, according to current research, hold for the reading of non-fiction (e.g. Jerrim & Moss, 2019).

All I can do is encourage those people to look to their peers, information experts who are respectful of research while understanding that researchers do not serve up immutable truths; we just give you the best knowledge that we have at the time. I can, and do, revise my position on my research all the time, based on new knowledge. For example, in my early papers on reading engagement, I tended to use the term *aliteracy* (e.g. Merga, 2014a) without problematising it, failing to appropriately establish that low reading engagement is about much more than just choosing not to read. I do a much better job of this in subsequent works (e.g. Merga, 2014b). As such, I have an ongoing commitment to be responsive to quality research data and to continue to learn, and share my knowledge with interested end-users.

Furthermore, a number of limitations apply to this book, not the least of which is that there is still a paucity of current, rigorous, peer-reviewed research to draw upon to explore the issues raised in the book. This means that, as with my previous book in this area, a limitation of the research sources informing this book

> lies in the fact that many of the supporting sources have not undergone peer-review. For example, some of the findings explored in this book that report on research conducted in Australia and elsewhere, were based on research reports. There is always a risk that such reports may not have been conducted with the same degree of rigour as academic research, and they may have been funded by bodies with a potential conflict of interest.
>
> (Merga, 2019b, p. 14)

While I have made every effort to use the highest quality sources of evidence possible, the reality is that we need more researchers producing empirical research in this space.

On a final note, I would like to thank you, the reader, for your interest in my research. I really appreciate it, and you have motivated my work in this area. Every kind message has been gratefully received, and every picture on my Twitter feed from where my ideas have been put into action by school library professionals has given me great happiness. You are honestly the best thing about my job up to this point, so please accept my sincere thanks. If this book helps even one school library professional protect their role and advocate more effectively for student reading engagement and wellbeing, I view it as well worth the time writing it and the years of conducting the research that informed it, so I really hope that it is helpful. If you have found this book at all useful and want to make my day, tag me into a Tweet that explains how you were able to use it in your library and school. I'd love to see this book support your practice and your advocacy goals, wherever you are in the world.

References

Adam, H., & Barratt-Pugh, C. (2020). The challenge of monoculturalism: What books are educators sharing with children and what messages do they send? *The Australian Educational Researcher*, 47(5), 815–836.

Bladek, M. (2021). Student well-being matters: Academic library support for the whole student. *The Journal of Academic Librarianship, 47*(3), e102349.

Drane, C., Vernon, L., & O'Shea, S. (2020). *The impact of 'learning at home' on the educational outcomes of vulnerable children in Australia during the COVID-19 pandemic*. National Centre for Student Equity in Higher Education, Curtin University.

Elliott, V., Nelson-Addy, L., Chantiluke, R., & Courtney, M. (2021). *Lit in colour: Diversity in literature in English schools*. Penguin Random House UK. https://t.co/SCHy033oBv?amp=1

Farmer, L. S., & Safer, A. M. (2019). Trends in school library programs 2007–2012: Analysis of AASL's School Libraries Count! data sets. *Journal of Librarianship and Information Science, 51*(2), 497–510.

Jerrim, J., & Moss, G. (2019). The link between fiction and teenagers' reading skills: International evidence from the OECD PISA study. *British Educational Research Journal, 45*(1), 181–200.

Leung, L. M., Chiu, D., & Lo, P. (2020). School librarians' view of cooperation with public libraries: A win-win situation in Hong Kong. *School Library Research, 23*. https://files.eric.ed.gov/fulltext/EJ1265783.pdf

Merga, M. K. (2014a). Are Western Australian adolescents keen book readers? *Australian Journal of Language and Literacy, 37*(3), 161–170.

Merga, M. K. (2014b). Western Australian adolescents' reasons for infrequent engagement in recreational book reading. *Literacy Learning: the Middle Years, 22*(2), 60–66.

Merga, M. K. (2014c). Are teenagers really keen digital readers? Adolescent engagement in eBook reading and the relevance of paper books today. *English in Australia, 49*(1), 27–37.

Merga, M. (2017). Do males really prefer non-fiction, and why does it matter? *English in Australia, 52*(1), 27–35.

Merga, M. K. (2019a). Collaborating with teacher librarians to support adolescents' literacy and literature learning. *Journal of Adolescent & Adult Literacy, 63*(1), 65–72.

Merga, M. K. (2019b). *Librarians in schools as literacy educators*. Palgrave Macmillan.

Merga, M. K. (2020). How can school libraries support student wellbeing? Evidence and implications for further research. *Journal of Library Administration, 60*(6), 660–673.

Merga, M. K. (2021a). Libraries as well-being supportive spaces in contemporary schools. *Journal of Library Administration, 61*(6), 659–675.

Merga, M. K. (2021b). How can Booktok on TikTok inform readers' advisory services for young people? *Library and Information Science Research*. https://doi.org/10.1016/j.lisr.2021.101091

Merga, M. K., & Mat Roni, S. (2017). The influence of access to eReaders, computers and mobile phones on children's book reading frequency. *Computers & Education, 109*, 187–196.

Merga, M. K., Mat Roni, S., Loh, C.E., & Malpique, A. (2021). Revisiting collaboration within and beyond the school library: New ways of measuring effectiveness. *Journal of Library Administration*. https://doi.org/10.1080/01930826.2021.1883370

Saunders, L., & Corning, S. (2020). From cooperation to collaboration: Toward a framework for deepening library partnerships. *Journal of Library Administration, 60*(5), 453–469.

Scholes, L., Spina, N., & Comber, B. (2021). Disrupting the 'boys don't read' discourse: Primary school boys who love reading fiction. *British Educational Research Journal, 47*(1), 163–180.

APPENDIX 1
Background and Methods of My Research Projects

This book includes discussion of findings from my research projects in libraries and literacy. In Table 1, you can find a list of these relevant projects; although I discuss some of the research work I've done in research communications in this book, I don't include those projects here to preserve the focus on libraries, literacy and wellbeing. If you want information about these research communications projects, please refer to my ResearchGate page: https://www.researchgate.net/profile/Margaret-Merga-2

Table 1 *Research studies in literacy and/or libraries*

Study	Years	Sample and size	Lead researcher(s)	Co-researchers and/or co-authors	Funder
Western Australian Study in Adolescent Book Reading (WASABR)	2012–2014	520 adolescents at 20 schools	Margaret Merga	Brian Moon	Australian Postgraduate Award
International Study of Avid Book Readers (ISABR)	2015–2016	1,136 avid readers from 84 countries	Margaret Merga	Saiyidi Mat Roni	Murdoch University School of Education Strategic Funding
Western Australian Study in Children's Book Reading (WASCBR)	2015–2017	997 children at 24 schools	Margaret Merga	Saiyidi Mat Roni	Ian Potter Foundation
Teen Reading in the Digital Era	2015–2017	555 adolescents at 13 schools	Leonie Rutherford	Michelle McRae, Katya Johanson, Margaret Merga, Lisa Waller, Elizabeth Bullen and Andrew Singleton	Deakin University Central Research Grants Scheme and Copyright Agency Cultural Fund
Western Australian Study in Reading Aloud (WASRA) (also known as For the Love of Reading project)	2016–2017	624 respondents involved with 21 schools 220 children (7 schools) 303 parents, 101 teachers (14 schools)	Margaret Merga and Susan Ledger	None	Collier Charitable Foundation

Continued

Table 1 Continued

Study	Years	Sample and size	Lead researcher(s)	Co-researchers and/or co-authors	Funder
Teacher librarians as literature and literacy advocates in schools (TLLLAS)	2018–2019	30 teacher librarians in Western Australian schools	Margaret Merga	Shannon Mason	Copyright Agency Cultural Fund
Supporting struggling secondary literacy learners	2019–2020	315 mainstream secondary English teachers in Australian public schools	Margaret Merga	Saiyidi Mat Roni, Anabela Malpique, Shannon Mason	Collier Charitable Foundation
Teaching writing for all in primary education	2020–2021	310 primary school teachers	Anabela Malpique	Margaret Merga, Deborah Pino-Pasternak, Susan Ledger, Debora Valcan	Collier Charitable Foundation
Writing for all: Studying the development of handwriting and keyboarding skills in the early years	2020–2022	To be determined	Anabela Malpique	Margaret Merga, Deborah Pino-Pasternak, Susan Ledger, Debora Valcan	Ian Potter Foundation
Building Readers for Life: A Sustained Silent Reading Program	2020–2021	Staff and students at one large K-12 Australian school	Gabrielle Mace	Rosalind Walsh, Catherine Phoon, Merrilyn Lean, Isaac Dargan, Kim Elith, Vanessa Collins, Anthony George. Specialist Mentor Margaret Merga	Association of Independent Schools of New South Wales (AISNSW) School Based Research Grant

Continued

Table 1 *Continued*

Study	Years	Sample and size	Lead researcher(s)	Co-researchers and/or co-authors	Funder
School libraries promoting wellbeing in Australian primary and secondary schools	2020–2021	School libraries at three Western Australian schools. Three library managers and 12 middle-years students	Margaret Merga	Anabela Malpique, Margo Pickworth, Kerry Pope, Saiyidi Mat Roni, Claire Gibson.	Bupa Health Foundation Grants
Library workforce project	2020–ongoing	Job description documents from Australia, the UK and the US. Literacy policy documents from Australia and the UK	Margaret Merga	Catherine Ferguson	Unfunded
TikTok and young people	2020–ongoing	Analysis of TikTok videos	Margaret Merga	None at this stage	Unfunded

I also provide further detail about studies that I have specifically directed the reader to within the book, where I have asked you to refer to Appendix 1 if you need more information around methods. I moved this information to this Appendix because I know that not everyone is that interested in methods, but they are important to me as a researcher, so I wanted to make sure that all of my interested readers and 'methods heads' could find the additional information about these projects.

I've assumed that if you're reading this section, you have at least a basic understanding of research methods, so I won't be explaining the basics (e.g. the difference between qualitative and quantitative approaches). I'm a pragmatic researcher who has set up camp between paradigms, not locked into any method or supporting theory, just using whatever theories or approaches best service my need to solve real-world issues and meet end-user interests. Sometimes I even contribute to the generation of theory (e.g. Merga, 2017), but only if I can see a pragmatic purpose for doing that (i.e. informing interventions for reading engagement).

I also wanted to add that where I have used direct quotes in this book, in some instances such as where grammatical errors were present, I have lightly edited the quotes for readability where needed and possible, while retaining the meaning.

2020 TikTok and young people

You've probably noticed that I'm really into hybrid content analysis, and I used it for the content from the 2020 TikTok and Young People project that I include in this book. I'm not going to go into detail about what TikTok is; if you want that content, please read my paper (Merga, 2021a), or install the application on your device and familiarise yourself with it from a user perspective.

Making the leap from document analysis to video analysis was relatively easy to achieve as I had extra time for background reading, due to the COVID-19 pandemic hindering my school-based research. For the long version on how I did this, refer to the original paper (Merga, 2021a); you can get a free copy of the pre-print from my ResearchGate account if you don't have institutional access.

For the short version (that is still longer than what I included earlier in this book), I did the following:

Lurking and learning

I spent the months in the lead-up to the project lurking on TikTok, familiarising myself with the language and common themes of the #Booktok community. I mostly did this in my leisure time. To be honest, I also watched a lot of unrelated content too, which turned out to be helpful/justifiable as there was thematic cross-over between communities, often flagged by use of the same sound. For example,

> the use of the sound Mr. Blue Sky by Electric Light Orchestra to provide a list of categories of member is not unique to Booktok, where it has been used by multiple content creators to depict types of readers as categories of person as will be explored further in the findings, and this sound has been used across various other TikTok communities to depict diverse categories of member of particular discourse communities to often humorous effect.
>
> (Merga, 2021a, p. 3)

I also emerged from my period of lurking with an Asian drama addiction (mostly Korean and Chinese, but also some Taiwanese) and as a KPop stan, so the lurking phase had a significant impact on me that I did not anticipate. This enabled me to learn about how TikTok uses my current interests to propose future interests to engage me in a plurality of communities with what TikTok must presume will be like-minded people.

Harvesting

Once I felt confident that I had strong enough background knowledge of TikTok, and #Booktok in particular, to be able to interpret videos and their supporting text content, I set up a new TikTok account exclusively for the purposes of collecting data.

If you are repeating this study, and you want to know if you have enough background knowledge, I saw myself as ready when I was able to:

- make links across TikTok communities
- understand what #Booktok related hashtags meant, even if they appeared as gibberish to outsiders (e.g. the commonly used #acotar to signify the book *A Court of Thorns and Roses* and/or the related series)
- recognise recurring TikTok trends.

Between 18 August and 1 September 2020, I collected 116 TikTok videos through search of the hashtag #Booktok. I stopped at 116 as I was starting to see the same content, with different content producers (CPs), over and over again. There is already a lot of duplication of themes within the sample, but that's also typical of TikTok; it's a space where appropriation (often with creative tweaks) is somewhat encouraged rather than shunned, though exact replication without providing credit to or 'Stitching' with the original is disparaged. Stitching is similar to Duetting: the stitch tool on TikTok 'allows users the ability to clip and integrate scenes from another user's video into their own', and 'like Duet, Stitch is a way to reinterpret and add to another user's content, building on their stories, tutorials, recipes, math lessons, and more' (TikTok, 2020).

Appropriation typically involves some degree of transformation, even if it's exactly the same sound being mimed and acted out in the same way by a different CP. Ownership and intellectual property simply do not exist in this space in the same way that they do in academia, that's for sure. Once I stopped seeing new content, I wrapped it up at 116, which seemed large enough for my purposes, given that there's no specific formula for determining the right size of sample for this kind of research, at this point in time. I also skipped a video if I had already captured that CP, so there's no duplication of CPs in the sample, even though some CPs were prolific.

I recorded the following information about each video:

1. view date
2. user name
3. nationality if provided
4. age if provided
5. assumed gender (female/male/other) though sometimes pronouns were explicitly specified
6. number of followers
7. number of likes
8. number of video likes
9. hashtags listed in the video
10. text included alongside the hashtags
11. books named
12. authors named
13. brief summary of the video's plot
14. the sound used.

Table 2 details the characteristics of the 116 CPs in the sample.

Table 2 *CP characteristics*

Characteristic	in sample (N= 116)	in sample (%)
Gender		
Female	101	87.1
Male	10	8.6
CBI*	5	4.3
Age Group		
Unspecified	67	57.8
13–15	4	3.4
16–18	16	13.8
19–21	20	17.2
22–24	7	6.0
25–27	2	1.7
*Nationality***		
Unspecified	88	75.9

Continued

Table 2 *Continued*

Characteristic	in sample (N= 116)	in sample (%)
Australia	5	4.3
Belgium	1	0.9
Canada	6	5.2
Germany	1	0.9
Iran	1	0.9
Netherlands	1	0.9
New Zealand	1	0.9
UK	10	8.6
US	4	3.4
CP Followers		
<10,000	51	44.0
10,000–50,000	46	40.0
50,001–90,000	11	9.5
90,001–130,000	5	4.3
130,001–170,000	1	0.9
170,001-210,000	1	0.9
210,001–250,000	0	0
>250,000	1	0.9

* cannot be inferred
** % greater than 100 as some respondents indicated multiple nationalities

(Merga, 2021a)

Analysing

I analysed the 116 videos to answer a number of research questions, but the focus I include in this book is around the themes. I used a hybrid version of content analysis to identify recurring themes, and how often they appeared in the sample. As such, this involved both qualitative and quantitative analysis, switching from inductive to deductive lenses (Merga, 2021a). The tricky bit comes from the fact that qualitative analysis is typically done with small samples that are not supposed to allow for statistical-probabilistic generalisability (Smith, 2018), but when you want to do counts *within the sample* by doing quantitative analysis as well, you need to go bigger. This means that you wind up doing in-depth qualitative analysis across often quite massive volumes of text, or in this case, more than 100 short videos. I actually found this approach wasn't too arduous when compared with analysis of large volumes of text. At the analysis stage, I was at the mercy of the accuracy of my brief summary of the video's plot; fortunately, Past Me anticipated Future Me's need and did a fulsome job!

2020 School libraries promoting wellbeing in Australian primary and secondary schools

As I explained previously in the book, in the latter part of 2021 I visited three schools to interview students and library managers (LMs) about diverse issues relating to libraries and wellbeing. In this Appendix, I also report on the specific semi-structured interview questions I asked the students and LMs. See Table 3 for details on the participants and their schools.

Table 3 *School and student descriptions*

School code	School and LM description	Student description (N=12)
School A	Secondary school (Years 7–12), ICSEA[1] in 1,000–1,100 range. >1,100 students. LM **Jane**.	**Felix** was a 13-year-old male in Year 8. **Jennie** was a 12-year-old female in Year 7. **Kai** was a 15-year-old female in Year 9. **Lacey** was a 13-year-old female in Year 8.
School B	Primary school (Years PP–6), ICSEA[1] in 1,100–1,200 range. >600 students. LM **Anne**.	**Chris** was a 10-year-old male in Year 5. **Josh** was an 11-year-old male in Year 6. **Rose** was a 9-year-old female in Year 4. **Sophia** was an 11-year-old female in Year 6.
School C	Combined primary and secondary school (Years PP–12), ICSEA[1] in 1,000–1,100 range. >1,600 students. LM **Veronica** worked in the primary school library, therefore all findings from this setting relate to the primary school library.	**Bob** was a 10-year-old male in Year 5. **Momo** was a 10-year-old female in Year 5. **Piper** was a 12-year-old female in Year 6. **Skyla** was a 10-year-old female in Year 5.

[1] Australian schools are categorised using the Index of Community Socio-Educational Advantage (ICSEA) (ACARA, 2015): 'the lower the ICSEAf value, the lower the level of educational advantage of students who go to this school' (p. 1), and the average is 1,000.

(Table from Merga, 2021b)

As I've explained, these data relate to a small sample qualitative sample of 12 students and three LMs at three schools that presented themselves as effective at using school libraries to promote wellbeing.

However, those of you who have an interest in methods are probably wondering how I went about recruiting 'exemplar' schools and 'avid user' students. This exemplar school self-identification was built into the recruitment materials for the LMs. The recruitment letter stated:

The project seeks to explore how school libraries may:

1 operate as safe spaces for young people;
2 promote and resource mental health and wellbeing initiatives in schools and their communities;
3 foster reading as a practice associated with enhanced wellbeing in young people.

It then went on to state that 'we are inviting library managers of school libraries that promote student wellbeing to take part in our study', and that 'we will recruit library managers that perceive that they have exemplar school libraries'. As well as consenting to be interviewed for 30–60 minutes, LMs also recruited avid user students, involving student respondents according to the following direction:

> Identifying four students from your school that you know make good use of the library, and who would be willing to take part in a 15–30 minute interview. These students should be in any of Years 4–9 as we are interested in perspectives from students in the middle years.

In addition to LM consent, informed consent for school involvement was collected from the Principal, as well as from both students and a parent in order to meet all ethics requirements.

Semi-structured interview questions relevant to Chapter 4

The following semi-structured interview questions were asked around reading engagement and wellbeing.

LMs

1 Do you ever recommend books to students based on issues they are experiencing in their lives? If yes, please describe.
2 Do you ever read books to students based on issues they are experiencing in their lives? If yes, please describe.
3 Do you ever have conversations or discussions with students about challenges characters face in books, and how they are overcome? If yes, please describe.

4 Do students use your library for reading for pleasure during class time? If yes, which year groups do you typically see? If yes, how frequently do they have this opportunity?
5 Do students use your library for reading for pleasure outside class time (e.g. before school, recess, lunch time, after school)? If yes, please describe what this library use typically looks like.

Students

1 Do you like reading books?
   a If yes, what kinds of books do you like reading? (Prompt: Why do you like these kinds of books?)
   b What is the best thing about reading?
   c **If no,** what do you prefer to do for fun?
   d Why don't you like reading books?
2 How does reading books make you feel?
3 Do you prefer reading fiction or non-fiction? Why?
4 Tell me about one of your favourite book characters. Why do you like them?
5 Does reading about a character's experiences make you think or feel differently about things? If yes, please explain.
6 Does your librarian recommend books to you? If so, what kinds of books do they suggest for you? (Prompt: Are they normally interesting to you? Explain).
7 Does your librarian read books to you? If so, what kinds of books do they read to you? (Prompt: Do you like being read to? Why/why not?)

Semi-structured interview questions relevant to Chapter 5

I asked the following interview questions, and reported on the findings. Students were asked these interview questions:

1 If you need information about your health or wellbeing, where do you usually get this information? (Prompt: do you usually ask someone or look it up in the library or online? Who do you ask/where do you go?)
2 Why do you get your information from this source (these sources)?
3 How do you know if this information is correct?
4 How did you learn to identify if information is correct? (Prompt: Has anyone taught you how to identify if information is correct?)
5 Does your library have any information about health and wellbeing?
   a **If yes**, do you know how to find it in your library?

LMs were asked the following interview questions:

1. Does your library collection include texts and resources on mental health and wellbeing?
2. If yes:
   a. what kinds of texts and resources do you have?
   b. how do you promote them to students?
   c. how do you promote them to staff?
   d. Are there any other members of the school community who use these texts and resources (e.g. school psychologist, leadership, parents etc.)? Please describe.

   If no:
   a. Are you taking any steps/measures to acquire texts and resources on mental health and wellbeing?
3. What are the mental health and wellbeing text and resourcing priorities for your particular school community?
4. Does your library play a role in teaching students to evaluate the quality of sources such as health resources? If yes, please describe this role.
5. Does your library play a role in teaching staff to evaluate the quality of sources such as health resources? If yes, please describe this role.
6. Do you provide support for students who have physical and/or mental health/wellbeing issues in the library? If yes, what kinds of supports do you provide?
7. Do you provide supervision and/or support for students unable to learn in the classroom (e.g. excluded students)?

As mentioned in Chapter 5, I also want to draw attention briefly to some of the ethics considerations related to this line of questioning. While this study had institutional ethics approval, it was *really* important to conduct it so that students did not feel that these questions were inviting personal disclosure about private information in relation to their own health. To this end, I made sure that I prefaced this section of the interview with the following statement:

> I am now going to ask you some questions about where you find information about health and wellbeing. By health and wellbeing, I mean physical, mental and emotional health, so it could include sicknesses as well as worries. I will not be asking you any questions about your health and wellbeing, only questions about how you find information about this.

I also reminded students that they didn't need to answer any of these questions if they felt that in answering them, they would inadvertently disclose information about their own health that would make them uncomfortable.

Semi-structured interview questions relevant to Chapter 6

Responses reported on in this chapter were to the following interview questions.

Students
1. What is your favourite place to be in your school? Why?
2. Do you like spending time in your school library?
   - If yes, why?
   - If no, why not?
3. A 'safe place' is a place where you feel secure and where you can relax and be comfortable. Is your library a safe place?
   - If yes, why?
   - If no, why not?
4. Do you have a preferred place to sit in your library?
   - If yes, why do you like that spot?
5. What is the best thing about your library?

(adapted from Merga, in 2021b)

LMs
1. If a 'safe place' is a place where you feel secure and where you can relax and be comfortable, is your library a safe space for students? Why do you/don't you think this?
   - If yes, is your library being a safe space intentional, or did this just happen? Please explain.
   - If no, are you taking any steps/measures to make your library a safe space for students? Please describe.
2. Have students provided past feedback to you around the library as a safe space? (This can be formal e.g. surveys or informal e.g. brief conversation).
   - If yes, what kinds of feedback have you received? Please describe.
3. In your view, what kinds of students gain the most benefit from the library being a safe space?

2020 Library Workforce Project

I again used hybrid content analysis for the library workforce project. I enjoy this methodological approach as it gives me the sense that I am shining a light onto issues of current and pragmatic interest. With interviews and surveys, there's often concern that satisficing will be at play, and that respondents are editing themselves and their responses to align with what they think my expectations are.

I go to some lengths to mitigate the likelihood of satisficing; you can learn more about satisficing in our 2020 book if you're interested, and we detail some of the steps and strategies we use to reduce satisficing (Mat Roni et al., 2020). However, the reality is that when you interview or survey humans, particularly where participation is voluntary as it must be for easy passage through the university's human research ethics committees, satisficing is unavoidable to some degree. While the documents that I analyse in hybrid content analysis are also crafted for specific audiences, they are not recrafted by the producer in response to me as the researcher; as such, I come across them communicating what they wished to convey, without my interference. This allows scope for a kind of potentiality for veracity that I cannot capture in my studies with library professional, student, teacher and parent respondents, so while I also enjoy collecting data from these respondents, I do appreciate the advantages of content analysis.

Of course, these advantages are also accompanied by disadvantages; for example, in an interview, I can follow up with a respondent on the spot or afterwards in some cases (if retrospective follow-up is part of the project and has ethics approvals) to gain further clarity around a project; however, documents lack this affordance.

Details on paper on Australian teacher librarians

Using job description documents (JDFs) as an indicator of the employer expectations of the role is a useful measure, and this book reports on findings previously published in a paper that analysed JDFs for the role of Australian teacher librarian (Merga, 2020a). Table 4 includes the data on the schools from which the JDFs were sourced online.

Table 4 Data on schools associated with job description documents

Characteristic	in sample (N = 40)	in sample (%)
Year		
2020	6	15.0
2019	11	27.5
2018	5	12.5
2017	8	20.0
2016	4	10.0
2015	2	5.0
2014	2	5.0
2013	1	2.5
2012	1	2.5
Sector		
Non-government	38	95.0
Government	2	5.0
Location		
Major cities	36	90.0
Inner regional	3	7.5
Outer regional	1	2.5
Place		
ACT	3	7.5
NSW	11	27.5
QLD	5	12.5
SA	7	17.5
VIC	11	27.5
WA	3	7.5
ICSEA*		
1,200–1,300	1	2.5
1,100–1,200	28	70.0
1,000–1,100	9	22.5
900–1,000	2	5
Whole-school type		
Primary	1	2.5
Secondary	11	27.5
Combined	28	70.0

* Index of Community Socio-Educational Advantage (ICSEA) shows the socio-economic status of the school and its immediate context. The average ICSEA is 1,000 (ACARA, 2012). It is based on currently available (2019) data collected in May 2020 from ACARA (n.d.).

(adapted from Merga, 2020a)

Analysis captured the overall scope of the role using a hybrid approach towards content analysis. This involved:

- Collecting as many JDFs as possible. A very wide range of keywords and search terms was used. The collection really slowed down after 35, and getting to 40 was a real challenge, so again, as per the TikTok paper, sampling became related to a kind of saturation in relation to access. Documents had to be from schools located in Australia, dated within the last decade (2010–2020), and be at least one page in length.
- Once I had my documents, I read through them many times. I then started my analysis with a conventional inductive approach (Kondracki et al., 2002), which involved going through the documents to identify facets of the role. Once these were identified in the documents through a process of iterative reading and coding, I returned to the documents again to quantify the number of times a role or responsibility appeared in the sample.
- I then homed in on all of the content in the documents that was relevant to teacher librarians as literacy educators, using an inductive approach again to identify seven key subthemes.

(Merga, 2020a)

Details on paper on UK school librarians

I analysed the JDFs for the role of school librarian in the UK (Merga, 2020b) shortly after the previous analysis of the Australian documents. Table 5 on the next page includes the data and role titles associated with the JDFs, illustrating their currency and applicability.

In the absence of norms around sample size for this kind of analysis, I decided to stop collection when I reached 40 JDFs, so that the sample could at least be comparable to my previous paper. The inclusion criteria were slightly different. Like the Australian documents, the UK documents needed to be context-specific (for positions located in the UK), and at least one page in length. However, due to the greater volume of available UK JDFs of recency, I was able to raise the currency criteria from ten years to eight (published within 2012–2020). As with the previous analysis, I read through all of the documents many times before commencing analysis, and the analysis was basically identical, except for the fact that I switched the order in reporting. In the Australian paper (Merga, 2020a), I presented the overall scope of the role, and then the literacy educator facets of the role. In the UK paper (Merga, 2020b), I started with my thematic analysis (from an inductive thematic approach) on the literacy-supportive role of the school librarian, followed by the hybrid analysis of the overall scope.

The biggest difference between the Australian and UK papers was the salience criteria applied to report on roles and responsibilities. While salience criteria for the Australian paper was set at 25%, in the UK paper, the salience

Table 5 *Data on job description documents*

Characteristic	in sample (N = 40)	in sample (%)
Year		
2020	22	55.0
2019	6	15.0
2018	3	7.5
2017	0	0
2016	3	7.5
2015	2	5.0
2014	1	2.5
2013	1	2.5
2012	2	5.0
Role titles		
School Librarian	14	35.0
Librarian	13	32.5
Senior School Librarian	1	2.5
Deputy School Librarian (E-Librarian)	1	2.5
Deputy Librarian	1	2.5
Reading Champion	1	2.5
Librarian/Learning Resources Centre Manager	1	2.5
Learning Resource Centre Manager	1	2.5
Information Centre Manager	1	2.5
Library Coordinator	1	2.5
School Librarian and Archivist	1	2.5
Library Manager	1	2.5
Library/Resources Manager	1	2.5
School Senior Librarian	1	2.5
Library Supervisor	1	2.5

(from Merga, 2020b)

criteria were set higher, at 40%, meaning that a role or responsibility needed to appear across at least 16 documents to be included. This decision was purely directed by the word-count limitations of one of the journals, and it definitely needs to be taken into account when comparing the two papers.

Details on paper on Australian and US school library professionals

This paper was different from the previous two because the research questions were focused on the aspects of the school librarian role in relation to supporting reading for pleasure (RfP). As such, the point of the analysis on this paper was to concurrently and comparatively analyse JDFs from Australia and the US in relation to the RfP supportive roles and characteristics of library professionals in these contexts (Merga & Ferguson, 2021). See Tables 6 and 7 for details on the documents.

Table 6 *Characteristics of job description documents in the US*

Characteristic	in sample (N=126)	in sample (%)
School type		
Unspecified/various	61	48.4
Elementary	43	34.1
High[1]	12	9.5
Middle	7	5.5
Middle/Upper combined	2	1.6
Junior High	1	0.8
Location[2]		
South	54	42.9
Midwest	28	22.2
West	23	18.2
North-east	21	16.7
Year		
2020	106	84.1
2019	8	6.3
2018	5	4.0
2017	2	1.6
2016	1	0.8
2015	2	1.6
2011	2	1.6
Role title[3]		
Library Media Specialist[4]	65	51.6
Librarian	18	14.3
Media Specialist	15	11.9
School Librarian	12	9.5
Teacher Librarian	3	2.4
Library and Digital Media Specialist	2	1.6
Library Media Teacher	2	1.6
Teacher Media Specialist	1	0.8
Library Media Specialist Teacher	1	0.8
Media Specialist Librarian	1	0.8
Library Media Education Teacher	1	0.8

Continued

Table 6 Continued

Characteristic	in sample (N=126)	in sample (%)
Teaching/Library Media Specialist	1	0.8
Lead Media Specialist	1	0.8
Librarian School Media	1	0.8
Library Media	1	0.8
School Library Media Coordinator	1	0.8
Coordinator Media	1	0.8
Library Media Technology Specialist	1	0.8
Instructional Technology Information Specialist	1	0.8

[1] Also includes Upper and Secondary
[2] Location in relation to census bureau-designated regions and divisions
[3] Where multiple possible titles were presented, both titles were used and therefore the full number of titles exceeds the N
[4] Or extremely similar e.g. Library and Media Specialist

(from Merga & Ferguson, 2021)

Table 7 Characteristics of job description documents in Australia

Characteristic	in sample (N=61)	in sample (%)
School type		
Combined[1]	37	60.7
Secondary	19	31.1
Primary	5	8.2
Location[2]		
VIC	20	32.8
NSW	18	29.5
SAU	8	13.1
QLD	6	9.8
WAU	5	8.2
ACT	3	4.9
TAS	1	1.6
Year		
2020	15	24.6
2019	18	29.5
2018	7	11.5
2017	10	16.4
2016	5	8.2
2015	2	3.3
2014	2	3.3

Continued

Table 7 Continued

Characteristic	in sample (N=61)	in sample (%)
2013	1	1.6
2012	1	1.6
Role title[3]		
Teacher Librarian	50	82.0
Library Coordinator	2	3.3
Head of Library and Information Services	2	3.3
Teacher Librarian Literacy Specialist	1	1.6
Lead Librarian	1	1.6
Library Manager	1	1.6
Library Resource Centre Leader	1	1.6
Librarian	1	1.6
Information Literacy Teacher Librarian	1	1.6
Information Specialist	1	1.6
Leader of Information Resources	1	1.6
Digital Innovation Specialist	1	1.6
Resource Centre Manager	1	1.6
School Librarian	1	1.6

[1] Includes primary (elementary) and secondary (middle/high school) years
[2] Location in relation to Australian states and territories
[3] Where multiple possible titles were presented, both titles were used and therefore the full number of titles exceeds the N

(from Merga & Ferguson, 2021)

Given that Australian JDFs are comparatively scarce, it took a very long time to get 61 Australian JDFs. We noted that 'the corpus for each was deemed sufficient at the current N (US N=126; Australia N=61), as beyond this point it became extremely difficult to source additional current job descriptions' (Merga & Ferguson, 2021, p. 8). It's also important to highlight the obvious: that the samples were not of comparable size. Documents needed to be for jobs located in Australia or the US, published within the last nine years (2011–2020), and not describing an adjunct staff role (such as library assistant or library technician). The same analytic approach was employed as outlined in relation to the other two JDF papers, and if you want to learn more about the coding exclusions, take a look at Table 3 in the original paper (Merga & Ferguson, 2021).

Details on paper on Australian and UK literacy policy analysis

This paper differs from its predecessors on this project as the data source is different. Instead of JDFs, I analysed literacy policy documents (LPs), though as you'll note from Tables 8 and 9, they had a lot of different names (especially in the Australian context), which made identifying them a painstaking process. As per the paper, in order for inclusion in the corpus, documents needed to meet the following criteria:

- Be published or created since 2010
- Be at least one page in length
- Be a document, not just website content
- Be focused on schooling years beyond very early childhood (preschool years)
- Have a detectable date of creation or publication
- Feature a clearly discernible school literacy policy or plan of at least one page in length.

(Merga, 2021c)

I wound up with 70 from each context as I wanted to analyse a comparable amount, and the search for Australian LPs reached the point where no further documents could be found. Though again there was a greater volume of UK documents available, I paused the search for UK documents at the same amount as the Australian maximum.

Table 8 *Australian document characteristics*

Characteristic	in sample (N= 70)
Year created	
2020	5
2019	5
2018	10
2017	3
2016	9
2015	9
2014	10
2013	6
2012	6
2011	4
2010	3

Continued

Table 8 *Continued*

Characteristic	in sample (N= 70)
School location	
ACT	2
NSW	3
NT	2
QLD	5
SA	22
TAS	0
VIC	17
WA	19
School type	
Primary	56
Secondary	8
Combined	5
Special	1
Document length (pages)	
1–2	17
3–4	22
5–6	6
7–8	6
9–10	3
11+	16
Document title	
Literacy Policy	16
Literacy Agreement**	6
Literacy Plan	6
Whole-School Literacy Plan	6
English Policy	4
Whole-School Literacy Agreement	3
Business Plan	2
Continuity of Learning Plan: Literacy	2
Literacy and Numeracy Policy	2

* only titles used by more than one school are included, and therefore the total is less than N=70
**or very similar

(Merga, 2021c)

Table 9 UK document characteristics

Characteristic	in sample (N= 70)
Year created	
2020	4
2019	11
2018	15
2017	8
2016	14
2015	5
2014	5
2013	1
2012	4
2011	3
School location	
England	49
Northern Ireland	17
Scotland	2
Wales	2
School type*	
Primary/Junior/Infant	41
Secondary	26
Combined	2
Special	1
Document length (pages)	
1–2	0
3–4	5
5–6	11
7–8	13
9–10	13
11+	28
Document title**	
Literacy Policy***	42
Whole-School Literacy Policy***	7
Language and Literacy Policy	6
English Policy	4
Literacy and English Policy***	4
Literacy and Numeracy Policy	3

* where UK schools were secondary apart from inclusion of Year 6 (e.g. UK63) they were classified as secondary rather than combined
** only titles used by more than one school are included, and therefore the total is less than N=70
*** or very similar

(Merga, 2021c)

For the analysis on this paper, I did the following, and because it was quite a complex method employed, I actually strongly encourage you to read the full version in the paper (Merga, 2021c) if you are thinking about replicating this study:

- Read the LPs many times
- Used a deductive approach to count the occurrence of libraries within the documents
- Used a deductive approach to count the kinds of libraries featured
- Switched to an inductive approach to explore the roles that libraries were positioned as fulfilling in LPs.

Again, while this Appendix provides further information on the methods far beyond what appears in the chapters of this book, it is still really scanty because you are probably realising that one could literally write a book just on these methods. Do take a look at the original reporting papers, all of which have been through the rigour of peer review at well regarded journals, if you need further information and background sources, or if you are still unclear on principles such as the difference between inductive and deductive orientation in analysis.

References

ACARA. (2012). Guide to understanding ICSEA. http://www.saasso.asn.au/wpcontent/uploads/2012/08/Guide_to_understanding_ICSEA.pdf

ACARA. (2015). What does the ICSEA value mean? http://docs.acara.edu.au/resources/About_icsea_2014.pdf

ACARA. (n.d.). My School. https://www.myschool.edu.au

Kondracki, N. L., Wellman, N. S., & Amundson, D. R. (2002). Content analysis: Review of methods and their applications in nutrition education. *Journal of Nutrition Education and Behavior, 34*(4), 224–230.

Mat Roni, S., Merga, M. K., & Morris, J. (2020). *Conducting quantitative research in education*. Springer.

Merga, M. K. (2017). What motivates avid readers to maintain a regular reading habit in adulthood? *Australian Journal of Language and Literacy, 40*(2), 146–156.

Merga, M. K. (2020a). School librarians as literacy educators within a complex role. *Journal of Library Administration, 60*(8), 889–908.

Merga, M. K. (2020b). What is the literacy supportive role of the school librarian in the United Kingdom? *Journal of Librarianship & Information Science*. https://doi.org/10.1177/0961000620964569

Merga, M. K. (2021a). How can Booktok on TikTok inform readers' advisory services for young people? *Library and Information Science Research*. https://doi.org/10.1016/j.lisr.2021.101091

Merga, M. K. (2021b). Libraries as wellbeing supportive spaces in contemporary schools. *Journal of Library Administration, 61*(6), 659–675.

Merga, M. K. (2021c). The role of the library within school-level literacy policies and plans in Australia and the United Kingdom. *Journal of Librarianship and Information Science, 41*(1), 39–50.

Merga, M. K., & Ferguson, C. (2021). School librarians supporting students' reading for pleasure: A job description analysis. *Australian Journal of Education*. https://doi.org/10.1177/0004944121991275

Smith, B. (2018). Generalizability in qualitative research: Misunderstandings, opportunities and recommendations for the sport and exercise sciences. *Qualitative Research in Sport, Exercise and Health, 10*(1), 137–149.

TikTok. (2020). New on TikTok: Introducing Stitch. https://newsroom.tiktok.com/en-us/new-on-tiktok-introducing-stitch

APPENDIX 2
A Place to Get Away from It All: Five Ways School Libraries Support Student Wellbeing

I've included this piece as an example of Plain English communication of research on wellbeing and libraries. On 30 September 2020, I shared this Plain English piece so that my school library professional friends could have an easy read that they could share with their school leadership, colleagues and school communities. Feel free to share the link at the end of the article if you think it could be useful for your school community.

Students in Australia and around the world have experienced significant challenges this year, including the COVID-19 pandemic and natural disasters.

Globally, as many as one in five young people may experience mental health problems (Dray et al., 2017). These can be exacerbated or even brought on by stressful life events, including economic pressures related to the pandemic.

We know teacher librarians and school libraries play an important role in supporting young people's reading (Merga, 2019a) and broader academic achievement (Lance & Kachel, 2018). But school libraries play a more diverse role in students' lives (Merga, 2020a), among which is to support their wellbeing (Merga, 2020b).

Here are five ways they do this.

1. They can be safe spaces

Creating a positive, safe and supportive school environment can help schools meet young people's academic, emotional and social needs (Kutsyuruba et al., 2015).

Whether students are victims of bullying or simply feel like they don't fit in, school libraries can provide safe spaces in sometimes challenging school environments. In some schools, the library is the only space intentionally created as a refuge for young people (Wittmann & Fisher-Allison, 2020).

Both the library as a whole, and spaces in it, can be adapted to be comforting sanctuaries. A quiet space with comfortable furniture can make the library a place to 'get away from it all' (Hughes et al., 2016).

In recent times the school library has been expected to cater to a growing array of diverse purposes such as sports equipment storage and meeting venues (Merga, 2019b), perhaps challenging its ability to be a safe space. It's important for schools to ensure, within these demands, students still have a special spot to come to for refuge.

2. They provide resources for wellbeing

When students are experiencing health and other wellbeing issues, libraries can have valuable resources to help them understand what they are going through and where to get help (Lukenbill & Immroth, 2009). School libraries can also potentially provide valuable health resources to the broader community (Adkins et al., 2019).

Teacher librarians curate resources (and weed out irrelevant ones) to ensure students get current, quality information (Kimmelman, 2018). Library staff may also work with teachers and school psychologists to ensure the school community is well resourced for meeting young people's needs.

3. They help build digital health-literacy skills

The World Health Organisation (n.d.) has emphasised the importance of health literacy and its potential to support better individual and community health outcomes.

Young people need these skills to prevent potentially dangerous misconceptions, such as those that have circulated during the COVID-19 pandemic (Vanderslott, 2020).

In a 2017 study, researchers worked with school librarians to improve young people's digital health-literacy skills. The study showed that while young people had good digital literacy skills when it came to searching for general information, they had poor knowledge when it came to evaluating the credibility of websites and health information (St. Jean et al., 2017).

School librarians are digital literacy experts. Supporting staff and students with their information skills is part of their job description (Merga, 2020a). School libraries can build students' digital and information health-literacy skills (Bröder et al., 2017), helping them evaluate online health information sources.

4. They support reading for pleasure

Reading for pleasure is associated with mental wellbeing (Clark & Teravainen-Goff, 2018).

School libraries facilitate reading for pleasure by providing comfortable reading spaces, as well as access to interesting texts. Visits to the library encourage young people to read more and have positive attitudes towards reading (Mat Roni & Merga, 2019).

Teacher librarians may also make recommendations and read books aloud, which is relaxing for young people (Merga, 2017a).

While much is known about the literacy benefits of reading (Merga, 2018), keen reading in childhood is also linked to healthy choices and fewer issues with behaviour in the teen years (Mak & Fancourt, 2020a, 2020b). Reading for pleasure can provide a valuable escape from the challenges of everyday life (Merga, 2017b).

However, the crowded curriculum can lead to RfP being undervalued in schools (Merga, 2020c). Students at schools with libraries do not always have regular access to them, which is something schools need to ensure is provided (Merga, 2019b).

5. They encourage healing through reading

Teacher librarians may also support students to engage with literature in healing ways. Known as bibliotherapy, which is 'healing through books' (Harvey, 2010), students can deal with issues challenging their wellbeing from a safe distance when they are experienced by book characters. They can also get guidance on how to cope from the experiences and perspectives of book characters.

Teacher librarians may select specific literature to support students encountering particular challenges (Harper, 2017). This is one of the numerous benefits of the literature expertise of teacher librarians.

School libraries and staffing are under threat and undervalued (Dix et al., 2020; Merga, 2019c). These resources are easy to take for granted, and school libraries often lose out in budget cuts (Softlink, 2020).

Where school libraries do not have the staff and materials they need, this can limit their ability to support student wellbeing (Great School Libraries, 2019). We need to better understand how our school libraries and staff contribute to student wellbeing so we can make the most of this valuable resource.

(This article is shared under Creative Commons Licence. It was originally published on 30 September 2020 at https://theconversation.com/a-place-to-get-away-from-it-all-5-ways-school-libraries-support-student-well-being-145180. The only alterations are the removal of hyperlinks which are replaced with references for this print version. Please feel free to tweet, post and share the original article, which can be accessed at this link.)

References

Adkins, D., Brendler, B., Townsend, K., & Maras, M. (2019). Rural school libraries anchoring community mental health literacy. *Qualitative and Quantitative Methods in Libraries, 8*(4), 425–435.

Bröder, J., Okan, O., Bauer, U., Bruland, D., Schlupp, S., Bollweg, T. M., & Pinheiro, P. (2017). Health literacy in childhood and youth: A systematic review of definitions and models. *BMC Public Health, 17*(1), 1–25.

Clark, C., & Teravainen-Goff, A. (2018). *Mental wellbeing, reading and writing: How children and young people's mental wellbeing is related to their reading and writing experiences*. National Literacy Trust.

Dix, K., Ahmed, S., Carslake, T., Gregory, S., O'Grady, E., & Trevitt, J. (2020). *Student health & wellbeing, systematic review*. Australian Council for Educational Research.

Dray, J., Bowman, J., Campbell, E., Freund, M., Wolfenden, L., Hodder, R. K., & Wiggers, J. (2017). Systematic review of universal resilience-focused interventions targeting child and adolescent mental health in the school setting. *Journal of the American Academy of Child & Adolescent Psychiatry, 56*(10), 813–824.

Great School Libraries. (2019). *Great School Libraries survey findings and update on phase 1*. https://d824397c-0ce2-4fc6-b5c4-8d2e4de5b242.filesusr.com/ugd/8d6dfb_a1949ea011cd415fbd57a7a0c4471469.pdf

Harper, M. (2017). Helping students who hurt: Care based policies and practices for the school library. *School Libraries Worldwide, 23*(1), 41–54.

Harvey, P. (2010). Bibliotherapy use by welfare teams in secondary colleges. *Australian Journal of Teacher Education, 35*(5), 29–39.

Hughes, H., Franz, J., Willis, J., Bland, D., & Rolfe, A. (2016). *High school spaces and student transitioning: Designing for student wellbeing. Research report for Queensland Department of Education and Training*. Queensland University of Technology, Australia.

Kimmelman, A. (2018). The wise whys of weeding. *Teacher Librarian, 46*(1), 20–22.

Kutsyuruba, B., Klinger, D. A., & Hussain, A. (2015). Relationships among school climate, school safety, and student achievement and well-being: A review of the literature. *Review of Education, 3*(2), 103–135.

Lance, K. C., & Kachel, D. E. (2018). Why school librarians matter: What years of research tell us. *Phi Delta Kappan, 99*(7), 15–20.

Lukenbill, B., & Immroth, B. (2009). School and public youth librarians as health information gatekeepers: Research from the Lower Rio Grande Valley of Texas. *School Library Media Research, 12*, 1–35.

Mak, H. W., & Fancourt, D. (2020a). Reading for pleasure in childhood and adolescent healthy behaviours: Longitudinal associations using the Millennium Cohort Study. *Preventive Medicine, 130,* e105889.

Mak, H. W., & Fancourt, D. (2020b). Longitudinal associations between reading for pleasure and child maladjustment: Results from a propensity score matching analysis. *Social Science & Medicine, 253,* e112971.

Mat Roni, S., & Merga, M. K. (2019). The influence of extrinsic and intrinsic variables on children's reading frequency and attitudes: An exploration using an artificial neural network. *Australian Journal of Education, 63*(3), 270–291.

Merga, M. K. (2017a). Interactive reading opportunities beyond the early years: What educators need to consider. *Australian Journal of Education, 61*(3), 328–343.

Merga, M. K. (2017b). What motivates avid readers to maintain a regular reading habit in adulthood? *Australian Journal of Language and Literacy, 40*(2), 146–156.

Merga, M. K. (2018). *Reading engagement for tweens and teens: What would make them read more?* ABC-CLIO/Libraries Unlimited.

Merga, M. K. (2019a). How do librarians in schools support struggling readers? *English in Education, 53*(2), 145–160.

Merga, M. K. (2019b). *Librarians in schools as literacy educators.* Palgrave Macmillan.

Merga, M. K. (2019c). Do librarians feel that their profession is valued in contemporary schools? *Journal of the Australian Library and Information Association, 68*(1), 18–37.

Merga, M. K. (2020a). School librarians as literacy educators within a complex role. *Journal of Library Administration, 60*(8), 889–908.

Merga, M. (2020b). How can school libraries support student wellbeing? Evidence and implications for further research. *Journal of Library Administration, 60*(6), 660–673.

Merga, M. K. (2020c). School libraries fostering children's literacy and literature learning: Mitigating the barriers. *Literacy, 54*(1), 70–78.

Softlink. (2020). *The 2019 Softlink Australia, New Zealand, and Asia-Pacific School Library Survey Report.* https://www.softlinkint.com/downloads/2019_APAC_School_Library_Survey_Report.pdf

Steffen, N., & Lietzau, Z. (2009). Retirement, retention, and recruitment in Colorado libraries: The 3Rs study revisited. *Library Trends, 58*(2), 179–191.

St. Jean, B., Greene Taylor, N., Kodama, C., & Subramaniam, M. (2017). Assessing the digital health literacy skills of tween participants in a school-library-based after-school program. *Journal of Consumer Health on the Internet, 21*(1), 40–61.

Vanderslott, S. (2020). How to spot coronavirus fake news: An expert guide. *The Conversation.* https://theconversation.com/how-to-spot-coronavirus-fake-news-an-expert-guide-133843

Wittmann, P., & Fisher-Allison, N. (2020). Intentionally creating a safe space for all: The school library as refuge. *Knowledge Quest, 48*(3), 40–49.

World Health Organisation. (n.d.). *Health literacy.*
   https://www.who.int/healthpromotion/health-literacy/en

Index

access to books 1, 16–17, 20, 22, 40–1, 65, 71, 73, 110–13, 118, 149–50, 193
administration 8, 14, 16, 27
American Association of School Librarians (AASL) 50, 101–2
American Library Association 144
anxiety 61, 88, 95, 110, 121, 125, 138
Australian Curriculum 14, 23, 37, 40, 44, 108
Australian Curriculum, Assessment and Reporting Authority (ACARA) 37, 174, 180
Australian Library and Information Association (ALIA) 2, 10, 136, 138–40, 144
Australian School Library Association (ASLA) 2, 4, 102
avid reader 35, 49, 84, 90, 94, 118, 124–5, 161, 167

Bangladesh 112
bibliotherapy 86, 193
Booktok 84, 87, 94, 130, 159–60, 170–1

Chartered Institute of Library and Information Professionals (CILIP) 3, 18
Chile 60
China 108, 160, 170
clickbait 106–7
collaboration 6–7, 11, 14–15, 22, 24, 128, 156–7, 159

collection building 2, 6, 17, 25, 45, 48
content analysis 4, 44, 87, 94, 158, 170–81, 186, 189
COVID-19 5, 24, 40, 96, 103, 106, 112, 130–1, 144, 155–6, 158, 160, 170, 191–2
Croatia 107, 112
curation 7, 45, 108–9

deprofessionalisation 138–9
dog (to support reading) 95, 108
dyslexia 63, 94–5

emotions 61, 84, 87, 123, 160
empathy 37, 91, 117
English as an additional language or dialect (EAL/D) 62–3
environment (of the library) 3, 6–8, 12–13, 15, 19–21, 26, 28, 45, 47–8, 50, 117–31, 148, 191
escape (through reading) 84, 86–8, 96, 120, 193
ethos (school) 10, 20
expired expectations 42

fiction 3, 7, 16, 25, 37–9, 45, 48, 83, 88–91, 109, 117, 162, 176
furniture 127–8, 192

health information 25, 34, 39, 101–14, 155, 176–8, 192
Hong Kong 135

Indonesia 92
induction (to library) 17, 40
Information and Communication Technology (ICT) 7, 10–11, 16, 19, 21, 26–7
information literacy 3, 6–10, 14, 16, 20, 22, 25–6, 68, 101–14, 140, 142, 149, 162, 176, 185, 192
 see also health information
initial teacher education (ITE) 61, 68
interpersonal skills 8, 17, 24, 27
intervention 21, 34, 51, 59, 61, 64, 69–77, 83, 88, 90, 95, 109, 143, 159, 169
introverts 28, 121–2

Japan 123, 135, 146
job creep 24, 29, 136–7
 see also other duties

Library Workforce Project 5, 43, 146, 169, 179–89

Matthew Effect 58
mentee 121–2, 125
mentor 19, 121–2, 125, 145, 159, 168
morale 137–8, 151

nomenclature 23, 57, 140–3, 151
non-fiction 39, 48, 104, 110–11, 113, 162, 176

online safety 7, 19, 105–6
orphaned responsibility 42
other duties 9, 11, 20, 29–30, 136–7

pandemic 5, 24–5, 34, 38, 83, 112, 144, 156, 158, 170, 191–2
 see also COVID–19
parent 6–8, 10–11, 13, 16–17, 19, 21, 24, 27, 35, 38, 41–2, 44, 49, 70–3, 75–6, 84, 94–5, 104, 108–10, 114, 161, 167, 175, 177, 179
perspective taking 7, 61, 88, 91–2, 96
professional development 9–11, 18–19, 21, 23, 26, 48, 68–9, 76, 113
Protective Behaviours 108

qualifications 2–4, 9–10, 18, 22–3, 28–9, 139–40, 159

reading aloud 65–6, 70, 72, 92–5, 167, 193
reading engagement 7, 16, 24, 33–52, 58, 66–74, 77, 83–96, 130, 150, 157, 159, 162–3, 169, 175
reading for pleasure (RfP) 3, 15, 26, 36–52, 66–7, 70, 75, 83–96, 117–18, 123, 176, 182–3, 193, 196
reading frequency 34–7, 51, 69, 74–5, 96, 149
research communication 43, 145–7, 167, 191
resilience 12, 18–19, 24–5, 89–90
role creep 29
 see also job creep
role model 6, 14–15, 35, 44–7, 49–52, 90–1, 96, 122
role requirements of school library professionals 2–30

safe environments 8, 11, 13, 15, 19–20, 28, 96, 113, 117–22, 126–30, 156, 175, 178, 191–2
school closures 5, 40, 96, 106, 130, 156
 see also COVID-19; pandemic
school culture 7, 15, 19, 24, 27, 37–8, 44–8, 50, 64–5, 124
School Library Association (SLA) 2–3
Singapore 96, 135, 149
struggling literacy learners (SLLs) 57–77, 147, 168
Sweden 39

TikTok 84, 87, 94, 130, 159–61, 169–74, 181
Twitter 145, 147, 163

weather 120, 125
Wikipedia 105, 107–8, 113